PLANNED ECONOMY FOR INDIA

PLANNED ECONOMY FOR INDIA

SIR M. VISVESARAYA

GYAN

Published by

Gyan Publishing House
5, Ansari Road
Daryaganj, New Delhi-110002
Phone: 011-47034999, 9811692060
E-mail: books@gyanbooks.com

Distribution Network
gyanbooks.com
India, USA, Canada, UK, Australia

ISBN: 978-93-7447-001-5 (PB)

First Published, 1934

2nd Impression 2026

Printed at: Gyan Press, Delhi.

PLANNED ECONOMY FOR INDIA
Author: SIR M. VISVESARAYA

PLANNED ECONOMY FOR INDIA

PLANNED ECONOMY FOR INDIA

BY

SIR M. VISVESVARAYA

K C I E , D Sc , LL D , M I C E

BANGALORE CITY

PRINTED AT THE BANGALORE PRESS, MYSORE ROAD

1934

PREFACE.

In this volume an attempt is made to present a brief but comprehensive view of the Indian situation in its economic aspects and to urge, in respect of the problems before the country, the adoption of certain courageous solutions based on recent world experience

A larger aim is to suggest the creation of opportunities and a course of action calculated to so strengthen the Indian in the business sphere that he may, within the shortest period possible, become, man for man, as capable a citizen, as strong a national and as broad-minded an international, as his compeer in America, Europe or Japan

The first step in this process is self-examination, that is, a survey and analysis of local conditions in India and a comparative study of the same with those of her prosperous contemporaries I have preferred an objective treatment of the Indian problem in this manner because it seemed to me the best way to impress the need for immediate action The Statistical Tables, given at the end of the book, have been specially prepared for this purpose A periodical self-examination like this is always beneficial to the moral health of any nation, and it will be particularly so, in the case of India in her present low economic position

The prolonged delay in constitution-framing and the absence of any move to grapple with the unemployment problem and other accumulated ills have intensified public anxiety in regard to the country's future. A cursory glance at the Tables is enough to convince the reader that the existing economic organization has failed us badly and that a modern and appropriate organization, modelled after the Economic Councils operating in European countries, is urgently needed

There have been no reasoned policies, no plan, no programme in the past to improve the income and wealth of the people A Ten-Year Plan is, therefore, suggested to cope with the situation and to carry out speedily many long-delayed reforms and developments

Both the organization and plan recommended are based on recent experience and they can be put in hand at once with a feeling of certainty that, under any reformed constitution, that may come into existence later, they will be pushed forward with accelerated speed

The country is in a position to-day—as it never was before—to advance to the front at a bound The people have most of the facilities required for a big step forward Enormous numbers of trained men and huge masses of uneducated population are waiting by the roadside to be picked up, drilled and put to work to increase production and service

An immediate beginning on the lines of the plan and organization will be most helpful to deal with the unemployment and other urgent problems and to relieve distress Since the Government of India appear to be thinking actively in the same direction for some time now, though they have not been able to reach any practical decisions yet, it is hoped prompt action will be taken to set the Government machinery in motion and put in hand the first year's work of the Ten-Year Plan

There should be no hesitation to proceed with the plan on the score of lack of funds Where a nation's prosperity is so closely concerned, money should be found somehow—by borrowing if necessary The credit of the

Government of India, which is also the credit of the people, is sufficiently high and the country is entitled to use all its potential resources for carrying out such a Plan No leading modern nation has reached its present prosperous position without being in debt during all the time it was building up its assets or wealth

It is hoped Government will co-operate with the people and, between them both, provide all the cash and credit and man-power and machine-power needed for *reconstruction* and *recovery* If, however, they show no inclination to make a start, it is up to the leaders and representatives of the people to concentrate attention on such of the measures recommended as may be immediately practicable, and take vigorous action to influence government policies on the one side and stimulate private effort on the other

A public statement by recognized leaders either of approval of the proposals urged in this book, or of any alternative recommendations, will go a long way to stop the conflict of views and waste of effort now going on in so many fields of economic endeavour In the former case, the way to practical action will be clear But in the latter, the action to follow may be determined at a conference of acknowledged leaders convened for the purpose

The book is based on information and ideas gathered during repeated visits to Europe, America and Japan, undertaken mainly with the object of studying how best the interests of a backward country like India could be furthered under the complex conditions of present-day civilization

In preparing portions of the book, I have kept in view the requirements of the general reader, the political thinker and the business man, who may care to use it for purposes of reference The figures in the Tables and the text have been checked and re-checked so as to run no risk of overstating the case

I have had the advantage of exchanging views on the problems dealt with in the book with a large number of representative men in the front rank of business and politics The views expressed in my own speeches and publications within the past two or three years have been freely drawn upon and I also wish to place on record my deep appreciation of the kindness of friends who read the manuscript as it was being sent to the press

M. V

TABLE OF CONTENTS.

GENERAL PLAN.

PART I ECONOMIC SURVEY.

PART I

ECONOMIC SURVEY

CHAPTER I.

INDIA IN A PROGRESSIVE WORLD.

World Changes—India under a Double Disability—Two Fundamental Measures—Survey, Analysis, Comparison, Self-Examination—An All-India Economic Organization—Lessons from Progressive Countries—A Ten-Year Plan—Scheme of the Work.

World Changes

We are living in a rapidly changing world There have been greater and more rapid changes within the past 40 years than were witnessed in the previous 300 years This is due partly to the many remarkable scientific discoveries and mechanical inventions to which this new era has given birth and partly to the World War from the effects of which we are not still free

In the political sphere the principal change has been the constitution of a League of Nations which originated with the Treaty of Versailles in 1920 The League is intended to bring the States and the peoples of the world closer together into one Commonwealth of Nations and to regulate their political and economic relations in conformity with the common advantage and safety of mankind

For well-known reasons the League is at the present time merely an advisory body and has little power to enforce its decisions It is said Geneva discusses much and concludes nothing But as the League was created to promote the permanent interests of humanity, it may be confidently hoped that it will grow in popularity as its aims become more widely known and appreciated, and that a World-State with real authority to enforce international co-operation will come into being in the fulness of time.

In the business world, mechanization and mass production methods are making rapid advance and the capacity of manufacturing and farm establishments to produce commodities has increased on a scale which could not have been thought possible a generation ago At the present time the producing power among industrial nations is said to be about 50 per cent in excess of the purchasing power of the consuming populations of the world If some method of securing an equitable balance between production and purchasing power can be devised, the living conditions for the average citizen are likely to undergo a radical change, his working hours may be reduced, his drudgery minimised and sufficient leisure found for him for culture and recreation But although the attention of the thinking public has been drawn to this question, no formula has yet been devised to secure this much-needed balance

The world has undergone and is still undergoing great changes in economic structure and outlook Amidst these world conditions, a disquieting change that is taking place in India is the rapid growth of population without a corresponding rise in production or income

The changes referred to are having a far-reaching effect on the welfare of the world population as well as that of India They have to be closely watched and the affairs of every country suitably adjusted to them from time to time in the interests of the local population. Such adjustments are taking place in every progressive country but so far as India is concerned there is no move in that direction The Government always put on a complacent mood whenever they speak of the economic condition of the people, while even a casual enquiry is enough to reveal a tragic state of things—

ignorance, inefficiency, dependence and a poverty which has no parallel in Western countries

INDIA UNDER A DOUBLE DISABILITY

Trade depression and economic losses have, for the past four or five years, afflicted India in common with the rest of the civilized world The population, insufficiently employed even in normal times, is experiencing acute distress at the present moment, owing to the phenomenal fall in prices and loss of purchasing power.

India is thus suffering at present from a double disability from which she has got to be rescued The countries of Europe and America are experiencing a temporary loss of efficiency through trade depression and monetary disorders, but India, under her non-modern economic order, is in a state of decay or partial paralysis, and if any redress is to come to her, her entire economic and political structure requires to be remodelled While, comparatively speaking, the States of Europe and America are concerned only with *recovery* from a temporary depression, India has need of *reconstruction* of her entire political and economic life

TWO FUNDAMENTAL MEASURES

Since the close of the War, two measures or developments are becoming popular among nations keen on rapid economic advance One is the establishment of a special Economic Organization and the other, a national Economic Plan, the object of both being to accelerate reforms and speed up developments which are in arrears. These two measures form the basis of the constructive scheme projected in this book

SURVEY, ANALYSIS, COMPARISON, SELF-EXAMINATION.

Indian economic problems are under constant

discussion in the press, in the central and provincial legislatures and elsewhere, but they are usually dealt with as isolated themes from a variety of standpoints often lacking sense of proportion, and often also militating against the permanent interests of the Indian nation as a whole Their treatment is without the background of a connected complete picture An attempt is made in this book to provide this background and explain matters in their right relation to enable the Indian reader to realize the true position occupied by his country in the business world and his own place in the scheme of things

It is the duty of every people and their government at regular intervals to take stock in this way of such economic factors as assets, income, occupations, business activities, equipment and education, in order to obtain an idea of how their country is faring as compared with other progressive countries, what resources are within reach for further betterment and how they may best be mobilised for the purpose

The Statistical Tables are intended to show how India stands as compared with some of the more advanced countries in economic activity and achievement The comparisons made are admittedly not under identical conditions in all cases, and in dealing with so wide a range of figures, it is impossible to claim that their appositeness and accuracy are in all cases above cavil Notwithstanding this, it will be seen that they turn the light of truth on many aspects of the economic situation not hitherto correctly appraised and point to some very striking conclusions

The survey in the first part of the book, taken along with the Statistical Tables brings into relief nearly all the important problems in the economic field which are a source of anxiety and concern to the

Indian public at the present time Defects have been located, causes traced, resources brought to notice, so that the reader may realize precisely what has gone wrong with this old country of ours, what remedies are called for and what readjustments are possible and necessary for strengthening and safeguarding the country's economic future

An All-India Economic Organization

India has long been at a disadvantage on account of her position as a Dependency of Great Britain The rule from that distant island, being akin to that of an absentee landlord, has taken away from the people some of their natural functions, some of the duties and services which they owe to themselves and their fellowmen, almost all the privileges connected with the initiation and control of high policies and the planning and regulation of their own economic order By keeping the people ignorant and by reducing their opportunities for work and initiative, the present administrative system has increased their dependence on foreign countries for many of the commodities which require technical knowledge and manual skill for their manufacture

India has a population which is about seven and a half times that of the United Kingdom and three times that of the United States of America Given the opportunity, the Indian population should be able to produce goods and services commensurate in some measure with the country's large size and vast resources. If the people are properly equipped with machinery and technical skill and taught to work regular hours and transact business under a modern organization—there is no reason why they should not and there is evidence available that they can—the productive power generated would be colossal. But the average Indian, as the survey will reveal, is ill-fed, untrained, undisciplined, while nine-tenths or more of the total population of India is illiterate There is no organization to remedy this state of things, none to see that the enormous human energy in the country is mobilised and put to work The public policies, not being directed by the people themselves, are not adapted to the eradication of these permanent disabilities and the result is an appalling waste of man power

There should be some one interested in the economic progress of the people, some agency to study their deficiencies and wants, some thinking centre to mould their thoughts and shape their future destinies It is suggested that one such should be brought into existence, by creating an all-India organization made up of a Central Economic Council, predominantly unofficial, working in close association with a Development Department of the Government of India, Provincial Economic Councils in similar relation with the Provincial Governments, and Local Economic Councils distributed at the rate of one at least for every city and district

If it is decided to bring order into our economic system, there is no lack of outside experience to guide us Within the past fifty years, countries like the United States of America, Canada, Japan and Sweden have worked tirelessly to develop their material resources, to stimulate industry and trade and to wrest wealth and power, in some cases, from very unpromising surroundings The author has had opportunities of discussing with the leading statesmen, economists and business men of those countries, the more pressing economic world problems in relation to their own country as well as India The experience of the countries named will, if utilized, be of immeasurable value in any attempt to rebuild life and polity in this country

LESSONS FROM PROGRESSIVE COUNTRIES.

The creation of an economic organization or agency to work out many much-needed developments and make up for lost opportunities will itself be a notable departure from administrative traditions The first duty of this organization should be to survey, analyse and carry on a comparative study of the economic conditions in India with those of the leading progressive countries of the world Such an investigation would reveal the deficiencies and wants under which the country is labouring, suggest remedies and developments that are within reach and draw attention to resources wherewith to meet them The comparative study would also suggest many new policies, measures and practices which have helped those countries in the past and which may be relied on to help India in her long wished-for rapid advance

A TEN-YEAR PLAN

The next step which the economic agency referred to should help government to take is the preparation of an Economic Plan—say, a Five-Year or a Ten-Year Plan—for dealing with the accumulated deficiencies and wants Such a plan is usually prepared by a small Commission consisting of economists, tried administrators and leading business men specially qualified for the work. The essential characteristics of the plan needed are outlined in Part II of this book

It is proposed under the Plan to bring all economic problems of India into one conspectus, to prepare an analysis of Indian conditions and examine how they stand in relation to foreign countries, to concentrate attention on increasing production and the use of modern tools and machinery, to obtain for this work all the guidance that can be had from foreign experience ;

to mobilize the country's resources in men and money to give effect to the plan, to review progress periodically and maintain a record from year to year Such, in brief, are the objects of the plan The Indian plan, should avoid *communistic* tendencies, its basic policy should be to encourage collective effort without interfering with individual initiative The developments should be more on the lines followed in the United States of America and in Turkey

The plan is capable of being put into immediate operation, if the Government and the people agree to work it and are prepared to make the necessary sacrifices demanded in their respective spheres

If the other measure, the economic organization brought into being for working out such a plan, is able to give results at a reasonable pace in these directions, it will automatically provide the mechanism for self-help and initiative needed for many other purposes in future and set free the imprisoned creative power of the people. In this way, the nation will be enabled to develop into a self-sufficient and self-improving organism

SCHEME OF THE WORK

Though the masses still continue to believe in *Kismet* and *Karma*, there is a general awakening in the country A new spirit is abroad People want to manage their own affairs How they should do this in the business sphere from the point of view of economic progress is the theme of this book The book is divided into two parts The first part deals with a survey of existing conditions and the second with the suggestions and conclusions based on the survey Under each phase of economic activity examined, the lines of appropriate future advance are indicated and, as far as possible, also the means of securing that advance. The numerous and necessarily detached suggestions and recommendations in the earlier chapters are gathered together towards the end, into six or seven specific schemes, which, in the aggregate, constitute the Ten-Year Plan proposed.

CHAPTER II.

INDIA COMPARED WITH ADVANCED NATIONS.

Inadequacy of Indian Statistics—Vital Statistics—Population Gainfully Employed—Education—Production—Trade—Transport and Communications—Finances—Defence—Output of Work—Income, Assets, etc

INADEQUACY OF INDIAN STATISTICS

THE comparisons instituted in these pages are of the nature of self-analysis from the Indian point of view If the results are to lay any claim to scientific accuracy, such comparisons should be made with the aid of statistics Ten abstract Statistical Tables have been compiled for this purpose, comparing India with half a dozen leading countries of the world in which statistics are maintained in a high state of efficiency, the countries being the United States of America, United Kingdom, Canada, Germany, France and Japan Statistics for India are incomplete and defective for a complete diagnosis of the situation, but every endeavour is made to interpret impartially such as are available, from local knowledge The method adopted in compiling the statistics and the sources of information consulted are explained in a Note attached to the Tables

A beginning will be made by presenting in this chapter a summary of known results The detailed investigations are embodied in later chapters and the appropriate reforms and remedies suggested towards the end in Part II of the book

"Economic progress can only hope to have a sound foundation when men are able to base their action upon facts instead of guesses Those countries which have learned to base their action upon authoritative facts will have a decided advantage over those who ignore such data" This statement appeared in a recent Government publication in the United States of America. Referring to the Statistical Research Bureau functioning since July 1933 under the Director-General of Commercial Intelligence and Statistics, the Viceroy of India, in his address before the Annual Meeting of the Associated Chambers of Commerce on 8th January 1934, said: "It has also been recognized that, if any programme of planned economic advance for India is to be undertaken, it is necessary to have in existence a trained organization for the analysis and interpretation of economic facts and phenomena" Statistics are unquestionably the basis of any solid structure of planned economy They furnish a record of what has been done in the past and they are indispensable as a guide to planning developments for the future They enable government to guide and control the trend of economic developments and to create wealth by judiciously conceived productive enterprises, plans of taxation and public expenditure

The following extract is taken from the recent Report of Dr A L Bowley and Mr D H Robertson, the two British experts, who have submitted a Scheme for an Economic Census of India —

"The statistics of India have largely originated as a bye-product of administrative activities, such as the collection of land revenue, or from the need of information relating to emergencies, such as famines....As a result the statistics are unco-ordinated and issued in various forms by separate Departments ..The only co-ordinated general publication is the Statistical Abstract, which omits some important statistics which must be searched for in other documents"

VITAL STATISTICS

World conditions are changing rapidly, most countries are busy adjusting themselves to the new situations, and their governments are developing new conceptions of duty to their subjects While every progressive country is actively engaged in strengthening its economic position by such measures as starting new industries, rationalising and re-equipping old industries, limiting imports, stimulating exports and accumulating gold, India has remained helpless, stolid and inactive She suffers, in the first place, from the initial low economic situation brought on by her century-old Dependency position, and in the second place, she shares in common with other nations the disadvantages of the present world trade depression Unlike Western countries and Japan, she has to recover lost ground due to the accumulated weaknesses and misfortunes arising from her two-fold disability The people here have no freedom, no opportunity to develop their own plans for the future, and no chance to put their house in order by their own collective effort

The population of India has been growing at a very rapid rate It has increased by nearly 100 million or 39 per cent in the fifty years between 1881 and 1931. Having regard to the rainfall, climatic conditions, present state of production and food supply, the population may be said to have outrun the means of subsistence Unemployment is rife and in many aspects of national development, India is dangerously weak at the present time It is obvious that no Government interested in the welfare of its people could afford to postpone an investigation into India's true condition or lose time in the application of needful remedies

The total area of the world is roughly 51 million square miles, and India occupies 1.8 million or 3 5 per cent of this total The area of British India is 1,096,171 square miles and that of the Indian States 712,508 square miles The total population of the world in

1931 was estimated at 2,025 million of which India held 353 million persons or 17 per cent The total population of India, according to the 1931 Census, was 352,837,778 of which 271,526,933 resided in British India and 81,310,845 in the Indian States In area India stands seventh in the list of countries of the world and in point of population she was hitherto considered second only to China

The *Census Report of India*, 1931, Vol I, Part I (p 29), states · "The actual figure of the increase alone is little under 34 million, a figure approaching equality with that of the total population of France or Italy and appreciably greater than that of such important European powers as Poland and Spain The population now even exceeds the latest estimate of the population of China, so that India now heads the list of all countries in the world in the number of her inhabitants This increase, however, is from most points of view a cause for alarm rather than satisfaction "

The density of population of India, as a whole, is 195 persons per square mile, that of British India being 248 persons to the square mile, and of Indian States 115 persons The density in some of the more fertile regions is very high , for instance, the province of Bengal (area 77,521 square miles) has 646, the sub-province of Oudh (area 24,154 square miles) 529, the province of Delhi (area 573 square miles) 1,110, and the district of Madura in the Madras Presidency, 817 The *Indian Census Report* of 1931 states that the density of population varies largely according to the rainfall and therefore in the densest parts, like Cochin, Eastern Bengal, the North-East of United Provinces and of Bihar, the rainfall is heavier than in any other part of India except Assam and Southern Burma The *Report* further states that the general density of the Cochin State is 814 2 persons per square mile and the density is at its highest at about 2,000 persons per square mile in some parts of the South-West coast. Similarly there are some tracts in Bengal, where a large population of 14 million is maintained at a mean density of 935 persons to the square mile The mean density of some of the other countries is England and Wales 685 persons to the square mile, Europe as a whole 127 persons, the United States of America 41, Japan 443 and China proper 200 to 220

The abnormal density noticed in parts of the country is doubtless due to the productivity of the soil and other features favourable to gainful occupations. A closer investigation may suggest the desirability of redistributing the population in particular regions by adjusting the density according to the sustaining capacity of each

The increase of population of India, as a whole, since 1911 has been 37 7 million or about 12 per cent. of the total In the decade ended 1931, the increase was 33 9 million persons or 10 6 per cent At this rate of growth, India in 13 5 years increases her population by an amount equal to the entire present population of the United Kingdom including Northern Ireland If calculation be made at the average rate of growth since 1911, the same increase will take place in about 24 5 years

The average death-rate in British India for the ten years ended 1930 was 24 5 per 1,000 of the total population The corresponding death-rate in the United Kingdom was 12 5, in France 16 3, in Germany 11 1, in the United States of America 11 3, and in Japan 18 17 The average birth-rate for British India was also high, being 32 9 per 1,000 persons for the decade ended 1930 The corresponding figures for other countries were · the United Kingdom 16 3, France 17 4, Germany 17.5, the United States of America 18 9 and Japan 32 35 The infant mortality (deaths under 1 year per 1,000 living births) in 1930 in British India was 18 The rate in the United States of America was 65, in the United Kingdom 63, Germany 85, France 78 and Japan 124

The demographic survey of India shows that the population has been growing very rapidly and that both birth- and death-rates have been high and infant mortality has been excessive The expectation of life in British India, according to the Census of 1931, is only 26 7 years, the latest figures available for other countries being—England 57 6, the United States of America 56 4, Germany 49 04, France 50 5 and Japan 44 5

According to the Census of 1931, the urban population of India numbered 38 98 million persons and the rural 313 86 million The urban population was thus 11 and the rural 89 per cent of the whole The corresponding percentages of urban and rural populations were in England and Wales 80 and 20 respectively, in Germany 62 and 38, in France 49 05 and 50 95, in the United States of America 56 2 and 43 8, in Canada 53 7 and 46 3 and in Japan 56 0 and 44.0

Population Gainfully Employed

Of the total population of India in 1931, the actual workers numbered 153,916,050 Of these latter, 152,071,213 were engaged in gainful occupations and the remaining 1,844,837 in unproductive ones The workers constituted a little over two-fifths of the total population and they were employed in a large number of callings which may be analysed roughly into the following classes —

Occupation	Actual workers (1931)	Percentage of total population
Agriculture, including fishing and hunting .. .	103,294,430	29 2
Industry including Exploitation of Minerals ..	15,697,953	4 4
Trade and Transport	10,235,003	2 9
Public Force and Public Administration .	1,836,758	0 6
Professions and Liberal Arts .	2 310,141	0 7
Domestic Service .	10,898,277	3 1
Other undefined occupations	7,778 612	2 2
Unproductive	1,844,837	0 5
Total Workers	153,916,050	43 6

EDUCATION

The number of literate persons in India, according to the Census of 1931, was 23,969,751 men and 4,169,105 women, or a total of 28,138,856 persons, representing a proportion of 8 0 per cent of the total population, which in that year amounted to 352 8 million The corresponding proportion based on population aged 10 years and over comes to 11 0 per cent in British India For other countries, the corresponding proportions, on the basis of population aged 10 and upwards, are Great Britain 92 5 per cent , France 94 1, Germany 99 7 or practically 100, the United States of America 95 7, Japan 96.0, Canada 94 9 and Australia 98 3 These percentages are based on the latest Census records available for each of the countries named, the year of such record for India and the United States of America being 1931 and 1930 respectively, and for the rest ranging between 1921 and 1926 Published reports show that Soviet Russia has reduced illiteracy from 83 per cent to 10 per cent since the revolution.

Just as in the distribution of the population, only one-ninth is urban, so in point of education only one-twelfth of the total population is literate Literacy was practically at a standstill during the past decade and ruralization has been on the increase These are grave national defects, prejudicial to the efficiency and progress of the nation No one, however, seems to realize that a radical change of policy in this respect is urgently called for The aim of India within the next ten years should be to reduce illiteracy, as rapidly as possible, to increase the urban population to about 40 per cent. and to bring down the rural to 60 per cent from the present proportions of 11 and 89, respectively

According to the latest statistics, the number of educational institutions in British India for the year 1930-31 was 262,068, and that of scholars attending them 12,689,086 This gives one institution for every 1,036 persons of the total population Taking elementary education alone, the number of schools was 204,384 and of pupils 9,362,748, giving a rate of one school for every 1,329 persons of the population

The number of persons attending educational institutions is very large in all progressive countries save India The figures in Table X—the latest available—show that the percentage of population attending educational institutions in British India was only 4 67, whereas that in Great Britain was 18 8, and in Japan 19, and in the United States of America and Canada, the proportions go up to the extraordinary figures of 23 7 and 24 4 respectively While in British India one in every 21 persons of the total population is attending educational institutions, the corresponding proportion in the United States of America and Canada is about 1 in 4 Including adult and vocational classes, one-quarter of the entire population of these two countries is at school In Soviet Russia in 1933, the population in school and college was computed to be about 26 million, that is, one in every 6 of the total population was under instruction This gives a tremendous pull in preparing their population for business life Money may be wanting for starting schools, but the least that the Government of the country should do is to carry on propaganda drawing attention to the vital importance of mass education and to the many ways in which private effort and enterprise may be enlisted in this behalf Money spent on education will in the long run prove a productive investment

The expenditure on education in British India for the year 1930-31 was Rs 28 32 crores This gives a rate of Rs 22 3 per head of school-going population and only a rupee per head for the entire population The corresponding figures per head of school-going population in other countries were Rs 58 in Japan, Rs 172 in Great Britain, Rs 199 in Canada and Rs 275 in the United States of America In Soviet Russia, in the four-year period in which the first Five-year Plan was completed, a sum of 11,290,000,000 roubles (roughly Rs 1,584 crores) was spent on education, giving Rs 158 per head of population under instruction Taking the expenditure per head of the entire population, the amount in Japan is Rs 11, in the United Kingdom Rs 32 4, in Canada Rs 48 and in the United States of America Rs 65 The amount spent on education per head in the United States of America is about equal to the entire income per head in British India

The total number of institutions connected with professional and technical education of the University grade in 1930-31 was 8 colleges of Agriculture, 7 of Engineering, and 7 of Commerce, and the students in these Colleges numbered 1,033, 2,129 and 1,727, respectively The lower grade institutions giving instruction in the same three subjects numbered 162, and the scholars undergoing training in them 9,172 It will be seen that the provision made in this country for professional and technical education is extremely meagre The number of scholars under professional and technical instruction of all grades in British India in 1931 was 94,610, whereas in Japan for the same year the number is reported to have been as high as 1,586,062

There were in 1930-31 in British India 1,708 newspapers of which 221 were dailies The number of all classes of newspapers and periodicals published was 4,468 or 16 4 per million of the population The number for the whole of India including Indian States comes to 12 6 per million The corresponding figures for other countries are—the United States of America 172, Japan 155, Canada 158 and Soviet Russia 100 The total number of printing presses in British India was 6,520, and the books published numbered 2,353 in English and European languages and 14,084 in the vernaculars

Production

The total cultivated area in British India in 1930-31 including current fallows was 278,732,854 acres, that is, 1 02 acres per head of the total population of British India Of this, the irrigated area amounted to 49,097,216 acres This gives a *per capita* average of 0 84 acre of dry crop and 0 18 acre of irrigated crop for the entire population of British India

The total agricultural production of all-India in 1921-22 was estimated at Rs 2,032 crores or about

Rs 64 per head of the population The corresponding *per capita* production for the United States of America may be taken at Rs 175, for Canada Rs 213, for Japan Rs 57 and for the United Kingdom Rs 62 The industrial production of all classes including minor and agricultural industries for 1921-22 was estimated at about Rs 408 crores for all-India, and this gives a *per capita* value of about Rs 12 There may have been a small increase since The corresponding *per capita* figure for the United States of America is Rs 721, for the United Kingdom Rs 412, for Canada Rs 470 and for Japan Rs 158 The industrial production of Japan has shot ahead within the past thirty or forty years by reason of the sound industrialization policies pursued in that country The total production of India from both agriculture and industries for the year 1921-22 may be taken at Rs 2,500 crores, which on the basis of the present population comes to Rs 71 per head On account of the prevailing depression, the aggregate value of production at the present time must be much lower than this figure

TRADE

At the present time trade is in an abnormally depressed condition Taking the year 1928-29, that is, the year immediately preceding the depression, imports of merchandise were valued at Rs 253 3 crores and exports at Rs 330 1 crores, giving a trade balance of Rs 76 8 crores in favour of India This gives a *per capita* value of about Rs 17 for the total trade of the country The corresponding figure for the United Kingdom in the same year was Rs 597, for the United States of America Rs 214, for Canada Rs 920 and for Japan Rs 90 Taking the latest published returns available, the average *per capita* trade was for all-India

Rs 7 6, for the United Kingdom Rs 324, the United States of America Rs 84, Japan Rs 47 and Canada Rs 304[1] The latter set of figures, however, relates to a time of phenomenal trade depression and cannot be regarded as normal

The total world trade in 1929, before the present trade depression set in, was about Rs 19,000 crores and in 1933 Rs 7,700 crores, a reduction of 59 5 per cent. in 4 years

Transport and Communications

The total mileage of metalled and unmetalled roads in British India in 1930-31 was 253,125 Of this, 27,339 miles of metalled and 21,294 of unmetalled roads were maintained by Government and 46,716 miles of metalled and 157,776 of unmetalled roads by the municipalities and other local authorities

The total length of railways in India for 1931-32 was 42,753 miles, giving a rate of 120 miles per million inhabitants in the country The corresponding figures for other countries were the United States of America, total length 261,816 miles and per million inhabitants 2,132 miles, the United Kingdom 21,162 and 460, Canada 43,173 and 4,318 and Japan 13,363 and 206 Japan, though a mountainous country surrounded on all sides by the sea and much of its trade is done by shipping, has a larger railway mileage per head of population than India

The tonnage of shipping entered into, and cleared

[1] These figures pertain to the years noted against each country named —

British India .. .	1932–33
United States of America .	1931–32
United Kingdom .	1932
Japan .. .	1931
Canada	1932

from, Indian ports during 1931-32 was 20 5 million The average for three years ending 1931–32 was 15 million tons The corresponding figures for other countries were the United Kingdom 161 million tons, Canada 66 million, the United States of America 146 million and Japan 110 million

In 1930-31, the number of vessels registered in India was 409 and their tonnage 0 27 million As against this, the following figures show the gross tonnage of merchant vessels in other countries the United Kingdom 19 7 million, the United States of America 13 4 million, Japan 4 3 million and Canada 1 5 million Owing to unfair competition and lack of a development policy, there is very little building of merchant vessels going on in India

The tonnage of shipping entered and cleared at Indian ports stood at 17 4 million in 1913 immediately before the War and it rose to 18 87 in 1928-29, showing that India has made no progress in overseas travel or communications In the same period, the tonnage in Canada rose from 26 2 to 52 9 million excluding that of the coasting trade, which was 87 73 million

In 1931-32, the number of post offices in India was 23,983 The total number of letters, post cards and money orders which passed through the post offices in that year was 1,014,592,000 The number of newspapers was 76,498,000, of parcels 14,110,000 and of packets 107,313,000, making a total of 1,212,513,000 This represents 3 4 articles per head of the total population In some of the other countries the corresponding rates were the United States of America 216, the United Kingdom 144 and Japan 87

There were 18 1 million telegraph messages delivered during the year 1931, or 51 per 1,000 persons of the population The corresponding figures for other countries, for one or the other years between 1927 and 1931, were 1,129 for the United Kingdom, 941 for Japan, 1,951 for the United States of America and 2,145 for Canada

The number of telephone connections in India was 55,850 in 1932, or about 1 6 for every 10,000 inhabitants in the country In Japan the corresponding number was 110, in Australia 830, in the United States of America 1,634, in the United Kingdom 446 and in Canada 1,410 These figures show that communications in this country are very inadequate and business activities incredibly low

FINANCES

The gross Government revenue in British India including the Provinces and Local Government institutions for 1932-33 amounted to Rs 268 crores, or roughly Rs 10 per head of the population Of this sum the revenue of the Central Government amounted to Rs 129 96 crores The corresponding figures for other countries, for one or the other years between 1931 and 1933, respectively were the United Kingdom Rs 1,334 crores, the United States of America Rs 2,732 crores, Canada Rs 205 crores and Japan Rs 459 crores (*Vide* Table III)

DEFENCE

The Defence Forces of India consist of

The Units of the British Regular Army,

The Indian Army,

The Royal Indian Marine, and

The Air Force

It may be mentioned that in the Great War (1914-18) the total contribution of personnel by India was 1,457,000 men, of whom, 1,381,000 served overseas This is equivalent to about 25 per cent. of the total forces

—5,704,000 officers and men—contributed by Great Britain The Overseas Dominions sent between them 12 per cent of the same total

In 1932, the strength of the Regular Army consisted of about 59,773 British and 162,600 Indian troops.

The other subsidiary forces were —

Auxiliary Forces .	30,200
Territorial Forces	15,400
Indian Army Reserve .	36 000
Indian State Forces	41,974
TOTAL	123,574
making a grand total of	345,947

The corresponding figures for Great Britain were 138,023 regulars actually in that county and a total of 198,334 in Great Britain, in India and abroad These figures do not include the strength of the Territorial and Reserve forces in Great Britain The army of all ranks in the United States of America numbered 133,200 in 1932, that in Japan 276,647 and in Canada only 3,800

There is no regular Indian Navy to speak of at present The Royal Indian Marine is now a combatant force consisting of four sloops, two surveying vessels and two patrol vessels The contribution made by India towards the naval expenditure of the British Commonwealth compared with that of the Dominions is as follows —

	£
India	167,400
New Zealand	100,000
South Africa ..	85,000
Australia	49,100
Canada .	10,800
Newfoundland . .	3,000
TOTAL .	415,300

If the Bill to create a navy for India, introduced into the Legislative Assembly in November 1933, is passed by that body, an Indian Navy will come into existence as a separate force

The Royal Air Force forms part of the defence services of India and is controlled by the Commander-in-Chief with the Government of India The total establishment consists of 244 officers, 1,850 airmen, 891 Indian officers, other ranks and followers and 464 civilians There are 8 squadrons, 7 of which are stationed along the North-West Frontier and one at Ambala

The military expenditure for 1930-31 was Rs 57 39 crores Including marine expenditure of Rs 90 41 lakhs, the total defence expenditure may be taken at Rs 68 29 crores This is reduced to Rs 50 92 crores according to the Budget Estimates for 1932-33 The corresponding total expenditure on defence in the United Kingdom was Rs 118 crores, in the United States of America Rs 169 crores, in Japan Rs 63 crores and in Canada only Rs 3 5 crores In proportion to her revenue, let alone other considerations, the defence expenditure of India is excessive While India till recently spent nearly half its central revenues on its defences, Canada spent practically very little No wonder that Canada has had ample resources to build up her prosperity

OUTPUT OF WORK

According to the latest figures available, the total capacity of electric supply plants in twelve of the leading countries of the world is estimated at about 79 million kilowatts Of this, the capacity of plants in India is estimated at about a million kilowatts, that in the United Kingdom at 5 8 million, in the United States of

America 31 6 million and in Japan 4 million The output of energy in thousand million units (kilowatt hours) in India is 1 8, in the United Kingdom 16 6, in the United States of America 115, in Japan 14 1 and the total output for the world is estimated at 260 billion kilowatt hours

The comparative output of work per person in the various countries of the world is estimated as follows [2]

China ..	1
British India .	1½
Italy .	2¾
Japan . .	3½
France	8¼
Germany	12
Great Britain	18
Canada . .	20
The United States of America	30

The differences in output arise from the liberal use of machinery and artificial motive power for production and other activities by the more progressive nations The above figures show that the United States of America and Canada, by reason of their large hydro-electric and other power plants and superior organization, are in advance of every other country in the world in the output of work per head of population India occupies a place practically at the bottom of the list because she continues to carry on all her field, farm and factory work by manual labour

INCOME, ASSETS, ETC

Table III gives the statistics of wealth, income and taxation of five of the principal countries of the world compared with India The figures given vary with the

[2] Thomas J Read, "The American Secret" in *The Atlantic Monthly*, March 1927.

production and prices from year to year, and also with varying rates of exchange, so the comparison can only be regarded as approximate Besides, they are not all for the same year Making allowance for all these, the average income for British India in a normal year may be taken at about Rs 82 per head of the total population In the present slump, it would be correct to take the average at about two-thirds of the normal, or Rs 55 per head

It will be seen from the same Table that the average income in Japan is Rs 271 *per capita*, in Germany Rs 634, in France Rs 636, in the United Kingdom Rs 1,092, in Canada Rs 1,268 and in the United States of America Rs 2,053 The income in the United Kingdom is thus nearly 13 times that of India and that in the United States more than 25 times The average *per capita* income in Japan is nearly 3½ times the corresponding income in India The Government and the people of Japan started late in their career to increase wealth but nevertheless have contrived by utilizing every opportunity, including scientific inventions and commerce, to raise production and income rapidly Less than sixty years ago, the conditions in Japan were on about the same level as they are in India to-day

The total wealth of the United States of America is estimated at Rs 112,315 crores as compared with Rs 12,000 crores in British India or about 9 times, notwithstanding that the population of India is three times greater The United Kingdom has property valued at Rs 29,432 crores or about 2½ times as large as that of India One of the leading economists in America, Mr Julius Barnes, stated a decade ago that America had amassed wealth aggregating $300 billion or Rs 83,333 crores, and Great Britain $170 billion or Rs 47,222 crores, out of the total wealth of the world amounting to about $1,000 billion or Rs 277,777 crores. The wealth of India as a whole may be taken at about Rs 15,500 crores and it will be seen that, with 17 per cent. of the world's population, India has only 5 per cent of the world's goods According to a later report, America, with only 7 per cent of world's population, has accumulated about 40 per cent of the world's wealth.

CHAPTER III
AGRICULTURE

Agricultural Data—Defects in Rural Areas—Agricultural Improvements Ordinarily Attempted—Occupations Associated with Agriculture—Agricultural Organization—New Developments in Agriculture—Training the Rural Population—The Problem in a Nutshell

AGRICULTURAL DATA

THE total area of land surface of India is 1 8 million square miles and that of British India alone 1 1 million square miles The land surface in British India thus forms 2 15 per cent of that of the entire world, estimated at 51 million square miles The cultivated or cropped area in British India is 261 9 million acres (409,240 square miles), equivalent to 37 5 per cent of its total area According to Government statistics, there is, in addition to this, an area of 154 million acres designated as "cultivable waste", not brought under the plough This represents 22 per cent of the total area of British India The question how much of the cultivable waste can be brought under cultivation by the application of scientific methods and machinery requires early investigation

The population of British India, according to the Census of 1931, is 271 5 million of which the agricultural population alone is estimated at 192 million persons, or 70 6 per cent of the whole This gives slightly less than one acre of cultivated land per head of the entire population of British India and 1 4 acres per head of the actual agricultural population

The total area irrigated in British India in 1930-31 amounted to 49.7 million acres of which, in round figures, 26 million acres were from canals, 6 8 million from tanks, 11.7 million from wells and 5 3 million more from other sources Of the total area, over 22 million acres were watered by Government irrigation works The capital invested on irrigation, including improvements to old works, amounted at the end of 1930-31 to Rs 136 44 crores The gross revenue and working expenses during that year amounted to Rs 12 09 and Rs 5 69 crores respectively, giving a net return of 4 69 per cent on the total capital invested

The number of cattle (oxen and buffaloes) maintained in British India in 1930-31 for cultivation, draught and milk supply came to 152 8 million, or 56 cattle per 100 persons of the total population, and 58 cattle per 100 acres cultivated

The acreage and yield of the principal crops in British India for 1930-31 were —

Name of crop	Area sown (Million acres)	Yield
Rice	80 6	33 2 million tons
Wheat	21 8	9 3 ,,
Other food grains[1]	78 3	18 4 ,,
Oil seeds	16 4	2 0 ,,
Sugarcane	2 9	3 2 ,,
Cotton	14 2	6 8 million bales
Jute .	3 4	11 2 ,,
Tea, Coffee and Rubber (1929-30)	1 04	448 million lbs

[1] Only those of which the yield is known

The quantity of food grains required to feed the population has been estimated at between 85 and 90 million tons per annum But the yield of food crops sown over about 203 million acres, in a normal year, amounts to between 60 and 70 million tons If allowance is made for the quantity required for seed, feeding cattle and export, the balance left will be barely 50 million tons, showing that the food supply of the population in a country deemed to be predominantly agricultural falls far short of the demand

In the year 1898, the Famine Commission estimated that the annual food grain production in British India was about 51 5 million tons and that its requirements were 47 million tons The population at that time was about 231 26 million and since then there has been an increase of over 40 27 million There is sufficient justification for the appointment of a committee to investigate these questions with a view to remove any uncertainties in respect of the food supply of the people The committee should give for each province the quantities of food crops in a normal year, as compared with the requirements of its people, and proposals and suggestions should be put forward as to how and from what sources the supply could be supplemented to ensure that there will be no food shortage in years of scarcity

The yield of crops per acre is low chiefly because cultivation in many parts of the country is still primitive. The following table shows the average yield of rice and wheat (two staple articles of diet) per acre in India, as compared with the yield in some of the countries where cultivation is intensive, or scientific and up-to-date. The figures are for 1931-32[4] —

[4] *Statistical Year Book of the League of Nations* (1932-33).

Country	Rice	Wheat
	(lbs)	(lbs)
Italy	4,001	1,241
Japan .	2,767	1,508
Egypt .	2,356	1 688
United States of America	2,112	973
United Kingdom	.	1,812
Germany .	.	1,710
India .	1,357	652

The annual income of British India from agriculture is estimated at Rs 1,568 crores which gives an average return of Rs 60 3 per acre cultivated including irrigated crops, and of Rs 59 per head of the total population The corresponding *per capita* agricultural income was Rs 102 in Sweden in 1931 and, as stated already, it was in the United States of America Rs 175 in 1929 and in Canada Rs 213 in 1930 This comparison is no indication of the relative values of production from all sources, since India is utilizing three-fourths of its man power on this one industry of agriculture alone, while in the three countries cited, the income from industries and other sources is considerably larger than from agriculture One writer on economics[5] estimates that "agriculture in India is only 86 per cent as efficient as the average production in the important countries of the world, but, compared with most of the European countries, it would be scarcely more than 50 per cent as efficient "

The agricultural population of British India has a debt variously estimated at between Rs 800 and

[5] Rajani Kanta Das, *The Industrial Efficiency of India* (1930), p 29

Rs 1,200 crores The actual debt is probably not under Rs 950 crores, or say, Rs 50 per head of the total agricultural population

DEFECTS IN RURAL AREAS

There are many grave defects in the organization and operations of agriculture in this country and in the policies governing its administration which account for its present backward condition A brief reference will be made to some of the principal defects noticed and the reforms considered necessary

All progressive countries in the modern world are moving towards industrialization In India, on the other hand, the tendency has long been in the opposite direction According to the Census of 1891, the population dependent on agriculture was 59 8 per cent It rose to 71 3 per cent in 1911 and to 73 per cent in 1931 These figures point to the progressive ruralization of the country They show that 3 out of every 4 persons in India derive their support from the land The true significance of this will be understood when it is remembered that it is "only in the non-industrialized, poverty-stricken countries of the East does the land hold and gain population "[6]

The following percentages indicate the proportion of population employed in agriculture in India, including Indian States, and in five progressive countries —

[6] L W White and E W Shanahan, *The Industrial Revolution and the Economic World To-day* (1932), pp 346, 347

Country	Year	Percentage of population employed in agriculture, fishing, etc., to the total working population
England and Wales	1921	7 1
United States of America	1930	22 0
Canada	1931	31.2
Germany	1925	30 5
France	1926	38 3
Japan	1930	50 3
India	1931	67 2

The chief reason of the backwardness of agriculture is the appalling extent of illiteracy noticed in the country Want of education keeps the people ignorant of the scientific practices and modern methods which Western civilization has developed for increasing production and income The people are still guided by old-time traditions They have no regard for time Co-operation is wanting There is much waste of resource, discipline is little understood, women who constitute about 50 per cent of the total population are employed only in the least gainful of occupations All these defects are in the main due to the absence of an active State policy to abolish illiteracy and to train the people to lead orderly and disciplined lives

With the growth of population, the land is being divided and subdivided from generation to generation and, at present, the holdings in many parts of the country are of very small size In 1921, according to the official reports, there were on an average 2 2 acres of cultivation per worker in Bengal and about 3 acres in the major provinces except Bombay, North-West Frontier Province and the Punjab where the average was said to be 10½ acres The holdings are so small that machinery and modern scientific methods cannot be profitably applied to increase their yield This arises from the absence of diversity of occupations and the concentration of overwhelming numbers upon agricultural land for their means of livelihood

It was pointed out by Mr H B Clayton, a Bombay Member in the Legislative Assembly, on February 6, 1934, that agricultural labour was so unorganized, that it had not a single official representative in any legislature in the country who could speak for it There were in India 70 per cent agricultural labourers as compared with only 3 per cent textile workers

The rural population is at present usefully employed only for 4 to 6 months in the year and, if suitable machinery and modern methods of production are utilized in cultivation, it is computed that all their work can be done in less than 90 days

Thanks to the introduction of machinery, power and scientific methods, in countries like the United States of America, Canada and Russia, it has been demonstrated that commodities could be manufactured more rapidly than at any time before It is estimated that, if all the work on peasant farms in Russia were organized as efficiently as that on State farms in that country, the 26 million peasant house-holders comprising a 100 million population could be displaced by 1,200,000 persons[7] In one sense this newly acquired capacity for rapid production is a great gain to humanity The problem that is now engaging the attention of statesmen

[7] Stephen Viljoen, *Economic Tendencies of To-day* (1933), p. 53.

and thinkers in many parts of the world is how to distribute the increased production in an equitable manner and to enable the entire population to share both the labour and benefits of rapid production

Sufficient diversity of occupations is lacking, modern machinery and scientific methods have not been introduced into the country on any appreciable scale to help in increasing production If there were a balanced structure of occupations, less than half the population now employed in it would be sufficient for agriculture In the natural course, the rest of that population should be provided with work in industries and other occupations It wants large-scale operations and the adoption of a multi-productional programme to do this Appropriate changes should be effected to safeguard the country's future interests in this respect

Another important handicap is what has already been referred to, namely, the indebtedness of the rural population, which comes to about Rs 36 per acre cultivated Measures for relief of this ever-growing evil are overdue, as also for bringing capital within the reach of the cultivator for normal agricultural operations and for carrying on cottage industries

The high rate of exchange maintained by Government in opposition to Indian opinion is also injurious to agriculture As about 80 per cent. of the expenses of cultivation constitutes the wages of labour, the farmer receives fewer rupees for his products sold in foreign countries, while the expenses of cultivation remain the same

Agricultural Improvements Ordinarily Attempted

The main object to be aimed at is to increase the quantity of the products and improve their quality The most remunerative products that can be cultivated in the area should be grown and the production of only those among them for which there is a demand should be attempted A large proportion will of course be the staple products used by the farmer and his family, that is, those most in demand for the support of the rural population generally

The following are some of the more important facilities needed in the normal course to improve the quality and increase the quantity of agricultural products —

Selection of good seed,
Application of fertilizers including artificial manures,
Protection from insect, vermin and fungoid pests,
Use of modern tools and implements,
Healthy live-stock,
Supply of working capital at reasonable rates of interest,
Cheap and rapid transportation, and
Favourable marketing facilities

The waste of natural manures which often takes place in rural areas should be prevented and their judicious use in cultivation at the proper time and in proper condition encouraged Artificial manures should be used under the advice of experts, wherever their application is found to be remunerative Live-stock should be maintained in a healthy condition for agricultural operations, milk supply and transport For perishable articles used as food, the transport in a tropical country like India should be rapid and for this purpose railways and motor transport should be increasingly availed of

For working capital, the cultivator is still largely dependent upon the indigenous money-lender Co-operative credit societies are giving some help, particularly to small farms But it is recognized that they only serve as a brake on indebtedness These societies need strengthening, and an independent organization is also necessary for the supply of working capital for large farms A few land mortgage banks have been started in Madras, the Punjab, Bombay, Bengal and Assam But their establishment is due to the enterprise of the local Governments under pressure from public opinion and not the result of any far-seeing policy on the part of the Central Government A suitable country-wide banking organization for supplying rural credit for both intensive and extensive development of agriculture is a desideratum In a recent Government resolution on the Provincial Economic Conference held in Simla in May 1934, it is stated that consideration was given to the possibility of establishing land mortgage banks and to the functions of the agricultural credit department of the Reserve Bank

The cultivators should be able to obtain advice regarding the chemical composition of soils and the plants or crops to which they are best suited Seed and modern tools should be available, as they are in countries like Italy, in local depots maintained by co-operative societies Sound information on current agricultural topics, on the best methods of cultivation, current prices, etc , should be disseminated through the medium of periodicals, bulletins, leaflets, lectures, cinemas, radios and travelling exhibitions

Agriculture is rightly described as a precarious occupation and it is particularly so in this country In the past, tens of millions of people have died of starvation during seasons of scarcity caused by scanty rainfall Happily the scarcities experienced since 1901 have not been so severe or frequent as the droughts and famines of the generation which preceded that year

It is hazardous for the rural population to be entirely dependent for their income on agricultural operations in a country where rainfall is so uncertain They should have, as already stated, a diversity of occupations, among these, cottage and home industries are the most important When he is under-employed, the cultivator should have opportunities of utilizing his slack time on some industry or gainful occupation, and, during periods in which agricultural operations are more or less at a standstill, suitable occupations should be found for him He should be induced to avoid debt, to practise thrift and to lay by sufficient savings to tide over bad times which unfortunately for him are too frequent

It is necessary to survey each province and region and to devise means of providing subsidiary occupations according to the circumstances of each locality In Japan, for instance, some districts are classed primarily as agricultural, and others industrial, according to the resources of each, and the people assisted and encouraged to follow recognized occupations Some such classification should be attempted both in the Indian Provinces and the States.

The following is a tentative list of rural, cottage and home industries which suggest themselves Most of these industries are practised at present in an unorganized haphazard form, their number is small and production extremely meagre The old village system which fostered these industries has given way under the stress of Western civilization and no modern or organized methods have as yet replaced it

Agricultural tools and smithing,
Live-stock raising and dairying,
Fruit culture,
Kitchen gardening,
Sugar manufacture,

Fishing,
Carpentry, furniture, woodwork and cart manufacture,
Hand-spinning and weaving,
Silk-rearing and reeling,
Ceramics and brick and tile making,
Copper and bell-metal ware, cutlery,
Match manufacture,
Leather work, boots and shoes,
Ropes, baskets, etc,
Cellulose industries such as plastics,
Embroidery, needle-work and socks,
Glass bangle manufacture,
Pastry and sweets,
Hand-made paper,
Toys, and many others

Reference is also invited to the list of cottage industries given on page 70 under Industries

OCCUPATIONS ASSOCIATED WITH AGRICULTURE

Certain special classes of occupations associated with agriculture will now be briefly explained

The most profitable form of cultivation under which crops of the highest value are grown is through irrigation. The supply of water for irrigation is either natural in the shape of rain or artificial when derived from tanks, canals, wells, etc As explained before, there are vast tracts of canal-irrigated areas in this country aggregating over 50 million acres, *i e*, the largest irrigated area in any country in the world

A large staff of experienced engineers and subordinates is employed on irrigation works and their duties include the protection of the land against over-irrigation or water-logging and salt efflorescence. From the time of the Irrigation Commission of 1901, there has been a rapid growth of new irrigation works by which scarcity and famine have been averted over large areas

The principal plantation industries are tea, coffee and rubber Tea is grown in Assam, Bengal, Madras,- Bihar and Orissa, the Punjab, United Provinces and Coorg The area cultivated in 1930-31 was 774,683 acres and the estimated production 391 million lbs Roughly over 80 per cent or the greater part of the tea grown in the country is exported chiefly to England, the value of the quantity so exported in 1931-32 being about Rs 19 crores Coffee and rubber are confined mostly to South India In 1929-30 the area under coffee was 163,000 acres and the quantity grown 352,000 cwts The export of coffee in 1930-31 was valued at Rs 1 92 crores The area under rubber in 1930-31 was 172,100 acres and the quantity grown a little over 24 million lbs

The area of forests in British India including Burma was in the aggregate over 249,710 square miles in the year 1930-31 But Burma has a large share in this, namely, 147,033 square miles Many of the forests are operated for timber supply The total outturn of timber and fuel in 1930-31 was 323 million cubic feet and the minor produce was valued at Rs 126 lakhs Bamboo forms an important part of the forest produce It has been demonstrated that, if bamboo is properly conserved and systematically cultivated, its pulp would provide raw material for the paper industry not only in India but for the greater part of the world The recent tariff protection for paper in India is based on this theory

Both forests and fisheries provide occupations to inhabitants of tracts along the boundaries of forests and sea-shore By proper organization and planning, there is room for considerable further improvement A satisfactory organization seems called for to utilize these two sources as a means of increasing occupations for the people

Agricultural Organization

The agricultural organization of the country consists of the Imperial Bureau of Agricultural Research and various agricultural colleges, schools and experimental farms in the provinces In some of the latter, demonstrations and scientific research are carried on and seed stores maintained

The officers of the Departments, both Central and Provincial, are doing solid work to spread scientific practices and information among the cultivators, but the impression made so far is inappreciable, except in the production of a few special crops like cotton, jute, wheat and sugarcane and on a smaller scale, rice and jawar The great drawback is that there is no organization for co-ordinated effort between Government officers and the farmers towards the solution of agricultural problems

There should be two parallel organizations, namely, one, composed of Government officials and the other, of agricultural associations consisting of leading farmers, experts and business men Representatives of these should have seats on boards committees and societies in each province, district and village group, respectively, as well as on a similar Central Agricultural or Economic Council The efforts of all these bodies should be suitably co-ordinated Reports and statistics for each area should be comprehensive, and all vital agricultural matters should be thoroughly elucidated, and sound policies and plans spread among the people to prevent waste in production and loss of opportunities

Such boards, committees and societies should be

closely associated with experimental and demonstration farms and research stations in the districts, as is done in the United States of America and Japan An organization of this sort will without doubt succeed, if administrative policies encourage co-operation of the people on a large scale

The district and provincial farms should be at all times prepared to solve the day-to-day agricultural problems referred to them by the cultivators The cultivators in each area should be advised by the board as to what is happening to production and prices in different parts of India and in competing countries outside it Cultivators should be able to obtain an analysis of soils from Government research stations and advice as to what crops could be best grown on them Besides the character of the soil the nature of the crops grown will depend upon water resources, demand for the product, and the working advance available for meeting the expenses of profitable cultivation

The organization and activities of the United States Department of Agriculture seem to be a model for India to follow The Department is described as a thoroughly business-like institution and it has an army of over 20,000 able workers of every kind The functions of the American Board of Agriculture are performed by 17 Bureaux which act as an Intelligence Department by providing agriculturists with valuable information of every kind Speaking of the functions of the Department of Agriculture, a recent English writer[8] states —

"The Department of Agriculture acts like a University A University has a two-fold purpose research and tuition. The United States Board of Agriculture acts like a gigantic University It carries out research by thousands of experts of its own In addition, research is carried on independently

[8] ...aker, *America's Secret* (1927), pp 213-215

by thousands of experts employed by the richly-endowed Departments of Agriculture belonging to the individual States. The results of these investigations and of the experiments made by private societies and individuals are collected, sifted and classified at Washington, and are then communicated to the agriculturists by means of pamphlets, books, etc . . The United States Department of Agriculture teaches not only by means of its publications—it might fitly be described as the greatest Correspondence School in the world—but also by lecturing, as does every University"

The Department of Agriculture of the Government of India controls the Imperial Council of Agricultural Research established with the object of promoting, guiding and co-ordinating agricultural and veterinary research throughout India There are a Governing Body and an Advisory Board The Council has investigated or has been investigating questions relating to cereals, sugarcane, hemp and other products of agriculture Efforts are being made to help special crops and problems, committees have been appointed for sugar, the locust problem, fertilizers and hemp, and special attention is being devoted to develop the Indian rice industry and tobacco The Imperial Council is also busy considering many questions connected with crops, soils, animal health and husbandry

In most provinces, as already stated, there is a Department of Agriculture, an agricultural college, a research institute, a civil veterinary department and an institute for veterinary research, animal husbandry and dairying Their defect at present is that their activities do not permeate to the lower strata of our farm population

Agricultural statistics, so far as details go, seem adequate But the economic implications of such statistics are either excluded or are absent from the reports of the Agricultural Departments Dr A L Bowley and Mr D H Robertson, in their Scheme already referred to, remark· "To put it briefly, the statistics even of crop production leave much to be desired, while statistical information about other important parts of agricultural income, such as the output of animal husbandry, are almost completely lacking, and statistics of industrial production are patchy in the extreme" Even the Royal Commission on Agriculture has found it necessary to comment adversely on this deficiency It should be possible to say from the Government statistics and reports how production of food supply in a province stands in relation to demand or consumption, what increases in products are necessary, how the needs in respect of raw materials for industries are met, and so on This omission will have to be supplied in future

There should be permanent agricultural museums established in every city and large town and also in a centrally situated village in a village group which has a local organization to promote the interests of agriculture Such museums should maintain books and pamphlets giving descriptions of the latest agricultural practices, specimens of farm products, tools and machinery They should also give demonstrations and hold annual agricultural exhibitions This might with advantage be done in connection with local festivities by the co-operative effort of the farmers and with the encouragement and support of Government The chief need is organization, the Government officials and the people should come closer together and take a live interest in promoting agricultural prosperity

New Developments in Agriculture

The art of cultivation is improving in several directions and various new methods are fast coming to be adopted for increasing and cheapening production.

Reference will be made here to the more important of these developments, leaving it to the cultivators of each local area to choose what suits them best and to seek detailed information from the Agricultural Departments and Colleges, Institutes, etc, of Agriculture in their respective provinces

Intensive cultivation is possible only where irrigation facilities exist Dry crop cultivation in many parts of the country is dependent on rainfall, which is confined to about four months in the year, and during these four months also occasionally there is drought and scarcity The Indian cultivator is, therefore, not prepared to take any large risks by spending money on expensive tools, machinery and fertilizers in areas where rainfall is precarious

The production of large quantities of crops is also rendered possible by the use of machinery worked by motive power In America, machinery to plough, sow and reap, is extensively used, the motive power being chiefly gasolene which is also produced cheap in that country The principal machines in use are the tractor, harvester, thresher and the combine

The combine cuts and threshes the wheat all in one operation A labourer who formerly ploughed one acre with a pair of horses is now able to plough at least twelve acres a day with a tractor By this quickening of agricultural practices, the human labour required is minimised One result of such reduction is that the total population engaged in agriculture in the United States of America has remained stationary since 1900, while the volume of production due to the use of new machinery and methods has undergone considerable increase Through these means, the growing population of America is kept abundantly supplied with food and other primary products Over half a million farms in that country are worked by machinery operated by electric power.

In Great Britain, too, a drive towards home-production is taking place by a larger use of machinery in agriculture with a view to making the country more self-contained

Soviet Russia is encouraging the use of tractors of which there are to-day about 200,000 in use in that country Till recently she was importing automobiles, tractors and raw cotton from America, but she has now become a producer of these commodities herself and has stopped importation She is reported to be manufacturing locally at the rate of 300 tractors and 650 motor cars a day, her plan for 1934 provides for the manufacture of 115,300 tractors and 72,000 cars

Both machinery and gasolene are dear in India. Tractors, steam-ploughing machinery, etc, are being slowly introduced The use of pumps and engines is increasing and electrical pumping for irrigation is resorted to in parts of the country like the Punjab, Mysore, etc

Production of huge quantities of commodities mainly by machinery and mass production methods is one of the new and most notable developments The new methods are very successful in the case of staple commodities the demand for which is considerable. One effect of such production is the lowering of costs. There have been occasions when wheat grown in Canada and Australia was sold at Karachi at prices cheaper than that grown by the farmers of Sind

In the United States of America the average size of a farm was 157 acres in 1930 With the use of machinery, the number of workers required for these farms is being reduced and it is computed that in the past 50 years the average size of the farm *per worker* has grown from 32 acres to 49 acres or nearly 50 per cent Mr Henry Ford of automobile fame has in his own estate encouraged the idea of carrying industries to farms, in other words, combining industry with agriculture He thinks that the future of agriculture is bound up with industrialization

Under communistic policies, in Soviet Russia, small holdings are grouped together and converted into large farms to enable farmers to pool their resources and get the best crops from the combined area This is known as collectivization The evil effects of excessive fragmentation of holdings may be countered to some extent by encouraging cultivation on a co-operative basis as is being attempted in the Punjab

The development of co-operative marketing, that is, the creation of marketing organizations to secure sales for products on a co-operative basis, is also one of the business tendencies of the day Co-operative marketing brings the highest prices possible to the small farmer in the same way that large-scale production leads to reduction of costs

TRAINING THE RURAL POPULATION

The man power required for direction at present is sufficient, so far as numbers go, for any conceivable expansion of agricultural activities, individual or national, in the country But the present poverty of man power arises from widespread illiteracy and want of training The rural population being uneducated is inefficient in many ways On an average, only one person out of every 12 in the country can read and write This deficiency and the attendant lack of specialized training are tremendous handicaps to the Indian in his struggle for existence

Mass education should be compulsory Adults

should be induced by suitable propaganda to learn the three R's The education given in the schools should include the essentials of home and farm accounts, in addition to instruction on agricultural products, cottage industries and occupations Lessons should be given in discipline, particularly on the value of observing regular hours of work, thrift and habits of frankness and truthfulness so that mutual trust may grow and joint effort in farming and village improvement may become universal

Also, for every four or five villages there should be a practical training class to supplement the education imparted in elementary schools, with instruction as to the manner in which agricultural operations should be carried on and farms managed Where possible, practical instruction should be given in cottage industries, smithy, carpentry, new methods of keeping elementary accounts, operations connected with co-operative credit societies, etc , so that young persons, after receiving such training, may at once enter upon practical work with profit Also the German and American methods of earning while learning should not be lost sight of

We have referred to the various classes of training which will benefit the farmer It will not be possible to provide all this training at once to every one who has a desire for it Here the requirements of the people are clearly explained , the actual provision made should be the best that local resources may permit At the outset a small sum should be spent on investigation and propaganda with a view to bring home to the village population a clear and correct idea of their educational and agricultural deficiencies and the means of remedying the same

The measures which have freed the Russian peasantry to a full enjoyment of the advantages of modern culture and education should be brought to the notice of our peasantry, at the same time the doctrines of communism should be discouraged as unsuited to the present conditions of India Information relative to the measures which are being taken to encourage the uplift of the rural population in various parts of the country should be gathered in pamphlets and leaflets and widely circulated

In the present circumstances of the village population, it will be difficult, if not impossible, to find the money and the teachers for all the training indicated But the people of each village group should do all they can by self-help, that is, through the activities of its more prominent leaders, or through *panchayets* or *ad hoc* committees to provide these facilities The first thing that a village should do is to form a society to promote education One such society should extend its activities over a number of villages so that the services of a sufficient number of intelligent men may be secured to carry on efficiently the duties expected of it If the societies are able to collect small sums of money and organize co-operative effort for promoting education, both theoretical and practical, Government and local bodies might be able to give small grants to supplement the funds locally collected

In order to encourage co-operation, Government should give small grants and prizes to villages which successfully practise teamwork Important developments such as irrigation, town planning, drainage improvement, water supply, forest plantation, cottage industries and other similar improvements may be promoted by the co-operation of large numbers of people under the guidance of government officials and the inspiration of leading citizens connected with the locality

The principle to be kept in view is first self-help

and individual effort, then co-operation between groups of individuals, and next large-scale co-operation between all the groups for common objects over a wide area Collective effort should be fostered without discouraging individual initiative The spirit of teamwork should permeate all groups and each group should recognize its dependence upon all others The people everywhere should join forces and develop capacity to advance common objects in every sphere, local, provincial and national, by co-operative self-help This subject is dealt with in the Scheme No VI, Chapter XV and also, in greater detail in a booklet issued by the writer in the year 1931

The Problem in a Nutshell

The Indian cultivator is the mainstay of the economic structure of the country at the present time and he gets very little sympathy or aid to improve his condition

His chief needs are education, instruction in modern methods of farming and an efficient organization for rural uplift Lack of organization has been the bane of agriculture as of so many other activities of national importance in India

The illiteracy of the ryot has been explained away hitherto on the ground that Government have had no money to spare for his education, but there has been no arrangement to spread knowledge and enlightenment in any other way The ryot has had no opportunity, no means of keeping himself informed of the more efficient methods of farming pursued in Western countries and Japan

The outstanding defects of rural life may now be summed up They are the excessive pressure of the population on land, the small size of holdings and their progressive fragmentation, the primitive methods of cultivation followed, the waste of farm manure, irregular hours of labour, insufficient and uneconomical utilization of women's services, the lack of finance for farm work, the old-fashioned character of the subsidiary occupations pursued, the crushing indebtedness of the ryot, short employment, universal illiteracy and phenomenal poverty

"If the inertia of centuries is to be overcome," says the Report of the Royal Commission on Agriculture in India (1928), "it is essential that all the resources at the disposal of the State should be brought to bear on the problem of rural uplift What is required is an organized and sustained effort by all those departments whose activities touch the lives and the surroundings of the rural population "

Given a suitable organization, efficient tools and instruction in up-to-date methods of farming, the Indian cultivator may be expected to rise to the same level of activity and enterprise as any of his enterprising brethren under similar circumstances in foreign lands All that is known about him ought to fully confirm us in this belief

CHAPTER IV
INDUSTRIES

Importance of Industries—Industrial Survey—Three Classes of Industries—Leading Industries and Manufactures—Industrial Structure Main Requirements, Subsidiary Requirements

IMPORTANCE OF INDUSTRIES

THE people of every country, whether progressive or backward, require the products of agriculture for their very existence, a certain proportion of the population will always be engaged in agricultural pursuits The tendency of all civilized nations to-day is for each to make itself as self-sufficient economically as circumstances permit Agriculture supplies certain indispensable primary requisites—food for the population, raw materials for industries and surplus products for export No country which aspires to be reasonably self-supporting can do without agriculture At the same time, no nation in modern times has grown rich through agriculture alone With the growth of civilization and multiplication of human wants, the occupations associated with industries and manufactures have increased in importance and are found to be more remunerative than those of agriculture, and industrialism has come to be regarded as a necessity and more or less as synonymous with civilization The recent practice in progressive countries has been to provide more work for their labour force in industries and subsidiary occupations and to limit the numbers employed in agriculture, it being recognized that the employment of more than a limited number of persons in agriculture tends to reduce the average income of the individual and the aggregate income of the nation as a whole This healthy practice has not yet obtained recognition in India

The number of industrial establishments in 1930 for which statistics are maintained was 8,148 in British India and 9,422 in the country as a whole Under the law governing the matter, the unit of an industrial establishment may consist of not less than 20 employees The total capital invested in them is not separately shown in the published statistical statements Including the capital of companies which, though registered in the United Kingdom, are working in India, the total capital of organized large-scale industries is estimated by experts at about Rs 700 crores The share of the Indian people in it is probably not more than Rs 300 crores In the United Kingdom with a population of only 13 per cent of that of India, the number of industrial and commercial establishments at work in 1928 was 107,500 The capital outlay on industrial companies alone in 1932 was Rs 7,067 crores or about 23 times the Indian capital The United States of America with a population 35 per cent of that of India, had 174,136 industrial establishments in 1929, with an invested capital of about Rs 23,000 crores or more than 75 times the Indian share in the industries of India Canada has a population of a little over 10 million or 3 per cent of that of India, and in 1929 she had 24,020 industrial establishments with an invested capital of Rs 1,445 crores or about 5 times the amount of India Japan in 1928 with a population 19 per cent of that of India, had 13,711 industrial corporations with an authorized capital of Rs 1,009 crores or more than 3 times what it is in India It is reported that the value of manufactured products in Japan increased seven-fold between the years 1914 and 1926 No such good fortune has fallen to the lot of India

The number of persons engaged in organized industries in British India was about 1 5 million in 1930, or roughly 1 per cent of the total working population, while for the whole of India it was 1 7 million The proportion of the working population engaged in all classes of industries including mining in India in the same year was 10 2 per cent, while in the United Kingdom it was about 47 2 per cent, in the United States of America 32, in Canada 25, in Germany 41 3, in France 33 3 and in Japan 19 5

There are twice as many people here dependent on agriculture, as there are in any progressive country of the world, and one of the problems with which this country is confronted is how to reduce this number to reasonable proportions and adjust the balance that ought to exist between agriculture and industries

The income per head of population derived from industries and agriculture, respectively, in India as well as in five of the most progressive countries of the world compares approximately as follows —

Country	Income *per capita*	
	Industries	Agriculture
	(Rs)	(Rs)
India	12	59
Japan	158	57
Sweden	384	120
United Kingdom	412	62
Canada	170	213
United States of America	721	175

These figures are rough estimates, but they are near enough to represent the relative position of income between agriculture and industries It will be seen that the *per capita* income from industries in India is insignificant, while in all the other countries mentioned, it is their principal source of wealth Having regard to the size and population of India, the average earning power of the Indian is the lowest among nations which have an ordered government

Great Britain was the first country in the world which raised the income and standard of living of its people by developing industries and manufactures. Other countries have followed in her wake In the United States of America, for instance, the income from industries in the year 1900 was about equal to that from agriculture But since 1900 the population engaged in agriculture has not increased on account of the comparatively unremunerative character of that occupation In 1900, the number so engaged was 10 4 million and thirty years later, *i e*, in 1930, it was still only 10 5 million, in spite of a large increase of about 47 million in the total population in the interval. The numbers employed in manufacturing and mechanical pursuits nearly doubled during the same period Canada, which before the War was predominantly agricultural, has since become an industrial country. Sweden is another country which in 1870 had only one-eighth of its population dependent for a livelihood on industries and commerce, to-day quite half of its population is maintained by these occupations The importance attached to industries in Soviet Russia will be evident from the fact that, while in 1913, industry formed 42 1 per cent and agriculture 57 9 per cent. of the total gross production of the Union, in 1932 the production changed to 70 7 per cent and 29.3 per cent. respectively

In none of the countries referred to above is the *per capita* income from industries less than that from agriculture, in one case, namely, that of Great Britain, it is more than six times In India, it is not even equal to that from agriculture but only about one-fifth of it

People at the present time buy from outside the country most of the manufactured goods that they need, including some of their staple wants like clothing, steel, sugar and salt—commodities which they once manufactured for themselves By doing this, not only have the people lost the direct benefits—increased skill, and higher purchasing power derivable from manufacture—but they have also had to pay for imported products out of the meagre earnings from the single precarious occupation left to them, namely, agriculture This arrangement is unsound because there is already excessive pressure of population on land and the cultivator's profit has been falling

Industrial Survey

Except in the case of organized industries, regular statistics of existing industrial establishments of all classes are not at present available The organized industries take into account only establishments employing 20 persons or more each, and the total number employed in them in British India in any year has been less than 1,700,000 persons There is a large number of minor or cottage industries employing less than 20 persons of which no account is taken in the figures recorded by Government The total number of persons *supported* by industries of all kinds, according to the Census of 1921, was 33,167,018 or 10 49 per cent of the entire population The corresponding figures for 1931 were 34 2 million and 9 7 per cent, respectively The number actually engaged in such industries is found from official reports to be 17,506,279 in 1911, 15,714,907 in 1921 and 15,351,953 in 1931, the percentage of total population, therefore, engaged in industrial pursuits during the three successive Census years was 5 6, 4.9 and 4 4, respectively These figures show that the country is receding in industrial activity In India, work and labour are not organized as in other industrially advanced countries and regular hours of work are not observed In many parts of the country, minor industries continue to operate along traditional lines without guidance or help from science or technical skill, and as a result they die out one by one as they become unremunerative in competition with modern mechanized industries

To obtain a clear idea of the true position of industries in this country, an industrial survey is a necessary preliminary and the first step towards it is to collect statistics of existing industries A reliable survey should be made of all the industries pursued, the quantities and values of products manufactured, raw materials utilized, number of persons employed, wages paid, motive power used and other particulars usually collected in advanced countries, and the results placed at the disposal of the public

Statistics are needed to show separately the size and income of factories and industrial establishments worked by the indigenous population to ascertain progress made by them from year to year At present the value of products of Indian industries including cottage and home industries and the gross income derived can only be guessed It probably amounts to one-sixth of the total value of products from both agriculture and industries

There has been no attempt at a systematic survey of the natural resources, such as has been carried out under the policy of "Conservation of Resources" by the Governments of the United States of America and Canada The natural resources in those countries have been by this means very carefully surveyed and mapped out Surveys of this kind have usually embraced resources under agriculture, irrigation, water power, forests, fisheries, mining areas, etc They ought to serve as models to us whenever the Government of India decide to undertake similar systematic surveys in this country

A third class of investigations required is an analysis of imports and exports, the imports to show the class of articles for which there is a home market, and the exports mainly to determine what materials, fit for providing occupations to indigenous labour and increase its purchasing power, are being sent out of the country in a raw or semi-finished state

The principal commodities imported into British India during 1931-32 together with their values, are given in the following table —

Name of Commodity	Value	Remarks
Exceeding Rs 1 crore in value	Rs (in crores)	
Cotton and cotton goods	26 19	
Railway plant and rolling stock	11 81	This figure includes Rs 2 81 crores on account of Government purchases

Name of Commodity	Value	Remarks
Exceeding Rs 1 crore in value	Rs (in crores)	
Machinery and millwork	12 06	Rs 1 14 crores is for Government purchases
Metals and ores .	9 78	
Oils . ..	9 72	
Sugar ..	6 16	
Vehicles	4 18	
Instruments, apparatus and appliances	3 69	
Provisions and oilman's stores	3 41	
Silk—raw and manufactured	2 73	
Dyes .	2 68	
Hardware ..	2 61	
Chemicals . ..	2 57	
Paper and pasteboard	2 50	
Liquors	2 27	
Rubber .	2 22	
Spices .	2 08	
Drugs and medicines	1 91	
Wool—raw and manufactures	1 62	
Fruits and vegetables	1 34	
Glass and glassware .	1 22	
Grain, pulse and flour .	1 18	
Total value of commodities exceeding Rs 1 crore each in value	117 31	

Name of Commodity	Value	Remarks
Exceeding Rs 1 crore in value	Rs (in crores)	
Total of all other commodities each costing less than Rs 1 crore .	25 09	
Government Stores not included above .	0 72	
Total value of imports	142 72	

The value of the principal commodities imported into British India during 1931-32 amounted to Rs 142 72 crores The bulk of these imports—over 80 per cent of them—are such as could be manufactured within the country Some of these products are already being manufactured but the number and magnitude of the related industries are wholly inadequate That the necessary industries have not been started is due to lack of organization, policy or attempts in that direction The latest figures from Russia show that, in pursuance of her policy of economic self-sufficiency, that country has already so developed her foreign trade that on an average 80 per cent of her imports consists of industrial raw materials or machinery and constructional materials and less than 15 per cent finished consumable goods

The principal commodities exported from British India during 1931-32, together with their values, are given in the following table —

Name of Commodity	Value	Remarks
Exceeding Rs 1 crore in value	Rs (in crores)	
Jute—raw . .	11 19	
Jute—manufactures .	21 91	

Name of Commodity	Value	Remarks
Exceeding Rs 1 crore in value	Rs (in crores)	
Cotton—raw and waste	23 78	
Cotton—manufactures	4 82	
Grain, pulse and flour	20 37	
Tea	19 14	
Seeds	14 59	
Metals and ores	5 17	
Leather ..	5 35	
Hides and skins—raw .	3 66	
Wool—raw and manufactures	3 37	
Paraffin wax .	2 32	
Oilcakes .	2 01	
Lac	1 84	
Total value of commodities exceeding Rs 1 crore each in value	140 13	
Total of all other commodities each costing less than Rs 1 crore	15 76	
Total value of exports	155 89	

The exports of the year 1931-32 were below the normal and amounted to Rs 155 89 crores The value of cotton manufactures exported was Rs 4 82 crores as against Rs 7 79 crores in 1898-99, or 33 years previously The raw cotton exported in 1931-32 was valued at Rs 23 78 crores against Rs 11 19 crores in 1898-99 Apparently, there has been a policy to encourage the growth of raw cotton, but none for the export of piece-goods and yarn The country has lost ground in the export of cotton manufactures within these 34 years Most of the commodities exported, except jute which is a monopoly of India, consist of raw materials and food products The export of these commodities should be encouraged only to the extent to which they are found to be in excess of the needs of the people The figures show, however, that there are many articles in the list which may be utilized, but are not, for giving employment to local labour, by converting them into finished or semi-finished commodities for internal consumption or for export

Many of the articles in common use, for the manufacture of which raw materials are available in the country, or which were being manufactured here at one time or another, are being obtained from abroad, showing that the country has been following policies which have made her dependent on foreign countries for some of her barest necessaries In recent years, there has been some improvement in the manufacture, particularly of cotton piece-goods and yarn, and there is a general determination on the part of the people to promote *swadeshi* enterprise, that is, to provide their clothing and other staple commodities which they need by employing local capital and local labour, as far as possible

It will be noticed that the people were used to making their own clothing from time immemorial The raw material needed for the manufacture of cotton piece-goods and yarn is available in the country and there is no excuse for importing them from abroad. The lack of organization and sound policies is a source of double loss to the country Workmen are deprived of their legitimate occupations and the money paid for the imported cloth, which the people can ill-afford to do, is withdrawn from internal circulation and sent out, rendering the country poorer thereby Cotton textiles of superior quality are a luxury which only the well-to-do classes can afford to buy No hardship will be felt, if their importation is restricted by heavy tariffs To so restrict in these circumstances is the primary duty of Government

Surveys under the three heads mentioned should be carried out for each Province and State as well as for the country as a whole The results, when recorded, will serve as a bench-mark or starting point from which to measure future progress They will also be of particular value for the preparation of a constructive programme or plan for future advance

Three Classes of Industries

Industries and manufactures of every description may, for convenience of organization, be considered, according to their size or the capital invested in them, under three classes, *viz*, (i) Heavy or Large-scale, (ii) Medium-scale, and (iii) Minor

These three classes of industries may be broadly distinguished by the amount of capital required for equipping and starting them Heavy or large-scale industries will be those enterprises which require, say, a capital outlay of Rs 30 lakhs or more each, medium-scale industries, between Rs 1 lakh and Rs 30 lakhs, and minor or cottage industries Rs 1 lakh or less This division on the basis of capital invested is perhaps unscientific and arbitrary, but it is adopted because the outlay required and the procedure to be adopted will depend upon the magnitude of the industry An industry like textiles may fall under any of the three classes and be practised in all the three forms

LARGE-SCALE INDUSTRIES.

Large-scale industries are important because, generally speaking, they include basic and key industries, require the use of developed machinery and technique, help mass production of staple commodities and represent the highest form of industrial enterprise The following dozen industries are typical of this class —

- Mining—coal, metallic ores and petroleum
- Iron and Steel—iron foundries and fabricated steel
- Engineering industries—manufacture of engines, pumps and machinery generally
- Railway plant including rolling stock
- Arms, ammunition and military stores
- Automobiles and aircraft
- Agricultural tools and machinery
- Hydro-electric and electrical appliances and machinery
- Cotton and woollen textiles
- Jute industry
- Chemical industries—heavy chemicals
- Ship and boat building

Heavy industries in their present stage of development in India require the earnest attention and the closest support of the Government, leading financiers and business men of the country They require large sums of capital and expert direction to establish and manage, and being sensitive to price changes and foreign competition, they need all the protection and assistance which the organized money power and political influence of the community, vested in Government, can give

When the Provincial Governments become autonomous, the representatives of all the provinces should meet, and in their common interest, evolve an all-India plan to bring into existence the more important large-scale industries mentioned above Each province should take upon itself the responsibility to start and maintain, even though at the risk of loss at first, two or three of the large-scale industries according to its resources and the aptitude of its people If the responsibility is shared in this way, no single province will feel it a heavy burden, while the country, as a whole, will be able speedily to bring into existence all the enterprises of national importance needed

Leading business men and large manufacturing firms in each province should be encouraged to start these industries with substantial help from Government Where sufficient private capital is not forthcoming, the Provincial Government itself should step into the gap, raise loans, just as the Central Government has done in the past, for constructing railway and irrigation works, and start enterprises in close co-operation with the people of the province In the more advanced provinces, prominent business men will in their own interest combine and come forward to start these industries, once they begin to feel that Government power and resources will be at their back in the event of severe foreign competition or other risks which may be beyond their power to face It is assurances of support of this sort that are wanted but are lacking to push forward a policy of industrialization If such support were forthcoming, India with its abundance of cheap labour and vast resources could be developed industrially in a very few years

Large sums of money are spent abroad every year for the purchase of railway plant and rolling stock, and arms, ammunition and military stores In some years, the money paid for them is as high as Rs 30 to 40 crores The value of stores purchased in 1927-28 by the railways alone amounted to Rs 36 crores If the money spent in a single year on these purchases is invested in equipping Government workshops with the requisite plant and machinery, and the necessary expert staff is engaged for a short period, the country can be made self-sufficient in respect of these supplies in a very few years The same object can be gained also, if large private local firms are subsidized and contracts for purchasing machinery and plant are placed with them for a reasonably long term of years

Medium-Scale Industries

Medium-scale industries are usually organized and carried on by companies working on the joint-stock principle, although many of them may also be privately owned Their first need is that the Provincial Government should, through the departments concerned or otherwise, give proof of its eagerness to see new industries started and co-operate to that end with the leading merchants and others interested in building up business or in floating companies The Department of Industries should readily place, at the disposal of the industrially-minded public, records of past surveys of the resources of the province

Business men among the local public should be invited to suggest schemes in which they are interested Chambers of Commerce and industrial associations should be asked to furnish suggestions When the character of an industry requires it, the Provincial Government should engage local or foreign experts to tour through the province and investigate individual schemes The experts should consult local business men and financiers and submit to Government preliminary schemes for new enterprises which, in their opinion, will prove remunerative Such a preliminary investigation, if undertaken in the diverse ways indicated, will rouse public interest and ensure co-operation, and half-a-dozen to a dozen industrial projects will emerge in each province for detailed investigation, and some of them for execution, in less than a year

The following are typical examples of medium-scale industries —

- Iron foundries
- Engineering industries for manufacture of engines, pumps and machinery
- Fabricated steel
- Metal works
- Cotton and woollen mills of moderate size, and artificial silk
- Cotton gins and presses
- Chemicals and dyes
- Sugar
- Paper
- Match manufacture
- Chemical fertilizers
- Food and drinks
- Alcohol
- Tobacco industry
- Soaps and candles
- Rubber and rubber products
- Tiles and bricks
- Ceramic industries, including cement, glass, stoneware pipes, etc
- Leather products, hides and skins—tanned and dressed
- Printing and publishing
- Photographic and cinema materials
- Clock and watch manufacture
- Manufacture of typewriters

Many of these industries are already in operation in various parts of the country Only their number is small, organization defective and production meagre. Under suitable protectionist policies and with the Government and leading business men working in co-operation, this class of industries can be made to multiply very fast

MINOR INDUSTRIES

In their transformation from the agricultural to the present manufacturing and commercial stage, industries have had to pass through the handicraft stage Minor and cottage industries were extensively practised in India before the British occupation, when the country had of necessity to be more or less self-sufficient But with the progress of communications and the opening up of the country to foreign trade, many of the older industries, such as iron, steel and salt, disappeared through sheer inability to compete with imported products Industries of the modern type are being slowly introduced, but not at the pace demanded by the size and the needs of the country or the rapidity with which the population has been increasing Minor industries of the older type which have survived are chiefly those associated with agriculture

There is thus considerable scope for the extension of minor industries, if a steady policy to encourage local industrial enterprise is pursued Such minor industries only should be encouraged, in the first instance, as supply staple products for which there is a demand within the country

Municipalities, local boards, village *panchayets* and local associations should encourage the establishment of industries in their midst by granting all reasonable concessions and facilities This will help not only to increase the money in circulation and the purchasing power of the community but also the revenues derived by the local government bodies It is the commonest practice in European countries for local authorities to attract capital and industries to their midst in this manner

The following is a list of typical handicrafts and minor and cottage industries which can be practised with profit by large sections of the population —

Metal works—smithing, agricultural tools and machinery
Manufacture of metal vessels—copper, brass, aluminium, etc
Hand-spinning and weaving, cotton ginning, silk reeling
Carpets and blanket making
Flour milling
Rice milling
Oil mills
Food products, fruit canning, drinks and aerated waters
Cigarettes and *bidis*
Brick and tile works
Furniture—chairs, tables, benches, boxes, combs, etc
Pottery
Mat-making, basket and rope-making
Shoe-making
Bee-keeping
Toys
Vegetable dyes paints, inks, etc
Pencil manufacture
Buttons
Soaps
Glass works—bangles, etc
Enamelled-ware
Printing
Book-binding.
House-building on modern lines.

Small-scale industries play an important part in the productive activities of countries like Germany and Japan It is recorded that 90 per cent of the industrial establishments in Germany are connected with small-scale industries and two-fifths of the entire population is employed on them Likewise in Japan, many of the industrial establishments are of very small size A recent publication[9] records that more than 50 per cent of the 55,948 factories listed in 1928 employed from 5 to 9 workmen and only about 0 5 per cent of these factories had as many as 1,000 workers or more

LEADING INDUSTRIES AND MANUFACTURES

The following is a list of the leading industries and manufactures practised in five of the principal industrially-developed countries of the world, namely, the United Kingdom, the United States of America, Canada, Germany and Japan —

Mining—coal, iron ore, etc
Textiles—cotton, wool, silk and jute
Iron and steel, and their products
Engineering industries
Machinery and tools including agricultural tools
Railway rolling stock
Automobiles
Electric industries including hydro-electric
Ship-building
Chemical industries
Paper
Fertilizers
Cement, lime and glass-ware
Artificial silk industry

Harold G Moulton, *Japa*
nomi (1932), p 132

Leather and rubber products
Food, drink and tobacco
Timber and wooden-ware
Metal works
Sugar
Clock and watch manufacture

Except for a few products, in respect of which some of the countries named above have a monopoly or special facilities, the description of industries in vogue is almost the same in every one of them Most of these types of industries have already been introduced into India in a small way More of them are required and, in many cases, larger ones and public attention should be concentrated on their development Some few, like the manufacture of machinery, automobiles, railway plant and rolling stock, which are most important, have not received any attention In any plan of industrialization, the foremost place should be given to these

INDUSTRIAL STRUCTURE--MAIN REQUIREMENTS

Industries have, for some years now, been a Provincial subject, although the Central Government retains the power *inter alia* of granting tariff protection, regulating banking facilities, adjusting railway freight, and directing commercial and financial policies, all of which vitally affect their progress The provinces have had little power and practically no funds to devote to industrial activities and, although nearly 14 years have elapsed since the control definitely passed into their hands, the Provincial Governments as a body have paid little heed to this national want

The Departments of Industries are not allowed to deal with the larger questions of policy and organization, and in some of the provinces their activity is limited to giving technical advice to minor industries and the supervision of the primary grades of technical and industrial education

Thanks to the enterprise of British and Indian investors and company promoters in the past, a few large-scale industries have sprung up since the closing years of the last century In some provinces industrial surveys have been partially carried out and in several others enquiries have been made into individual schemes, either existing or proposed But the scope of such enquiries has been strictly limited No organic relation is maintained between the few large-scale industries in operation and the Departments of Industries No effort is made to secure uninterrupted progress on the scale which the magnitude of the country's interests demands and, though a matter of fundamental importance to the country's welfare, industries are a no man's child at present

A sound organization or fabric should be set up in the country to create a healthy atmosphere for the growth of industries It should provide for the following half-a-dozen major requirements —

(i) *A general organization* composed of representatives of Government and business, who by mutual co-operation, shall maintain an atmosphere favourable to the rapid growth of industries

(ii) *A Local organization* or council in cities, districts and rural areas to encourage local activities in this respect

(iii) *Tariff protection*

(iv) *Banking facilities*

(v) Maintaining *statistical information*

(vi) Up-to-date legislation in regard to the *Companies Act* and the *Managing Agency System.*

Other *contributory facilities* needed are:—

(vii) Exhibitions and Commercial Museums

(viii) Experimental and Demonstration Stations.

(ix) Industrial Research

(x) Education—Technical, Commercial, etc

(xi) Indian Trade Commissioners in foreign countries and Commercial Intelligence

(xii) Transport and freight facilities

Provision should be made for all these dozen facilities in any complete programme of industrial development A few explanatory notes will now be added under each of these heads

General Organization

A suitable general organization should consist of an active Development Ministry in the Central Government and a Central Economic Council which would meet and deliberate once a quarter at the seat of that Government The latter should contain representative economists, industrialists and financiers, drawn from the chambers of commerce and business associations throughout the country and representing every sphere of the country's economic life The Economic Council will have an office at Delhi and there will be frequent consultations between the Ministry of Industries and the executive officials of the Economic Council The Council should be able to put forward, as required, proposals and measures from time to time for promoting industries throughout the country

A Provincial Economic Council should be established similarly in each province to work in close association with the Provincial Minister in charge of Industries With each of these Provincial Councils should be associated committees of experts to investigate questions and submit results and schemes to Government for practical action The Central Economic Council and the Provincial Councils should enunciate policies for the guidance of unofficial bodies in the country and should work in close association with the Government of India Both the Central and Provincial Governments will have to strengthen their establishments for this purpose

An All-India Industrial Conference should be held at the head-quarters of one or the other of the provinces once a year It may be remarked that at one time Industrial Conferences were held along with every session of the Indian National Congress The Canadian Manufacturers' Association has, for many years, maintained such activities in Canada with great advantage to the industrial interests of that Dominion

Local Organization

For the purpose of this organization, each city and district should be constituted into a unit area and provide itself with a Local Economic Council, a working committee of the Council and an executive staff maintained from funds raised within the area In countries like Italy, business men who join such councils or associations subscribe towards the up-keep of their executive Although the rates of subscription are fixed by resolutions of the councils or associations, Government undertake to collect and hand them over to the bodies concerned

Any area—even a small group of villages—may be allowed to constitute itself into an independent unit, if it is able to provide itself from its own resources, with a council and an executive staff All such councils should receive grants from municipalities, public bodies, business firms and citizens interested in industrial development

In each unit area, there should be representatives of the Government Department of Industries, working whole or part time in close co-operation with this unofficial Council of Industries

Industries are the concern of the people Under the organization proposed, there will be two parallel agencies constituting the industrial structure of the country—one, to represent the Government and the other, the public and local economic interests,—both working together in close co-operation in each area so that, in the event of slackness or neglect at any time, one of them at least may be effective and the industrial interests of the area may at all times be adequately safeguarded Great importance is attached to these local Economic Councils because they can be established and worked by the people themselves And it is here that numbers of our educated unemployed can find an opening for their activities and for eventually engaging themselves in occupations not only profitable to themselves but also of vital importance to the country's industrial future and this, they should do even if no help is forthcoming from Government They will teach the people to work together for common benefit and help to multiply the number of minor and cottage industries which can be undertaken with profit and take part also in the investigation of medium-scale industries The members will be familiar with the resources of the locality as regards capital, men of ability, raw materials, etc The Councils will endeavour to encourage the production of commodities for which there is an assured market either within or outside the area of their influence Each Economic Council should start, before the commencement of a new year, with a definite plan and programme for the year and a provisional plan and programme for at least three years in advance They should do everything possible by propaganda, lectures, pamphlets and otherwise, to educate the public as to the importance of industries for the economic regeneration of the area and the value of co-operative effort for promoting common interests

The work to be done in each unit area by the local Economic or Industrial Council may be summed up under the following twelve heads —

(1) To encourage and give every help in its power to promoters who have resources or ability to bring new industries into existence

(2) To make representations to Government and appeals to the public men, when necessary but otherwise to be non-political in character

(3) To be on the watch that no existing industry, that is otherwise sound and is under honest management, fails or suspends operation, by reason of unfair competition or through lack of reasonable banking or other facilities

(4) To perform the duties of a financial corporation until an industrial bank or banks are established in the region

(5) To help in marketing products for some of the industries, if required

(6) To help in providing technical and financial advice at a reasonable fee to concerns in need of it

(7) To help in correcting defective administration or management of existing concerns

(8) To carry out an industrial survey and investigate new schemes (The resources of the region should be under constant investigation and study)

(9) To collect and maintain statistics of industries and production

(10) To render methods of company formation, banking, etc, familiar to the public of the area.

(11) To watch the collective interests of industrial concerns and render help in individual cases, when help is asked for (Each individual industry will raise capital and carry on business on its own responsibility)

(12) To watch, with the aid of its technical staff, the world movements in trade and industry and advise companies and firms likely to be affected by them

In addition to these essential duties, the Local Council will arrange for conferences, lectures and propaganda and take all other measures that it may consider necessary to further the industrial interests of the area

TARIFF PROTECTION

Most countries reserve their home market to themselves by levying heavy and, sometimes, prohibitive duties and freight rates against imports There is a move to lower tariffs by international understanding but, till that consummation comes about, the most important help which industries in India require is tariff protection, that is, a preferential claim to dispose of the products of local industries in the home market, with the two-fold object, as previously stated, of saving the money that would go out of the country, were products of foreign manufacture purchased, and of giving employment to local labour Protection is needed primarily to enable new and infant industries to compete successfully with long-established foreign rivals

The tariff protection at present afforded in this country is inadequate The tariffs imposed are not high enough, the period of protection in many cases is far too short and there is no provision for prompt action to prevent dumping The enquiries by the Tariff Board are too elaborate and prolonged So long as foreign competition is keen, protection only discriminatory and subsidies are practically unknown, new industries have small chance of making headway Higher tariffs and more substantial protection are essential to inspire confidence and induce people to risk money in industries The present tendency in all progressive countries is to reduce imports and encourage the use of local products, even if foreign ones could be obtained cheaper

Since its establishment, the Tariff Board has examined about twenty industries and the Government of India have sanctioned effective protection in the case of five or six large-scale industries and moderate protection in a few others Even this small concession has materially helped to make the country self-sufficient to an appreciable extent

Every modern State has built up its industrial prosperity by tariff protection Great Britain herself originally developed her industries in this way India has suffered enormous losses all these years in conducting her foreign trade on a free trade basis to the dictation of England But since England herself has gone back to a protectionist basis, it is hoped India will henceforward be at liberty to follow her own special interests in this respect, till all the staple products required for her population are supplied from her own manufactures

That India, given the necessary freedom, will be able to produce manufactured goods for export, is evident from the fact that during the War, when there was little or no competition from Europe, she sent out more manufactured articles than either before or after the War Further, the eagerness with which sugar and match factories have been started the moment effective protection was afforded to these industries, is conclusive proof that the country is hungry for industries and it is only Government co-operation that is wanting to enable her to go full speed ahead

BANKING FACILITIES

Complaints were heard before the recent Indian Central Banking Enquiry Committee that existing banks did not afford sufficient financial facilities to local business men The enquiries of the same Committee recorded the fact that "there are 659 branches in India against 13,000 in the United Kingdom, or one for every 440,000 persons in India as against one for every 3,500 persons in the United Kingdom "

On account of lack of sound policies and organization in this country, the co-operation between commercial men, industrialists and bankers is feeble and the economic activities have no relation to the magnitude of the interests involved

The success of Germany and Japan in their industrial policies is largely due to the efficiency of their banking systems in relation to industry and trade An effective credit fabric is a *sine qua non* for the rapid growth of industries and, in a lesser degree for operating those already in existence Unless industrial banks are brought into existence and form the backbone of our industries, the problem of obtaining finance and working capital will remain just as acute as it is to-day, because no bank of the present type can afford to tie up its capital on long-term loans which industries would really require If Indian industries are to thrive, the banking organization should be brought up to the level maintained in self-governing countries like Germany, Japan and Canada

STATISTICAL INFORMATION

As stated before, the statistics of the Indian industries published at present are very meagre They are available only for organized industries which, in the aggregate, employ less than 1,700,000 persons Even for these, such essential information as value of products manufactured, of products exported, of raw materials used, value added by manufacture, wages paid, etc, is not available Business associations and the public have long been complaining of the inadequacy of this class of information

A census of production should be taken at least once in five years, embodying a record of productivity of the various industries in full detail, as is done in the United States of America and Canada and, in recent years, also in the United Kingdom and in Soviet Russia Russia, as is well known, is maintaining an elaborate system of statistics on the American model Variations in the estimates of production from year to year should be published for the information of the public

Legislation Re Companies Act and the Managing Agency System

Most industrial undertakings in advanced countries at the present time are organized and worked on the joint-stock company principle The company system of management was first started in England and is now in universal use In the United States of America, the term "Corporation" is used in place of "Company". The present Indian Companies Act stands as it was last shaped by amendments in 1913 and 1914 before the War It was based on the English Act in force at the time As the English Act itself has since been revised, a revision of the Indian Companies Act is now overdue Most industrial concerns of the world to-day come under the joint-stock company organization The working of the Act in India should be examined with the help of public bodies and business men who have studied the question and steps taken to remedy the defects noticed Similar enactments in countries like Canada and Japan should also be examined and the experience of those countries taken into consideration before a revised measure is placed on the Statute Book

A form of working public companies in India is the Managing Agency System, which has grown up as a result of local needs and conditions For a long time British companies, registered in England, have carried on business in India , and, as the London companies wanted some responsible agencies to look after their interests here, they appointed certain established European firms in India as their agents This system was extensively copied by Indian companies which managed the textile industry in Bombay and other centres Managing agents have done yeoman service in the past but for lack of scrutiny various abuses have crept into the working of this system The existing law gives too much discretion to the Managing Agents and too little scope for control or check by any public authority or by representatives of shareholders in the event of mismanagement or even of corruption For all practical purposes, the Agents appoint directors from among their friends and relations, instead of at the choice of the shareholders, or in the best interests of the business with which they are connected Some Managing Agency firms charge commissions on both purchases and sales even during years in which shareholders get no dividend Latterly, the Agencies have come to look upon themselves as hereditary establishments and upon their remuneration as part of their family income

In order to do away with these evils, the Indian Central Banking Enquiry Committee (1931) has suggested that "an attempt should be made to make industrial enterprise in India less dependent on the Managing Agency System for future development and to establish direct friendly relations between companies and commercial banks" It is stated that, if investors in India could be induced to put their loanable capital in joint-stock undertakings, then the managing agency system can be easily dispensed with The whole question requires to be threshed out by a committee of influential business men familiar with local conditions before a change in the law affecting the system is effected

Industrial Structure—Subsidiary Requirements

The major requirements for the organization and development of industries have been described There are needed, however, at least half a dozen more subsidiary facilities which should not be ignored in this connection

Industrial exhibitions are happily becoming a common feature in various parts of India Every large city, district head-quarters and business centre should have an industrial and commercial museum, which should interest itself in holding exhibitions and fairs, in providing practical education, in propaganda work and in stimulating local effort in the field of industries generally In a sense, these museums may be held responsible for securing the necessary contributory facilities for promoting industries and industrial efficiency among the population in their respective areas There are two large commercial museums in the cities of Calcutta and Madras, but they do not appear to be associating themselves with industrial activities The responsibility for financing periodical industrial exhibitions should be shared by municipalities and district boards in every part of the country At the present time, propaganda through *swadeshi* journals is being conducted with a certain amount of zest and its object is solely to increase production, promote technical skill in the working population and reduce the money spent on imported goods

Industrial experimental stations should be established by the Government Department of Industries in large cities and other industrial centres, to give practical instruction in at least half-a-dozen minor or cottage industries in order to bring employment to, and produce the commodities needed in, the immediate neighbourhood At these stations, experiments, either full size practical, or on the unit operation basis, should be conducted to instruct managers of small factories and train apprentices to manufacture products of high quality at minimum cost according to local needs and the resources available Such experimental stations are operated with great benefit in cities like Osaka in Japan.

Investigation of business conditions and scientific research should be continually pursued in relation to every important industry in order to improve the quality of the products, reduce costs of manufacture and maintain its competitive strength Such improvements are necessary in themselves and certainly indispensable in the face of foreign competition The Balfour Committee on Industry and Trade in England (1928) has stated that the amount spent in the United States of America upon industrial research annually was approximately Rs 22 5 crores The British Government provided for the year 1932-33 a grant of £ 296,620 (over Rs 40 lakhs) for research and development through the Empire Marketing Board

Unfortunately, the application of scientific research to industries, as compared with progress in theoretical science, is very backward in this country If industries of the same class would work together, they might all subscribe towards a common fund to carry on research. The Universities should be able to supply the necessary scientific equipment and trained intelligence for the purpose Research problems pertaining to industries might in this way be distributed, as is done in Germany, among the various institutes of science and university colleges of engineering and chemical technology Such distribution should become a common feature of the Indian Universities and institutes of science

It has been explained that Universities should be able to provide the necessary equipment and the graduate personnel needed for industrial research They should recognize that the country is over-populated, that the income of the people is miserably low, and that their first concern should be to equip the great majority of young men and women who pass through their portals with the training needed to earn a living The animal wants of a community are fundamental, when these are lacking, culture, recreation, refinements are a mockery.

The Universities should also give special prominence to degrees in technology, commerce and agriculture. At the Tokyo University in 1919, the largest number of under-graduates were preparing themselves for a degree in commerce More recently even greater prominence has been given in that country to training in technical arts It has been remarked that the cotton and other mills in Japan are to-day wholly manned by young men who have had higher training in textile, mechanical and other types of engineering As things stand at present, practical proposals of this kind, if put forward, are liable to be received with indifference or positive ridicule in University circles

There should be a large number of special business institutes and schools in the country at which arts graduates and middle-class business men might receive the finishing touches of training needed to manage a factory, farm or shop Industrial and technical institutes and Universities should arrange for popular evening classes in all industrial towns to enable practical men to improve their knowledge and qualify for more responsible positions in their own business

Other educational facilities needed are the deputation of students to foreign countries, changing the character of education in public institutions so as to provide an industrial bias, and provision of mass education and adult education on an extensive scale

The majority of the rural population should, as in the United States of America, receive training in mechanics and mechanical pursuits to give them a *machine sense* and make them efficient producers This will bring the education of the masses to the requisite practical standards for industrial life

It is reported that in many an educational institution in Soviet Russia models of locomotives, aeroplanes, automobiles and other machines are exhibited to serve as toys and games and to rouse in the scholars ambition for higher performance Wherever it was possible, schools have been linked with the factories associated with the dominant industrial tendency of the district The basic principle of all instruction in that country is to bring its recipients into close contact with processes of production

There is a Commercial Intelligence Section in the Commerce Department of the Government of India, but it is shaped on a modest scale and very little is heard of the department's activities outside Calcutta The Dominion of Canada has, in normal years, a total trade of about the same value as India and is maintaining more than 34 Trade Commissioners abroad These officers report to their Government from month to month all the important happenings and developments in industries and trade in the countries to which they are accredited and the reports are published in the *Commercial*

Intelligence Journal of Canada, a publication issued by the Department of Trade and Commerce for the benefit of Canadian business men Similar arrangements are overdue in the interests of industries and trade of this country

Freight rates on railways have to be examined and readjusted from time to time according to the needs of industry and commerce The existing arrangements, in spite of the appointment of the Railway Rates Advisory Committee, have not given satisfaction to Indian industrialists An impression prevails that there are concession rates for imported goods but that the rates and fares from and to industrial centres within the country impose a burden on industry The interests of industry demand that the rates for coal, cotton and other raw materials to industrial centres and for finished products from those centres to internal markets should be the lowest possible The adjustment would be easy if Government were guided in such matters by an All-India Economic Council

CHAPTER V

DEVELOPMENT OF INDUSTRIES

Management of Industries—Recent Industrial Trends—Facilities given in Progressive Countries—Need for a Bold Policy

MANAGEMENT OF INDUSTRIES

THE preliminary enquiries, which should be undertaken when a rapid development of industries is desired, have been explained In spite of tariff protection, industries are liable to lose ground heavily on account of keen international competition and eventually may come to be shut down Except a few, like cotton and woollen mills, industrial undertakings, particularly medium-scale and large-scale ones, require considerable forethought and skill to mature and put into operation Before launching a scheme, it is an advantage to possess a good practical knowledge of the working of similar undertakings in foreign countries

A country like the United States of America is fully organized for industrial development If a man has, or is assured of, the necessary capital and desires to start an industry, all his requirements are readily met. He can get expert advice, a qualified manager, skilled labour and raw and semi-finished materials if he is able to pay for them Even in such a country, out of every 100 undertakings started, only about 60 survive at the end of the year This is as much as to say that uncertainties and risks have to be constantly faced. Risks must be taken, venture should be made if people wish to earn profits and win prosperity This aspect of the matter is not fully understood in India where business men, who have money, want safe investments and will not invest in industries, unless there is an assured prospect of earning a dividend at least equal to the current bank rate of interest A nation which wants to prosper through industries should risk money and effort from time to time in order that a reasonable percentage of effort may succeed If the net result of bringing every year a number of industries into existence is that a majority of them get established, the owners of the industries and the nation as a whole reap the benefit, there is more employment all round, more money and more purchasing power in the country and the general standard of living is appreciably raised.

Leaving out the environment and the circumstances amidst which it has to be carried on, the normal requirements of an industry may be taken as seven in number —7 M's—namely —

(1) Money,
(2) Market,
(3) Management,
(4) Machinery,
(5) Motive power,
(6) Materials, and
(7) Men

The abundance or scarcity and the cheapness or dearth of many of these elements of production are influenced by a variety of factors, local and foreign, and the conditions of the world trade

Money or capital required for starting an industry is usually collected by subscriptions from the public by floating a joint-stock company The company may be a private body, if the capital is contributed by a small number of persons who wish to retain sole control, or it may be, as it usually is, a public company The banking system of the country, when reorganized, should be of great value for promoting local business enterprises of every kind Confidence in the political outlook of the country is also needed to enable its frozen wealth to become available for this purpose

At the present time the chief problem in industrially advanced countries is how to secure a market for their finished products In India, however, we have for the next 15 or 20 years at least, an assured market within the country for the great majority of industries that may be set up

A good manager is an acquisition It is not industry, education, or technical ability merely that makes a competent manager but a capacity—a sort of virtue—that enables him to obtain the largest and most favourable results from the resources at his disposal The qualities that go to make an efficient manager will be referred to later There are a sufficient number of trained engineers, chemists and other experts who have specialized in various industries and professions and who, with a little preliminary training, can promote or operate any industry Quite a number of these have received training in foreign Universities at great expense

Machinery is imported under the advice of experts or firms of consulting engineers chiefly from two or three countries, namely, England, Germany and the United States of America, which are industrially advanced and have specialized in this class of manufacture

As regards motive power, which of the sources—coal, oil, wood-fuel or hydro-electric power—would be most suitable and economical for any particular industry, in a given region or locality, should be settled only by local investigation This subject is dealt with more fully in Chapter VI—Transport and Power Supply

There is no dearth of raw materials for industries Huge quantities of these are being exported from India to European countries and Japan where, in the act of converting them into finished products, employment is provided for their labour population The export of primary products may be continued after meeting the local demand by producing more raw materials by the aid of machinery and mass production methods, as is done in respect of cotton in the United States of America

There is no organization or agency in the country to provide employment to young men trained in our Universities and none to encourage the manufacture of the enormous number of simple machines in demand in the country—machines which require little superior skill to construct Labour is for the most part illiterate and unskilled, and there is no organization to provide employment or training for our huge labour population

The preliminary enquiries to be made in starting a large or medium-scale industry are indicated in a general way in the account given in the previous Chapter under the head "Three Classes of Industries" Large-scale industries are to a great extent dependent upon Government help, medium-scale industries only less so, minor and cottage industries can be developed by the people themselves to a very large extent, Government help being needed only in regard to tariff protection in some cases and in providing a suitable industrial structure for the country

When a new industry, large- or medium-scale, has to be started, the promoters discuss the subject among themselves, collect data, consult specialists and obtain rough estimates of the size and initial cost of the undertaking and its probable financial results The actual working of undertakings of similar size is studied where possible, and advice obtained regarding the location of the factory in relation to water supply, proximity to a railway station, working costs, production value, market prices and other matters, before satisfying themselves of the remunerative character of the undertaking

When the project looks hopeful, the promoters form themselves into a provisional committee, raise funds among themselves for preliminary expenses and employ a competent consulting firm or expert or experts to make further detailed surveys, collect more exact data and complete other necessary enquiries The questions connected with the location, buildings, plant and other equipment of the factory, raw materials, water and power supply are all considered and a detailed scheme is drawn up, indicating in a rough way the capital cost and the probable remunerative character of the undertaking judged by the data so collected

Thereafter, a provisional prospectus and a memorandum of association are drawn up for the promotion of a company, a responsible chairman and directors are appointed as a temporary measure, and subscriptions invited towards share capital

While funds are being collected, careful consideration is given to the selection of a manager and other heads of the principal functional divisions of the work, such as, the engineer, works superintendent, sales manager, accountant and chemist as required

The scheme is further revised, if necessary, by spending some more money and consulting more experts with the aid of the principal members appointed on the staff, and, when the estimates are considered satisfactory and reliable by the majority of experts and business men consulted, the undertaking is finally approved, the necessary legal documents are drawn up in final form and the execution of the undertaking decided on Land is acquired, buildings are raised and the necessary machinery and plant obtained and installed

An undertaking is usually started, if a number of

competent business men and financiers approve of it But it often happens that these men have had no practical experience of the difficulties in the particular industry approved by them At the investigation stage, enquiries should be instituted into the minutest detail and money and effort should not be stinted for the purpose Sufficient provision should be made or assurances obtained for meeting the working advance during the operation Industries have failed in this country in the past mostly because they were begun without sufficient preliminary enquiry, or because the management was not sufficiently efficient and wide-awake

(i) *Efficient Management*—Management is defined as the arrangement of details of the operation of an industry in such a way that it will work harmoniously to produce the desired result Each department or section of the industry should be properly co-ordinated with every one of the other sections and with the management at the top, and great judgment should be exercised in choosing a competent man or men to the charge of the department To ensure a high level of efficiency, men of capacity should be chosen for the managerial staff and for all appointments requiring knowledge and skill

An efficient manager is a great asset and in many countries nowadays he is paid a higher salary than in almost any other profession A good manager may save considerable sums for the company by his vigilance and capacity, an inefficient one is likely to cause losses which, though imperceptible, may in the long run bring ruin to the company Under efficient management, strict discipline is maintained, the duties of the staff and workmen are regulated according to clearly defined rules, materials are utilized economically and costs cut down to the minimum Every part of the plant and every stage of the production are inspected at regular and irregular intervals to ensure discipline and rectitude of conduct on the part of the men concerned The Board of Management, when there is one, and the departmental head should be held responsible to regulate promotions by merit and ability and to give every incentive to the members of the staff to improve their knowledge and skill

(ii) *Departmental System of Management*—The best way to manage a large-scale industry is on the departmental system The operation and management of an industry should be divided into a specific number of branches or departments and each department treated and worked, as far as possible, as if it were a separate unit by itself Each such department should strive constantly to increase its production, improve the quality of the product and reduce costs Progress should be watched and the costs and other results compared from month to month In this way the success of the operation is assured by taking care that none of the departments is allowed to fall below a reasonable stipulated standard The entire concern will be satisfactory from the point of view of efficiency and finance, if both are taken care of in the detailed working of its various individual departments

(iii) *The Committee System of Management*—In large industries in the United States of America the committee system of management is found to be very efficacious and growing popular Under such a system all important questions connected with the management, future developments and improvement of departments are decided, after discussion and consultation among a number of members of the staff, mainly heads of departments and experts, and not on the sole responsibility of the over-worked general manager There will be a monthly committee meeting at which the working and financial results of individual departments of the previous month are reviewed by the general manager and the heads of departments, and the work of the ensuing month planned out

Committees are also appointed to watch the future developments of the concern Departmental committees are appointed to watch the working of individual departments, where the nature of work done is complicated In this way the committee system helps to concentrate many minds on a department or a subject, the members of the staff are set to think, faults are readily detected, right men will come to occupy positions they are entitled to and the air will always be thick with improvements and developments Each working department will develop into a self-improving organization and the management at the top will be automatically relieved of much of its anxiety and responsibility Under this system the manager becomes a co-ordinator instead of being an autocrat, and the committees will form a training ground for members of the staff to grow into future managers and experts of business

One of the chief difficulties in starting industries in India is finance This arises from the fact that the money power of the country is under the control of the Government which, as we have seen, does not see eye to eye with Indian leaders in regard to industrial policies. Banks under the control of Indian business men are very few and many of the larger banks are either under the influence of Government, or are branches of British and foreign banks

The amount of capital required will depend upon the size of the concern and the capacity of the market for its products, and, once the capital is fixed, the capacity for production becomes more or less limited. Capital has to be raised chiefly from subscribers to a joint-stock company or collected from private financiers. It is ordinarily required for three purposes, namely, fixed capital to promote a new industry, short-term capital to keep an industry going, and capital for extensions, developments and research from time to time, as occasion demands

In an efficiently-managed undertaking it should be possible to fix in advance the quantity of production, its value and the expenditure to be incurred by departments or sections of the business from month to month If this departmental expenditure and results are properly controlled, a firm grip will be maintained over the trading position of the undertaking And if, in addition, the management takes care to adjust the volume of business and methods of operation to the changing trends of the market, the smooth progress of the undertaking will be assured

The formal accounts to be maintained for an undertaking are prescribed by the Indian Companies Act and the Articles and Memorandum of Association of the Company concerned Along with the monthly accounts should be submitted to the directors a brief standardized report, clearly explaining all important phases of the operation and commercial position, together with explanatory notes on points which particularly affect the month's results

The accounts should be examined not only from the accountant's point of view but also from that of the manager The working of a concern should be analysed and reviewed under three heads, namely, (i) the business position, (ii) the trading position, and (iii) the financial position The business position depends upon the orders received, orders under execution and invoices issued. The trading position and the financial position are revealed by the *interim* balance sheet and profit and loss account The details of the business position should be available before the end of the first week after the close of the month, and those of the trading and financial positions by about the third week

In recent years on account of the financial dis-equilibrium brought on by War debts and other causes, industries have not been operating as smoothly, steadily and successfully as before the War In India, too, the older industries have not been giving satisfactory dividends and, barring sugar and textiles, no new large industries have been started Besides, both in Europe and America, machinery and plant are constantly undergoing improvement and change necessitating additions to the plant and increase of capital outlay Changes are constantly taking place in the values of products, methods of management and working costs, and rapid decisions are continually demanded to adjust the operation to the changing world conditions

In these circumstances, constant research and investigation have to be maintained to ensure that no faults in operation are allowed to remain undetected and no new data or discoveries likely to benefit the undertaking are ignored In addition to research, there should be carried out from time to time a thorough account audit from the point of view of expenditure and receipts, and an efficiency audit from the point of view of management For this purpose, the management should collect and maintain all worthwhile commercial information and data This may be done by deputing expert members of the staff to foreign countries, by corresponding with foreign agencies and by taking extracts from technical journals and other sources

Records of such information should be filed and indexed The leading members of the staff and many of the junior members also should be encouraged to study constantly and utilize the material so collected, as occasion demands, and be on the look-out for all new material that may aid the efficient conduct of the industry

Recent Industrial Trends

It seems necessary at this stage to refer to certain recent developments and tendencies noticed chiefly outside India, in order to stress the importance attached to industries in progressive countries and the relatively neglected condition of the same in this country

Through scientific discoveries and inventions, rapid changes are being made in methods of operation of industries with the object of reducing costs and obtaining the largest amount of production and income Most progressive countries are aiming not only to be self-sufficient in respect of manufactured products, but also to provide other countries with such products India is receiving such service and, in the case of certain staple commodities, what were once her best exports are now converted into leading imports

There is a growing force of nationalism in industrially developed countries and in India, too, the *swadeshi* spirit is growing strong and it must grow Nationalism and industrialism should develop hand in hand, if industries are to bring an adequate income to the country, but since India is still held and treated as a Dependency, and nationalism is not encouraged, industrialism has also suffered Industrialism can be either capitalistic or socialistic, or a combination of, or compromise between, both Progress in industrialism is a matter of co-operation and combination If industries are to thrive, there should be co-operation between the Government and the people on one side and between the owners of industries and the labour population on the other

In what follows, recent trends under the following five heads will be briefly explained —

Mechanization and mass production,

Trusts, combines, mergers, and cartels,

Rationalization,

Marketing organizations, and

Labour unions and combinations

Since the close of the War and partly as a result of War experience, great improvements have taken place, notably in the United States of America, in the mechanism and methods of industrial production Machinery is more largely used, motive power from coal, oil or water is on the increase, and management and methods are more scientific, more economical and efficient

In progressive countries modern management of large industries like steel and the automobile has reached a wonderful state of perfection The raw material is put in at one end of the factory and the finished article taken out at the other, the whole of the production being carried out by means of automatic machinery assisted by a minimum staff absolutely required for the few operations which the machinery cannot do for itself

Finding that large-scale plants as a rule produce commodities cheaper than small ones, the size of industrial undertakings is being continually enlarged Products in common use, such as clothing, are being standardized Standardization and mechanization combined lead to economical production of commodities and their supply at the least cost to the consumer Industries in this way are able to increase their selling power and profits and pay higher wages to their workmen

It has been seen that large industrial units produce commodities at cheaper prices than small ones There has therefore been a tendency in America towards the formation of trusts or economic combines under a single corporation or set of men by the amalgamation of enterprises engaged in the manufacture of the same product A similar tendency is noticeable in Germany where the process is known as "cartel" In America and Japan the terms used are "amalgamations," "trusts," "mergers," or "guilds" Large trusts have developed in America by this process of combination and consolidation undertaken in order to regulate prices and avoid internal competition

The trusts are usually of two classes, namely, (i) horizontal trusts, leading to the amalgamation of a number of establishments which manufacture the same product, and (ii) vertical trusts or integrations, representing a combination of industries which manufacture different stages of the same product In either case, the tendency is to bring the industries under one highly developed, technical and financial supervision leading to very appreciable economies in production

Under the "cartel" system, manufacturers of the same product in different parts of a country or in a number of neighbouring countries combine for the purpose of marketing A few years ago there was a cartel which represented a combine of the producers of steel in Germany, France, Belgium and Great Britain Such combines are able to sell a commodity at reduced prices—even below cost price—in some parts of the world where there is severe competition, and raise the prices in other parts and on the whole maintain an average price well above the costs Sometimes, after the rival industries are crushed by competition, prices are again raised to the prejudice of the consumer Semi-monopolies of this sort are some of the menaces to industries in undeveloped countries like India against which both the State and the people have to be constantly on the watch.

A combination of all measures, devices and processes which help to secure the maximum of output with the minimum use of raw materials and human labour in any industry is known as *rationalization*

Some of the measures taken to produce the desired result are—(i) control of a whole industry by one set of hands or by a single firm to eliminate wasteful production, (ii) changing machinery when any portion of it becomes obsolescent, (iii) making purchases of raw materials and stores in large quantities so as to be able to obtain them at the lowest rates, (iv) manufacturing commodities or semi-finished products in those places where on account of any special facilities they can be produced cheap, (v) standardizing products, and (vi) forming associations or cartels for the sale of the same.

The size of a plant may often be enlarged with profit after its products are standardized

Higher efficiency in the *staff* is secured by keeping its members supplied with up-to-date information and engaged in investigations and research problems connected with the industry, and wage-earners' efficiency is improved by giving them direct training

Till the beginning of this century, some countries specialized in industries and manufactures and others were content to grow primary products and there was exchange of goods between them But, with the rapid spread of industries in various parts of the world, countries which are industrially developed are finding it increasingly difficult to dispose of their products In agriculture, co-operative marketing organizations have facilitated the sale of agricultural produce to some extent In the case of manufactures also, new merchandising methods are being developed If for any reason the market is oversaturated, production is checked leading to shut-downs, depression and panic.

For these reasons, there is need in India for organizing sales activities on modern lines to withstand world competition The Indian market should, as far as possible, be reserved for Indian goods It behoves Indian industrialists not to shut their eyes to what is happening abroad in regard to the production and sale of commodities in which they are interested, but to adopt the up-to-date sales methods practised by their competitors

We have cheap labour in India, but, due to lack of mass education and training, the labour force is placed under grave disabilities In Europe, where there is universal mass education and workmen understand their rights, labour has learnt to organize and protect itself against any arbitrary acts of its capitalist employers or of government.

In India, too, the example of European labour organizations is being copied and workmen have begun to organize strikes with a view to enforcing their collective will, but the misfortune of India has been that these combinations have sprung up before industries themselves have gained a firm foothold The country is as yet industrially undeveloped and mutual quarrels between capital and labour are only having one effect, namely, of depressing the local industry and benefiting the foreign producer

Relations between capital and labour are undergoing readjustment both in England and in the United States of America but no formula is universally accepted so far The one country in which close co-operation between capital and labour was conspicuous until quite recently is the United States of America and the American example may be usefully followed in the case of large-scale industries For small industries, which are so much more numerous in India, the practices followed in countries like France, Japan and Belgium will be more suitable.

FACILITIES GIVEN IN PROGRESSIVE COUNTRIES

Convinced how intimately industrial growth is associated with prosperity, every modern country is striving its utmost to develop industries It may be of interest in this connection to recapitulate the efforts which some of the modern progressive governments have been making in this respect

Since the close of the War, the Government of Great Britain has given direct assistance to industries in various ways by levying anti-dumping duties and by investing public funds in national enterprises like the Cunard Steamship Company, the British Dyestuffs Company and the Home-Grown Sugar Company According to a statement of Mr J M Keynes in 1927, two-thirds of the capital invested in large-scale undertakings was in enterprises of a State capitalist character, *i e*, enterprises either in State hands or subject to some form of State regulation and control The British Industries Fair in London and Birmingham is a regular annual function under Government auspices A yearly grant was till recently being made to the Empire Marketing Board, that for the year 1932-33 being £300,000 The Trade Facilities Act and the subsequent Export Credit Insurance Scheme were designed to assist industries and trade which were adversely affected by the War So recently as on July 3, 1934, Mr Walter Runciman announced in the House of Commons that Government had agreed to a defensive subsidy not exceeding two million sterling, limited to a twelve month, for the relief of British tramp shipping which was suffering from subsidised foreign competition

The United States of America built up its industries by raising a high tariff wall against foreign goods In the year 1900 the income from industries in the United States was about the same as that from agriculture

Since then, particularly since the close of the World War, the United States has so extended her industries that the value of products obtained from them is now more than three times that derived from agriculture. Through this means and also by reason of its size and vast natural resources, the United States has attained the chief place in the world's industry and finance Very recently the Senate of the States went to the relief of industries by creating a 2,000 Million-Dollar Corporation to make advances to railways and other financial utilities which could not otherwise secure credit The Corporation also facilitates export of commodities by American agencies Enormous sums are spent on surveys, research and technical education The President of the United States under the Industrial Control Bill is vested with unprecedented powers to enforce, if necessary, sweeping regulations in industrial output, wages and prices for two years

Before the year 1911, the Dominion Government of Canada, in spite of that country's immense agricultural potentialities, built up its iron and steel industries by granting bounties for a long period of 28 years in addition to tariff protection It was the War that gave industries in Canada a stimulus and converted her into a manufacturing nation Her diversity of resources and manufacturing activities have so far increased her export trade that the value of that trade *per capita* now ranks first among the countries of the world This was brought about by many years of silent preparation by the Dominion Government In the interests of business and for securing profitable employment for its people, the same Government also takes infinite pains to gather and publish commercial and industrial statistics and information

Infant industries in Soviet Russia are protected

by high tariffs Many of the raw materials which were formerly being exported are now utilized for internal industries Automobiles and motor trucks which were being imported till recently are now manufactured locally The economic revolution in Russia is essentially an attempt to industrialize that country She is undergoing great privations and hardships due to her determination to realize that ideal It is reported that between 1921 and 1930 the total production of industry increased twelve-fold *The World Economic Survey*, 1931-32, published by the League of Nations, states, "Russia is one of the chief prodigies of the time From extreme backwardness it has advanced at a stride to the forefront of mechanical development" In the words of the Russian leader, Joseph Stalin,—Russia is going full steam ahead and becoming "a nation of metals, of automobiles and tractors"

When she started modernizing about the year 1870, Japan was in the same position industrially as India was The money she made from early enterprises she went on investing in extending and expanding industries and trade The subsequent progress has been extraordinarily rapid, particularly during and after the War The income from manufactures rose from Rs 206 crores in 1914 to Rs 937 crores in 1925, an increase of over 355 per cent The income from industries in 1925 was about double that from agriculture Government themselves financed many pioneer business undertakings and also set up factories which were afterwards sold to private individuals or companies They give subsidies and subventions to private enterprises and send out special investigators to foreign countries to learn new processes and efficient methods of operating industries In one of the author's visits to the Bureau of Standards at Washington, the business heads of that institution informed him that not a week passed without some representative from Japan visiting the Bureau to gather information in some department or other

In progressive countries like Great Britain, Japan and Germany, the Governments keep a close watch on the growth of industries and make suggestions and initiate measures calculated to advance the interests of owners of such undertakings The ministers and departmental heads, charged with the duty of promoting industries, adopt confidential policies not fully known even to their own nationals who implicitly confide in them When the people know that the duty is done better and more efficiently by the Government themselves, they merely follow the Government lead

Need for a Bold Policy

We find an altogether different state of things in this country Sir Basil Blackett, a former Finance Member of the Government of India, speaking before the Royal Society of Arts in London, on January 10, 1930, said, "The effect of the West on India, and, in particular, the reaction upon India of the industrial revolution in Great Britain and the consequent influx of machine-made goods, had during the nineteenth century seriously impaired the village economy of India and had reduced the output and the value to India of many of the indigenous manufactures previously exported, for which India was famous" "The Indian Government," he went on to say, "was dominated by the ideas of the Manchester School and restricted its intention in economic spheres and its taxation to the minimum needful to maintain law and order" It is apparent from this that in an industrial age, the Government policies of this country have tended to reduce employment in industries and to restrict the people to the one precarious occupation of agriculture

The suggestions made in these pages are in accordance with world practices to-day Sir Arthur Salter of the Secretariat of the League of Nations, who was consulted by the Government of India in June 1931 on these questions, also recommended the early establishment of Central and Provincial Economic Advisory Councils almost on the lines herein set forth "Indian industries," he remarked, "while already important enough, are at present small in comparison with her agriculture, and small also in relation to the future extension which they are no doubt destined to achieve" This is another way of saying what has already been expressed in plainer language, that India is not utilizing to her own full benefit her abundant resources and unequalled opportunities for industrial development.

Mr Roberson Taylor, Chairman of the Punjab Chamber of Commerce, at an Annual Meeting of that Chamber, said "India possesses in abundance all the conditions natural for a great industrial future," and "unless the country in the years to come can provide a wholly unprecedented industrial development, the level of subsistence of the country which is now dangerously low will become much worse" It is not necessary to give the opinion of any representative Indian economist in this connection because it will be difficult to find any one known as such to-day who will advocate a policy of "hasten slowly" in this important matter of industrial development

CHAPTER VI

TRANSPORT AND POWER SUPPLY

Population and Transport—Roads—Railways and Tramways—Shipping—Air Transport—Posts and Telegraphs, Telephones and Radio—Power Supply—Future Programme

POPULATION AND TRANSPORT

FOR over half a century, railways in India have had practically a monopoly of internal long-range traffic The advent of motor vehicles has challenged this supremacy, although railways must continue to be the main carriers of heavy goods and all long distance passenger traffic The growth of automobile traffic has also given an impetus to trade and commerce by bringing village produce closer to markets in point of time and distance The motor bus plying along village roads has inculcated habits of travel amongst the rural population even in remote corners of the country It is also having a distinct educative value in the villages Towns and markets which are frequented are rendered familiar to the villager, who has learnt to secure better prices for his products than before Cheap motor transport has to some extent done away with the wide fluctuations that existed in different parts of the country in the prices of food grains, cotton piece-goods and yarn

On account of the economic depression and the fall in prices of agricultural produce, traffic in passengers and goods over railways has decreased considerably. There has been little increase in railway communications in recent years, partly owing to competition from automobile traffic and partly also to lack of capital Considering the extent of the country and the population served, progress in the construction of new roads has also been slow Passenger shipping traffic has been steadily on the increase as a result of gradual disappearance of religious and social objections to ocean travel and with the increasing desire on the part of well-to-do Indians to visit foreign countries for business, education or pleasure Commodity traffic by ships, as in the case of railways, has been hard hit There is a striking advance in air traffic in India since the end of the Great War, not only have aero-clubs been started in a few important cities and towns giving the civilian population the "air-sense" but also regular postal and passenger air services have been installed between some of the principal stations in India and these are connected with the out-going and in-coming foreign mail steamers and foreign air services Communications by post and telegraph have become popular and their institution as a national service is widely appreciated both by the various departments of Government and the general public The use of the telephone and the wireless has not attained anywhere near the popularity they deserve, however, the rapid strides in the use of wireless telegraphy and telephony in other civilized countries are having their repercussions in India and business men are realizing that distances could be annihilated by the use of the radio-telephone Overseas radio telephone services have recently been inaugurated linking London and other cities of the world with important cities in India A beginning has thus been made for utilizing the opportunities created by the tremendous developments in modern methods of communication, and this is bound to react favourably on the industrial and economic regeneration of India

Roads

An economically sound development of the commerce and industries of a country depends, to a large extent, on a carefully planned and co-ordinated system of its transportation facilities Road mileage in India has not increased to the extent necessitated by the advent of the automobile The Indian Road Committee has felt it necessary to point out the incongruity of a large country like India having over 42,000 miles of railways with only less than 60,000 miles of surfaced roads It has been computed, that if India, excluding the Himalayan regions, the Indian desert and Burma, were as well served per square mile with public roads as is Great Britain, she would require nearly 3 million miles of road way The actual mileage of surfaced roads in India is only about 2 per cent and the total mileage of both metalled and unmetalled roads about 8 4 per cent of that figure There are, however, about 200,000 miles of unmetalled roads in rural areas which are managed by district and local boards, and which just answer local requirements. Even the development of such roads has been hampered through want of funds Expenditure from provincial and local revenues on the construction and maintenance of roads in British India during the four years ended 1926-27 was Rs 20 crores, while the corresponding expenditure in the United States of America, calculated on the basis of the outlay of the previous ten years, was the huge figure of Rs 1,100 crores In a single year (1927-28), such expenditure in the United States aggregated Rs 160 crores, constituting the chief item of expenditure of State Governments, without taking Federal grants into account

The bullock cart is the vehicle most in use for the carriage of goods in the interior of the country and for feeding the goods traffic on railways Modern lorry transport is, to an increasing extent, replacing the bullock or buffalo cart, but the latter mode of transport will continue under the conditions prevalent in India, where farmers need bulls and buffaloes for agricultural purposes but have little use for them for a good part of the year when farm work is slack or at a standstill

Rickshaws drawn by human labour are popular in certain hill stations and towns in India, in spite of the criticism levelled against them on the score of the inhumanity of using men for draught purposes, rickshaws will continue to be popular to a limited extent in view of their simplicity, cheapness and comfort for passenger traffic They are extensively used in Japan and in the Far East generally

Automobile transport gives employment to large numbers of people, and the manner in which it adds to the amenities of life and the capacity it has to open up areas for trade and industry are being slowly but steadily realized in the country The number of automobiles registered in British India at the end of March 1932 was a little over 200,000 Of the world total of about 39 million motor vehicles in 1930, the United States of America owned 26 8 million, United Kingdom 2 3 million, while India had only one-fifth of a million This means that in the United States of America, one person in every 5 owns an automobile; in the United Kingdom, one in every 20, and in British India one in every 1,300 It is said that the United States of America with her 26 8 million motor vehicles could transport her entire population inside her autos with 5 persons seated in each During the year ended 31st March 1930, India imported 32,700 motor cars and buses worth over Rs $7\frac{1}{2}$ crores, the bulk of which came from the United States of America and

Canada There is, therefore, considerable scope for the growth of the automobile industry in the country, but there are, as yet, no signs of any attempt to develop its local manufacture Such an industry would not only prevent a huge drain of India's wealth, but would also give employment to many thousands of her people It is bound in due course to become a factor of first rate economic importance to India

RAILWAYS AND TRAMWAYS

Railways have been allowed to be constructed in India, presumably for strategic reasons, side by side with and parallel to roads There are, for instance, about 13,000 miles of motorable roads in this country, running parallel to or in the neighbourhood of railways and it is estimated that the loss to Indian railways as a result of competition from motor vehicles is about Rs 1 9 crores per annum It is now realized that the money which is being spent on the upkeep of metalled roads running in the same direction as the railways could be used to greater advantage in the making of rural roads connecting village producing centres and markets with the railways

The Government of India and the Provincial Governments have had, so far, no co-ordinated rail and road policy Generally speaking, the railways are the concern of the Government of India, while roads are maintained by Provincial Governments and Local Bodies About Rs 800 crores have been invested in Indian Railways After discussing matters at a Railroad Conference, the Government of India have proposed to set up an All-India Central Board of Communications to be responsible in future for the development of all forms of vehicular transport. Such a Board, when constituted, will, it is hoped, study transportation problems of every kind and settle upon a comprehensive rail and road programme for future action

It is estimated that in 1931-32 the Government realized a total of Rs 13 crores from motor vehicles made up of import duties and provincial and local taxes, while the total expenditure on roads based on the figures for the two previous years was only about Rs 7 crores; and when it is realized that new roads also contribute to the economic development and trade of the country, apart from their other public uses, the significance of the absence of a policy behind road development in India becomes striking

Although the Indian Empire is more than twenty times the size of Great Britain, its railway mileage is only about twice as large as in Great Britain, and only about one-sixth of that in the United States of America

Railway development in India has not proceeded on modern lines There are four different gauges of railway track in the country, they prevent interchange of carriages and wagons, causing considerable inconvenience to traffic of both goods and passengers The management and administration of the Indian Railways is expected to be handed over under the proposed Federal Constitution to a Statutory Railway Authority, whose powers are at present under discussion They are now controlled and managed by a Railway Board A separate railway budget is maintained since 1925, which is independently considered and approved by the Indian Legislature Railways, in all countries of the world, are found to be generally a source of profit In India, an annual contribution of Rs 6 crores was being paid to the Central Exchequer till recently from the Railway revenues Competition with motor traffic has decreased railway earnings everywhere, and in many countries just now the problem of improving Railway finance is receiving close attention In the United States of America, for instance, the American Railway Association has set up a number of Regional Advisory Boards, representative of the shippers, producers and bankers concerned with the movement of freight in their districts. A programme of the country's freight requirements is made from the seasonal estimates of these Boards and published in advance for the information of traders and business men The United States has also recently appointed a Federal Co-ordinator of Transport, whose duties will consist, amongst others, of fostering internal commerce by maintaining an adequate national system of transportation

The Indian Railway administration has not so far, in spite of the country's "pilgrimage-ridden" tendencies, improved the financial position of its railways No organized attempt has been made to determine the demand for railway wagons or the economic necessity for reducing or varying the freights, according to local conditions, for the transport of agricultural products and manufactured goods The policy underlying future extensions should be examined, and the needs of the trade and traffic, and not the interests of the Railway Management, should be the paramount consideration in sanctioning the construction of new lines

In the matter of equipment and supplies for railways, as in the automobile industry, India is almost completely dependent on outside manufacturing countries And this, notwithstanding that India has the fourth largest railway mileage in the world Provision for advanced study and training of Indians in mechanical and electrical engineering to fit them for railway engineering work is most inadequate Instances have occurred where qualified Indians with advanced theoretical training were denied facilities for practical training on foreign railways and their engineering workshops The remedy lies in making provision for complete training in mechanical and electrical engineering in India itself in collaboration with railway engineering workshops. A new policy and an up-to-date programme are urgently needed in order that all our major railway requirements may be met from railway workshops and Government and private factories built in India, and that complete training in railway engineering and technique may be given to Indian students within the country itself Thus should India be enabled to meet her day-to-day wants The definite aim should be to make the transition from a stage of almost complete dependence, as it is at present, to one of self-sufficiency as early as possible

Electric tramways were once a useful form of passenger transport in many cities of the world but their development has been arrested by the advent of the cheaper and quicker motor bus transport Tramway companies, which have sunk capital on permanent way and tramcars, find it a problem to compete with motor buses Some of the companies are running bus services themselves side by side with tram service to keep themselves alive as transport agencies

SHIPPING

Next only in importance to roads and railways, shipping transport plays a vital part in the development of the commerce and industry of a country In spite of its intimate connection with a supreme maritime nation for the past 150 years, India has not become even a third-rate maritime power, its long coast-line and other geographical advantages notwithstanding In fact, the country has fallen from the position it once occupied as a maritime nation when Indian merchandise was carried to other countries in Indian bottoms

There is at present no shipping worth the name in India More than 99 per cent of India's sea-borne trade is carried by vessels not owned by Indians Before the Chino-Japanese War (1894), Japanese vessels carried about 8 per cent of that nation's foreign trade, ten years later, they carried 37 per cent of that trade, while in 1928, 72 per cent of the export and 63 per cent of the import trade were carried in Japanese liners This is an example of what a national government can do The tonnage of Indian-owned vessels is about 272,000 while the United Kingdom has over 19 7 million, the United States of America 13 4 million and Japan 4 3 million This most unsatisfactory position of Indian shipping is not due to the absence of interest or initiative on the part of Indians to create a mercantile marine or navy for their country

Every attempt on the part of Indians to reserve at least India's coastal trade to Indian-owned vessels has met with stout opposition from British Shipping Companies The Government of India has, in this struggle between Indian and European commercial interests, shown no inclination to aid the growth of Indian shipping The latest attitude of Government is reflected in the reply of Sir Samuel Hoare to a question in Parliament, namely, that it was not contemplated to reserve Indian coastal trade to Indian shipping No Indian Company, however strong, can hope to thrive in the teeth of competition from powerful vested interests with their accumulated reserves without the backing of a national government The history of the efforts of Indian shipping for a proper share in India's sea-borne trade and for the privilege of carrying Indian goods in Indian bottoms will be recorded as one of the country's hardest fights for existence against such well-organized interests It is reported that 27 of the 32 maritime nations of the world have reserved their coastal trade to their own nationals, the 5 that have not so reserved are possibly those that are strong enough to withstand competition Not only has the proposed reservation of coastal traffic in India to Indian-owned vessels been negatived by the attitude of the Government and British shipping interests, but the training of Indians as Officers and Engineers in sea-going vessels has also been practically ignored The Government have not visualized the necessity and the ultimate advantages of having an up-to-date mercantile marine and an Indian navy in Indian waters and have, in fact, shown no initiative in the matter, the solitary instance of the provision of the training ship "*Dufferin*" as a result of much public agitation, being too insignificant to be reckoned as an earnest attempt in this respect on their part

In 1929, Japan had 71,762 men possessing certificates of competency as Captains and Engineers, of these, only 132 were foreigners, among whom only one non-Japanese held a captain's rank The number of Indians qualified as captains and engineers in vessels carrying India's huge foreign trade is probably nil

The total number of shipping companies started in India was 32, of which 23 languished and went into liquidation through lack of Government support and *unfair* competition from non-Indian interests Of the remaining 9 companies, the Scindia Steam Navigation Company is the largest, having a fleet of 10 steamers of 43,076 total gross tonnage The largest British Shipping Company plying in Indian waters is the British India Steam Navigation Company, which has a fleet of 128 ships of 757,210 total gross tonnage The Scindia Company, under prudent management, with no Government support, has been carrying on its trade under sufferance between certain coastal ports in India Very few of the Indian Shipping Companies, however, find it profitable to carry passengers across the seas as attempts to do so are promptly scotched by competition from foreign companies It is learnt that so far only one Indian company has for the first time been granted the privilege of carrying mails in the Bay of Bengal

Under the new Government, in spite of the opposition from vested interests to which India's public men have by now got accustomed, special attention will have to be paid to encourage Indian shipping in the many ways it is done by national governments of other countries The Japanese Government's Ocean Service Subvention Law permits subsidies to ships built by a company in which the partners or shareholders are all Japanese subjects The Government of that country now pay a subsidy of Rs 75 lakhs annually to Japanese shipping The preamble to the Merchant Marine Act, 1920, of the United States of America contains the following significant words "It is necessary for the national defence and for the proper growth of its foreign and domestic commerce that the United States shall have a Mercantile Marine of the best equipped and most suitable types of vessels sufficient to carry the greater portion of its commerce and serve as a naval or military auxiliary in time of war or national emergency, ultimately to be manned or operated privately by citizens of the United States, and it is hereby declared to be the policy of the United States to do whatever may be necessary to develop and encourage the maintenance of such a mercantile marine" In Germany, from a small tonnage of 600,000 that was left to her by the Versailles Treaty, the ship-owners and the Government in that country have jointly increased it to over 3 million tons in a short period of 5 years.

India's dependence on foreign ships reduces her trade to one of absolute helplessness in times of war or other national emergencies A start should be made without delay with a programme of ship-building in India, with a view ultimately to form a maritime fleet at least of the capacity of that of Canada In 1932, in Canada, there were 8,895 vessels with a tonnage of 1,475,000 To carry out this policy, a Shipping Board should be constituted whose members should be Indians actively interested in India's trade and commerce The policy of such a Board should be along lines set out in the preamble to the U S A Merchant Marine Act quoted above There can be no question that the requisite talent has long been available for the purpose in the country

Waterway transport in India could not attain any importance commensurate with the number of large rivers in the country, for the reason that most of them are unfit for navigable purposes, and those that are fit, are only so for part of their courses In Bengal, there are 6 important navigable canals and receipts from them during 1929-30 amounted to nearly Rs 10 lakhs In Burma, where the river Irrawaddy, its tributaries and the delta creeks are eminently fitted for navigation, river transport plays a very important part Practically the whole of such transport is in the hands of a British Company, *viz*, the Irrawaddy Flotilla Co, Ltd Since irrigation canals are being extended in various parts of India, waterway transport through canals could be improved in future to some extent for the carriage, mainly, of agricultural and forest produce The Shipping Board, mentioned in the last paragraph, should initiate and encourage river and canal transport, wherever possible

Air Transport

Air transport has developed enormously in recent

years No achievement of man has ever made such rapid progress in so short a period as man's conquest of the air India, the country of long distances, has, by its geographical position as a focal point of aviation for Central Asia, been drawn in to take an important part in this development The Civil Aviation Department of the Government of India came into existence in 1927 The Government have permitted private enterprise to provide the country with air services and a few Indians are allowed training in Civil Aviation The aero-clubs that were started in many Indian cities are, however, only intended for the recreation of the few who could afford to become their members As is the case with other economic services in India, few, if any, facilities are afforded to the youth of the country to obtain instruction in aeroplane engineering or training as commercial pilots In Europe and more particularly in America, commercial aviation is rapidly assuming increasing importance For instance, investments in aviation enterprises are reported to have amounted to Rs 300 crores in America In France, a Supreme Air Council to control all air policy has been established, the Council, it is said, is to develop given routes, direct training and technical research, and promote the building up of an effective system of inspection and maintenance and *be responsible for economic results* Local governing bodies, chambers of commerce and agriculture, railways and shipping companies and seaports are to be associated with the State in this enterprise

Efforts on these lines should be made in this country to popularize the use of the aeroplane as a quick means of transport for mails and passengers The municipalities should be enabled to provide suitable landing grounds for air-taxis and the more important of them should arrange under adequate supervision for the training of young men as pilots and engineers The development of air transport, unlike that of ocean transport, has fortunately no vested interests to encounter, and the encouragement of the Government, in the shape of advice and bounties, can therefore be expected, if there is a sustained private effort in the country

The Indian Government have already provided landing ground, wireless and meteorological services, etc, on the Australian route through India The Standing Finance Committee of the Indian Legislative Assembly approved in August 1934 the Government proposals for the development of air routes in India. The proposals involve a total expenditure of Rs 92,57,000 spread over three years, of which aerodromes and landing grounds will absorb Rs 76,70,000, wireless facilities Rs 10,21,000, and the remaining Rs 5,66,000 will be employed on improving meteorological information now available for pilots Even with these measures, it is a question whether the Government have proved themselves sufficiently responsive in encouraging local services. The Imperial line passes through Karachi, Delhi, Calcutta and Rangoon A second line is that run by Messrs Tata Sons, Ltd, of Bombay between Karachi, Bombay and Madras which will be extended to Colombo as soon as the Government of Ceylon provide an Aerodrome there An attempt is at present being made by the same firm to start a direct service between Bombay and Calcutta *via* Nagpur, but Government response has been feeble A local passenger service is maintained daily between Calcutta and Dacca by Messrs Indian National Airways who also operate a weekly service between Calcutta and Rangoon A service started between Madras and Calcutta was for a time discontinued for want of adequate support but it is again revived There is demand for a line between Karachi, Lahore and Kashmir The training of local talent for pilot service seems altogether ignored.

Experts are of opinion that, unless night flying is arranged for, air transport will not attain its full value Further capital outlay is undoubtedly required for providing the above-mentioned requirements The Government can encourage private enterprise by paying subsidies or by giving mail contracts at rates of payment which will enable the transport to be self-supporting If sufficient encouragement on these lines be forthcoming, it is expected that air transport in India will pay itself in about ten years' time

Posts and Telegraphs, Telephones and Radio

Considering the comparatively small amount of business done in India, the number of post offices in the country may be said to be fairly satisfactory, although if regard is had to the population it must be pronounced very small For instance, for every 10,000 of the population, there are in Canada 12 post offices, in the United Kingdom 5, in the United States of America 4, while in India the number works out to less than 1 In the matter of telegraph offices, the number per 10,000 of the population in each of the countries in 1931 was Canada 4, the United Kingdom 3, the United States of America 2, Japan 2, while India had barely 1 for every 30,000 of its population

The use of the telephone is still reckoned a luxury in India to which only a big business man or official is entitled The total number of telephones in India during 1931 works out to 1 7 per 10,000 of the population, the corresponding figures for the other countries were, Japan 105, the United Kingdom 429, and Canada

1349 while the United States of America has the high figure of 1,637 This means that one person out of every 6 of the population in the United States owns a telephone, even as one in every 5 owns an automobile in that country

The use of the radio (or wireless) in India has potentialities of a far-reaching character, if proper efforts are made to develop it The educational value of broadcasting and its use as a means to supply information on agricultural and trade topics to the villages, to remove misunderstandings about Government policies and measures amongst illiterate people and, above all, to provide healthy recreation like popular lectures, music, etc , to people in rural areas are not sufficiently well realized In a land where the greatest handicap to progress is illiteracy and ignorance, education of the rural population by broadcasting in the vernacular from central towns has not been attempted, in spite of the recognition of its efficacy by numerous organizations in India Unlike many other proposals for the improvement of rural conditions, there are no financial difficulties in carrying out a comprehensive scheme of rural broadcasting According to the scheme prepared on behalf of the Indian Village Improvement Association, of which Sir Francis Younghusband is the Chairman and certain eminent retired British Indian officials are members, an area of 500 villages, each with an average population of 400, could be served from a central transmitter operating on a fixed wave-length, each village being equipped with a receiver and loud speaker ; and for each village comprising this area, the financial liability for the installation could be liquidated by a contribution of Rs 120 per year for the first 7 years, and a maintenance charge of Rs 60 per year thereafter. The following extract from a recent pamphlet issued by the Association giving details about the use of the radio for similar purposes in the Soviet Union will be found instructive —

"The Soviet Union, from the rural point of view, bears a close resemblance to India There is in Russia the same enormous extent of country, with a predominantly peasant population, the greater proportion of whom have been hitherto illiterate, though this is now rapidly changing There is almost an equal variety of languages, in many parts Russian is only understood by a small section of the people in the same way as Hindustani is more or less known in the villages of Northern and Central India A broadcasting service to be effective among such a rural population, must be based on relatively small units of area, and be of such a character that it is interesting and helpful to peasants and to more or less illiterate populations This is achieved by the establishment of a large number of local broadcasting centres, with public receivers in a large proportion of the villages in each language area In Russia no charge is made for the use of a receiving set, but by far the greater part of the rural population uses the public receiving set which is installed in one or more public meeting places either in the open or in a building in the village, as well as in the school The programmes are mixed, and include music, humorous items, material relating to hygiene, the care of children, agriculture, co-operation, new plans of rural development, and such schemes of rural organization as the authorities wish to bring to the notice of the village people As with all things in Russia, the whole work is organized on an official basis, but the development of the system proves that there is really no technical or other difficulty in producing and broadcasting programmes which are acceptable to a rural population not widely dissimilar to that of India "

In India, at any rate to start with, the Government should be the agency responsible for this scheme of broadcasting in villages, for, in that case, Government officials of the several departments connected with the nation-building activities could get a direct "hearing" from the villagers whom they are intended to educate and guide, and propaganda of a contentious or unhealthy type through the medium of the radio may be eschewed by official control A village of normal size will have no difficulty in raising the small sum of about a rupee per year per family to obtain the funds for the service of the radio, and the collection could be simplified by making it a part of some local cess to which the villagers are accustomed

Power Supply

While examining the resources in transport and communications in the country, a reference to the supply of power for transport and other purposes may not be out of place Coal, where available in sufficient quantities, has for long been the fuel for the generation of machine-power In the year 1931, the production of coal in the United Kingdom amounted to 223 million tons, in Germany 119 million tons and in France 15 million tons, while in the United States of America, it was more than the combined output of these three countries In India (including the States), the quantity of coal produced was only 22 million tons or a twentieth of that annually made available in the United States. Indian coal is not widely distributed and is generally of poor quality, but as forests are abundant, wood fuel is cheap and has often proved a profitable substitute. Since the War, the use of mineral oils has been on the increase as a source of power There has been keen competition for the control of the world's oil wells among the leading commercial nations In 1931, the principal countries of the world in the order of their yearly production of oil were the United States of America 117 million tons, Russia 22 million tons, and Venezuela 17 million tons Persia produced nearly 6 million tons while India and Argentine each a million tons The Russians had planned for a 85 per cent increase in oil output in 1932 over their 1927 figures, their oil resources, still mostly untapped, are believed to be by far the greatest in the world The petroleum produced in the oil wells of India (including Burma) during 1930 was worth Rs 5½ crores, of which Burma alone contributed Rs 4¾ crores. Practically the whole of Burma's exportable surplus of oil, worth over Rs 3 crores, apart from Rs 5 crores worth of kerosene, was sold to India; India, in addition, imported during the same year over Rs 2 crores worth of fuel-oil and about Rs 6 crores worth of kerosene, from foreign countries India, like most other countries, is dependent for her supply of oil on Burma, Persia, America and Russia

In recent years, some progress has been made in India in the generation of hydro-electric power, but the output compared to that in progressive countries is almost negligible

The waters of Indian rivers can be harnessed in places for power generation but, as the fair weather flow in them is small, expensive storage reservoirs will be necessary In some situations, water used for power generation may be later utilized for irrigation This might compensate in some degree for the heavy expenditure needed for storage

It is estimated that India has total potential power resources of 27 million horse-power, while the power actually developed is only 0 8 of a million or 3 per cent This latter figure is likely to increase to 1¾ million horse-power in the near future About half of this is being developed in the Western Ghats of the Bombay Presidency If India is to progress, consumption per head must grow Canada, for instance, consumes 450 watts *per capita* while the corresponding consumption in India is only 1 watt

The following figures will show how inadequate Hydro-electric development in India is as compared with the leading countries of the world —

Water Power Resources

Country	In million horse-power		Percentage to total
	Potential	Developed quantity	
United States of America	35 0	11 7	33
Canada	18 2	4 5	25
France	5 4	2 1	37
Japan	4 5	1 7	37
Spain	4 0	1 0	25
Italy	3 8	1 8	47
Switzerland	2 5	1 8	72
Germany	2 0	1 1	55
India	27 0	0 8	3

The foregoing table, with the exception of the figures for India, is taken from the *World Almanac*, New York (1932) The figures for India are not authoritative but approximate estimates

No reliable figures exist of the total production of

electricity in this country, it is believed that the total from all sources is about 1 8 billion kilowatt hours In the year 1931, Japan produced 14 billion k w h, of which 13 billion was hydro-electric In the United States of America, in the same year, 115 billion k w h was produced, of which 27½ billion was hydro-electric. The production of electricity in America is 45 per cent of the total world production

In India, the use of electricity has made some headway in a few industrial centres like Bombay and in lighting important towns, but its use for industries and manufactures is not being fostered according to a pre-determined plan While other countries are actively prosecuting well-thought-out schemes, this country seems to be merely looking on For instance, Italy electrified 3,000 miles of railways in 1929 About 75 per cent of the industries are electrified in the United States of America, about 70 per cent in Germany and Canada and 50 per cent in Great Britain No statistics, as far as we are aware, are available to testify to the use of electric power in India

An article in the *American Economic Review* for March 1933 on the daily output of work by the different countries of the world gives the following illuminating figures —

The World's Daily Output of Work for 1929

Country	Million horse-power hours					Daily output *per capita* (H P Hours)
	Human	Coal	Petrol	Water	Total	
India	106	34	8	3	151	0.47
United States of America	40	1001	181	121	1613	13.38
Canada	3.3	55	17.6	59	134.9	13.03
Great Britain	15	270	28.3	4	317.3	0.65
Germany	21	333	0.5	13	376.[illegible]	6.04
France	14	127	12.3	21	177.[illegible]	4.35
Japan	21	52	7	30	110	1.75

It is apparent from this table that human or manual labour, as opposed to mechanical labour, is used in India as nowhere else in the world and that the daily output of work *per capita* is on that account distressingly low It should be the task of the leaders of the people in the coming years to organize themselves and utilize to the best advantage the technical results of modern science and thus pave the way to the removal of the reproach conveyed by the low position occupied by India in this table

FUTURE PROGRAMME

The existing means of transport in the country may be summed up in round figures as follows .—

1 (*a*) Roads—74,000 miles are metalled and 160,000 miles unmetalled

(*b*) Automobiles—in use approximately 200,000.

2. Railways—mileage 42,000
3 Shipping—9 indigenous companies with a gross tonnage of 200,000
4 Posts—24,000 Post Offices carrying annually 1,210 million articles
5 Telegraphs—13,000 offices with a total of 18 million messages dealt with annually
6 Telephones—300 Exchanges with 56,000 connections
7. Radio—31 wireless stations maintained by Government, apart from a few broadcasting stations in the principal cities, their number being unknown

These services, for a country with an area of 1 8 million square miles and a population of 353 million, are miserably meagre as compared with what are available in modern countries In any future programme of transport and power extension in this country, the following developments should find a place —

(1) An All-India Board of Communications should be constituted, as early as possible, representative of all transport interests in India This Board should make a study of the transport requirements of the country in general,—together with a survey of the country's future road programme in particular,—and should evolve practical proposals for financing the schemes The Board should also be an expert advisory body for Provincial Transport Committees The present total length of roads in India is less than 300,000 miles The programme should aim at increasing the same to at least 1 million miles within the next five years

(2) Automobile industries should be started in important centres in India and arrangements made to increase the number of vehicles registered in India (nearly 200,000 in 1931) to at least 350,000 within 5

years, thereby providing in the first instance, 1 automobile for every 1,000 of the population

(3) Immediate steps should be taken to provide full and complete training in Mechanical, Electrical, Railway, Marine and Mining Engineering for Indian students in India A big start should be made in the manufacture of machinery and materials required for Indian Railways in workshops built in India, and the country should be made independent of outside assistance in the matter of her railway requirements within the next 5 years

(4) Renewed efforts should be made by suitable legislation and otherwise to freely permit Indian ships to carry on trade between coastal ports in India and with ports of other countries, adequate protection being given from economic wars with vested interests A programme of ship-building should be chalked out by a Shipping Board, by carrying out which the maritime fleet of India may attain a strength of at least 1 5 million gross tonnage in the near future Shipping companies regularly operating in Indian waters may be obliged by statute to employ Indians to at least 50 per cent of their superior staff within a period of 5 years, this will give an excellent impetus to maritime training for Indians

(5) The Aviation Department of the Government of India should devise effective methods of popularising the use of the aeroplane as a means of transport For instance, every city or municipality with over a lakh of population should be asked to provide suitable landing grounds for air-taxis, to arrange for regular courses of instruction for Indians as pilots and mechanics, the Government sharing the expenses by bearing the cost of the landing grounds and aerodromes and the pay of expert instructors.

(6) The Provinces of India should be parcelled out into several units, each unit covering an area of about 500 villages in which the same vernacular is spoken or understood Each of these units should be provided with a central radio transmitter and each village served by it with receivers and loud speakers Daily broadcasting from these centres on education and popular topics should be arranged with the co-operation of the local citizens and local Government officers, the Government being responsible for the conduct of the service

(7) A comprehensive scheme of development of electric power in India should be launched immediately with a view ultimately to supply cheap electric power for domestic use as well as for industrial and public utility undertakings in the country No effort should be spared until at least 50 per cent of the potential 27 million H P available is actually developed and brought into operation

CHAPTER VII

TRADE AND COMMERCE

Review of World and Indian Trade—Exports—Imports—Inland Trade—Sea borne Trade

REVIEW OF WORLD AND INDIAN TRADE

THE value of the total trade of the world increased from an average of Rs 11,000 crores during the three pre-war years to Rs 19,000 crores in the year 1929 Since 1929, there has come over such a huge wave of economic depression that trade in the year 1933 fell in value to 40 7 per cent of that in the former year Trade flourishes on mutual good-will and confidence But the lessons of the Great War and the provisions of the Treaty of Versailles put confidence between nations to a severe strain Creditor nations insisted on repayment of their loans in gold, instead of in goods, in order to conserve their own gold stock The debtor nations being unable to pay in gold for imported goods, soon found it essential by recourse to tariffs and economic plans to increase their own production The policy of "economic nationalism" with the resultant increased production has found favour in most industrial countries in recent years and led to a heavy fall in the prices of agricultural commodities This in turn has resulted in the reduction of the purchasing power of countries which formerly imported manufactured goods Efforts to improve prices of primary commodities, such as crop-planning and wholesale destruction of food-grains in certain countries, while millions of people in less advanced countries have been almost on the verge of starvation, have proved more spectacular than beneficial Other expedients also like exporting more while importing less, depreciation of currencies and manipulation of exchanges have been found to be mere palliatives

The more progressive nations of Europe, while particularly mindful each of its own interests, have made several attempts at co-operation among themselves with a view to bring the world trade back to normalcy and prosperity During the fifteen years following the Treaty of Versailles, over 50 international gatherings and about 28 economic conferences were held, but the remedies proposed have not succeeded in reviving international trade or restoring prosperity of the participating countries The decline in trade has continued The huge experiment of the United States of America in co-ordinating all branches of national activity under the Recovery Plan put into force by its present President is being watched with keen interest and expectation

The trade depression since 1929 has adversely affected business conditions in Great Britain London was hitherto rightly considered the centre of the world's international trade and finance Rumours of an adverse balance of trade led to heavy withdrawals of foreign funds invested in that country At the same time the demand for products exported from Great Britain also fell The effect of both these factors was that Great Britain departed from its gold basis and adopted a policy of protection for her manufactures by means of tariffs The reaction of such a policy on Indian trade has been that gold of the value of nearly Rs 200 crores was exported from this country up to July 1934 Great Britain's other efforts in the way of encouragement of inter-Imperial trade with the Dominions, India and the Colonies by the trade agreements arranged at Ottawa and other pacts have to a small extent helped trade revival among some of the Empire countries but the general position, at the time of writing, continues to be unsatisfactory

The future outlook appears to be that trade between nations will be steadily restricted to luxuries and indispensable commodities and to special products of which individual countries happen to have a monopoly. The volume of trade will show a tendency to decrease, keeping pace with the growth of the new economic nationalism

Indian trade, as may be expected, has expanded slowly, but its reaction on the country has not been favourable to its people India, not being dependent on other countries for its primary commodities, should be expected to have a satisfactory trade position But she has to maintain year after year a heavy balance of exports over imports to pay towards service and debt charges, profits on foreign investments, foreign trade and business gains, and other visible and invisible imports

If the movements of gold and silver, which in recent years have been heavy, are left out of account, the values of imports and exports of merchandise for 1932-33 were Rs 133 crores and 136 crores respectively, leaving a favourable trade balance of Rs 3 crores The corresponding figures for 1929-30 were Rs 241, 318 and 77 crores respectively Making the requisite allowance for the fall in prices and calculating on the basis of the values in 1913-14, the total trade in merchandise in 1931-32 was Rs 343 crores as against Rs 452 crores in 1929-30 and Rs 327 crores in 1913-14, the pre-war year The normal *per capita* foreign trade of India may be taken at Rs 18 per annum, which is the lowest figure for any nation in the world

Thirty years ago, India's trade was over twice that of Canada and over three times that of Japan, now it is less than that of either of those countries When the European nations were engaged in the world war, the United States of America, Japan and Canada took the opportunity to develop their resources During 1929-30, the total trade of Canada, with less than 3 per cent of India's population, was 15 per cent more than that of India, whereas in the pre-war year, 1913-14, India's total trade was 63 per cent better than Canada's. The *per capita* trade, during the same war-period, increased in Canada from about Rs 44 to Rs 105 and in the United States of America from Rs 132 to 276, while that in India remained practically stationary at about Rs 18 The expansion in the above countries was brought about by pursuing a vigorous policy of pushing industrial and agricultural production, building up of new transport, marketing and other economic services, and creating fresh banking and other trade facilities India did not take advantage of her opportunities to expand her trade even in the years that followed the war Indian business is carried on without the help of any proper organization and without any recognized policies, it is left to individual tradesmen and firms to develop it as best as they can in the face of severe foreign competition

Discussing India's industrial development in a speech made at Hamburg in 1929, Mr H A F (now Sir Harry) Lindsay, His Majesty's Indian Trade Commissioner, said that there were co-existing in India, but not yet properly co-ordinated, those three great forces which were essential to all industrial prosperity—materials, money and men There is an additional important force that stimulates production—namely, markets, in spite of such facilities for expansion of trade, possessed perhaps by no other country in the world, there is in existence no suitable machinery to foster trade commensurate either with the size or the importance of the task, neither has industrial development shown any appreciable progress

Agricultural production also has shown no appreciable progress to-day compared with the pre-war years. India produces 40 per cent of the world's supply of rice and 10 per cent of the world's supply of wheat The export of 8 per cent of her production of rice makes her the biggest rice-exporting country in the world, if her teeming millions eat enough and increase their consuming capacity by a small margin, the country will not only need all the food-grains now produced but considerable increase in production will be necessary, before it can resume its rôle as an exporter of staple food products And the same result will follow, if her population keeps on increasing as rapidly as it has done during the last decade

The country can meet its heavy foreign obligations in future years only by a substantial increase of production both from industries and agriculture Increased production in industries will reduce imports and the same in agriculture will increase exports, together, they should maintain the essential favourable balance How to arrange for the co-ordinated development of these two occupations and for a planned internal consumption and external marketing is the trade problem confronting the country at the present moment

EXPORTS

The total exports of merchandise from India during the year 1932-33 amounted to Rs 132 crores, the principal items being —

Jute and manufactures	Rs	31	crores
Cotton and manufactures	,,	24	,,
Grain and pulses	,,	16	,,
Tea	,,	17	,,
Seeds	,,	11	,,

These together contribute three-fourths of the value of the total export trade, the balance being accounted for by hides and skins, lac, oilcakes, rubber, spices, timber and other miscellaneous articles There was, in addition, the export of gold and silver to the total value of Rs 70 66 crores,—the highest figure on record of the export of precious metals from India Inclusive of this export, the *per capita* export trade of India was Rs 5 7

Exports of merchandise dropped in value from Rs 313 crores to Rs 132 crores within the last 3 years, *i e*, by 58 per cent, the fall in jute and cotton alone contributing Rs 97 crores to this decrease

The main feature of India's export trade is that the country is an exporter of tropical food-stuffs and of raw materials for foreign manufactures, these exports consist of products derived from primitive methods of cultivation, and are low-priced and unremunerative, while the export of manufactured goods from India is dwindling A favourable trade balance can be maintained only so long as the exportable goods find a market Of these markets, the United Kingdom and Japan are the most important, they being consumers of India's cotton, wheat and tea, Continental Europe affords a market for oil-seeds, hides and skins We are assured of our export trade in jute, because it is produced in no other country in the world, and India has a monopoly of that product The export of rice and wheat which accounts for 93 per cent of the total quantity of food-grains exported from India is bound to diminish in future, for, vast areas of land in South America, Africa, Italy and Japan, possessing similar climatic and soil conditions, are rapidly increasing their production of these food-grains by the use of machinery and the application of scientific methods of cultivation For instance, exports of rice to Japan from India (including Burma) decreased from Rs 418 lakhs in 1924-26 to Rs 10 lakhs in 1928-29. The export of wheat from India has fallen from over a million tons in pre-war years to 2,000 tons in 1932-33. The recent Japanese boycott of Indian cotton has shown that it is easy for Japan to go without buying Indian cotton for her manufactures, as the United States of America is a successful competitor in this commodity with India These considerations point to the danger of India's export trade diminishing in future years, unless special efforts are made in the interval to sustain it If the national policies and effective tariffs, referred to in the sequel, are followed, there will be a stimulus for increased consumption, the increase in indigenous manufactures and the consequent decrease of imports of the same could then be set off against the threatened decrease in export trade

The export of jute and tea from India stands on a different footing, in 1932-33, it amounted to 23 per cent. and 13 per cent, respectively, of the total export trade of the country The production, control and trade in these commodities amounting to over 40 per cent of India's total export trade are organized and managed by British business men This part of the export trade of India is likely to remain unaffected by changes in the trade policies of other countries

It must be realized, however, that a general increase of India's export trade does not necessarily mean increased wealth for the nation Such increase in the case of a country like the United Kingdom would bring in increased imports of raw materials for its industries and thus add to her productive wealth, a similar increase of exports of agricultural commodities in the case of India to pay for imports of manufactures which could, with greater advantage, be made within the country itself, with the raw materials available at our very doors, is an economic loss

Three main considerations emerge with regard to India's export trade in the near future Firstly, the country must maintain a large excess of exports over imports to pay for India's heavy external obligations enumerated in Chapter IX Secondly, the commodities which are now being exported in large quantities like food-grains and cotton (the production of which is increasing in other countries), may not find a profitable external market in future years, production of raw materials for manufactures and cultivation of new crops should, therefore, be correlated to the needs of the home and assured export markets Thirdly, in order that we may be enabled to get ready markets for exports, intensive and scientific agriculture on modern lines, for which climatic and soil conditions are quite favourable in India, and organized grading and marketing should take the place of the primitive methods of production and sales now common among our agricultural population If national policies are directed with these ends in view, an exportable surplus essential for India's stability and growth will be assured

IMPORTS

In years previous to British supremacy in this country, India was the principal exporter of cotton goods and sugar, it is recorded that small quantities of steel were also exported from South India about the year 1860, the organized growth of industrial activity in other countries has now made us the principal importers of these goods The value of cotton goods exported annually from India remained practically stationary (at Rs 90 lakhs) in the period 1814-1914; while imports of cotton goods increased from Rs ½ lakh to Rs 66.30 crores in the same period. The export of sugar from India *decreased* in value from Rs 103 lakhs to Rs 4 lakhs in the period of 70 years following 1860; while, in the same interval, imports of sugar increased from Rs 23 lakhs to Rs 15 78 crores!

The total imports of merchandise during 1932-33 amounted to Rs 133 crores, the principal items being cotton and cotton goods Rs 34 crores, machinery Rs 11 crores, oils Rs 8 crores, metals and ores Rs 10 crores, sugar Rs 4 crores and automobiles Rs 4 crores This gives a *per capita* rate of Rs 3 8 for imports into the country in that year The value of the total imports during the year dropped to 55 per cent of that in 1929-30, the value of imports of textiles and sugar alone dropping to 54 per cent and 25 per cent, respectively, of the pre-depression figures Such a heavy fall in the import trade was caused chiefly by the lowering of the purchasing power of the agricultural population, by the increased indigenous output of cotton goods both in mills and handlooms and also to some extent by the recent tariff protection policies Among other causes may also be stated the recent political unrest and the non-co-operation movement which led virtually to the stoppage of imports, cancellation of orders, and even the refusal to take delivery of goods of foreign manufacture received in India It has also shown how unnecessary it was and is for India to import textiles and sugar

The *per capita* consumption of mill-made cotton goods in the country in 1913-14 was 13 yards, of which about three-fourths was imported, while in 1931-32, the consumption was only 10 yards, of which a fourth was imported The difference, *i e*, about 3 yards per head, may have possibly been made up by *khaddar* and handloom products, or part of it may represent a real decline in consumption. At any rate *khaddar* production increased in value from Rs. 9 lakhs in 1924 to Rs 53 lakhs in 1929, excluding the relatively larger production of handwoven cloth in villages for which no figures are available

An increase in the import trade of India not correlated to the nature of the imported commodities and their economic necessity for India, is also not, in the country's present state, a desirable feature In the case of the United States of America, for instance, which in point of size and population is comparable to India, increased imports would mean an increased consuming power and a better standard of living for the people, which will be paid for by the nation's income from foreign investments, sale of manufactured goods and by shipping, insurance and other services rendered by their nationals to foreigners The same is true of Japan to a lesser extent, where there is usually an excess of imports of merchandise over exports Still, Japan has reduced its usual excess of imports from Rs 13 crores in 1931 to Rs 3 crores in 1932, in spite of the heavily depreciated yen In the case of India, however, increased imports have to be paid for by export of agricultural produce (the growth of which has, as we have seen, barely kept pace with the increase in population and which is hardly sufficient for the requisite internal consumption), or gold The recent payment in gold for imports is a very unsatisfactory index The country has to continue to import articles like machinery and other manufactured commodities which it does not produce at present The proper policy for this country in the immediate future should be to steadily reduce the volume of imports by increased industrialization and by restricting imports to luxuries and essential commodities only With a general increase of prosperity and the earning power of the country, the demand for increased imports would be automatically revived

The three main considerations as regards the future of import trade of India are firstly, a gradual elimination of such imports as cotton manufactures and refined sugar, for the production of which there are already adequate and fairly well-established machinery in the country, as also the necessary raw materials, secondly, the restriction of the imports into India to the extent to which she is able to pay by her own exportable surpluses of raw materials and food-grains, without entailing any substantial drain on the gold and other resources of the country, and thirdly, the introduction of an effective policy of protection to new industrial enterprises in India, which should be so regulated that it does not, by reason of costliness, entail a burden on the teeming masses of consumers in the country

INLAND TRADE

India's foreign trade is stated to be 7 per cent of her total trade There are no statistics maintained to determine the volume of internal trade in the country. The total of this trade is, however, estimated at about Rs 2,500 crores annually The inadequate banking system in the country and the heavy indebtedness of the agriculturist will be referred to in detail in another part of this book, save in the case of cotton, the farmers are obliged to dispose of their produce on the threshing floor at ruinous prices to the broker or the middleman, who is often also the pressing creditor No organized attempt is made in the country to build public warehouses, where grain could be stored for marketing on advantageous terms, as is done in progressive countries. The Japanese Government, for example, enacted the Agricultural Warehousing Law in 1917 and granted subsidies to associations interested in agricultural trade development That Government established 52 rice warehouses with a 4 million bushel capacity; agricultural and co-operative societies, with government aid, increased the number of warehouses to over 5,000 with a capacity of 30 million bushels by the year 1929 The agriculturist in India should be helped by a marketing organization which will furnish him with up-to-date information on markets and prices within and outside the country, and, if the banks also supply the needed credit, the present handicaps and losses suffered by agriculturists and the village tradesmen will become things of the past and a great impetus will have been given to internal trade leading to the prosperity of the ryot

To determine India's frontier trade, there are records of trade traffic in certain selected articles at some railway, riverine and other stations on or close to important trade routes The volume of total trade in those articles is known, but the figures do not give any idea of the actual value of the total land-frontier trade Till 1924-25 statistics were kept of the land-frontier trade, which showed that this trade was about one-twentieth of the sea-borne trade, averaging Rs 35 crores for the four years 1921-25

The chief countries with which the frontier trade is carried on are Persia, parts of Afghanistan, Central Asia, Turkestan, Tibet, Nepal, Sikkim, and Bhutan The imports consist mainly of rice, other food-grains and oil-seeds, while the exports are cotton piece-goods, wheat, salt, tea, sugar, petrol, machinery and treasure In 1929-30, imports of merchandise from these countries amounted to 50 lakhs of maunds, and exports to 77 lakhs of maunds

In 1930-31, the total value of coastal trade in Indian and foreign private merchandise and treasure in the several Maritime Provinces of British India including

Burma was Rs 88 9 crores of imports, of which private merchandise amounted to Rs 87 8 crores and treasure to Rs. 1 1 crores, while the exports amounted to Rs 82 2 crores, of which merchandise was Rs 81 2 crores and treasure Rs 97 4 lakhs

As regards the coastal trade between India proper and Burma, the chief items of import into India are rice (about 1 million tons), kerosene (about 100 million gallons), petroleum (about 50 million gallons), and timber of the approximate value of Rs 2 crores The total value of all imports in pre-war years was Rs 12 crores, it rose to Rs 28 crores in 1929-30, but fell to Rs 21 crores in 1931-32, due to decline in prices The chief items of exports to Burma are coal (500 thousand tons), cotton piece-goods (44 million yards) and gunny bags (50 million) The total value of all exports averaged Rs 8 crores in the pre war year, it rose to Rs 14 crores in 1929-30, but was only Rs 11 crores in 1931-32 due to fall in prices

The balance of trade between India proper and Burma was favourable to Burma by Rs 4 crores in the pre-war years and, favourable again, by Rs 14 crores in 1929-30, in spite of depression, the balance continued to be favourable to that province and amounted to Rs 10 crores in 1931-32 India is, therefore, a very desirable market for Burmese products

Sea-borne Trade

An examination of India's trade with the United Kingdom, the Dominions and foreign countries will show in what directions India's future trade can advantageously grow, assuming that the country is afforded adequate facilities for such growth

India carries on more trade with the United Kingdom than with any other country of the world In the year 1932-33, imports from and exports to the United

Kingdom were Rs 49 crores and Rs 38 crores respectively, they formed 37 per cent and 28 per cent. respectively of India's total imports and exports for the year India's total trade with the United Kingdom amounted to 40 per cent of her total foreign trade in the pre-war years, it decreased to 32 4 per cent in 1932-33, the trade with the British Empire as a whole also *decreased* from 55 4 per cent in the pre-war period to 45 per cent in 1932-33, while that with the foreign countries *increased* from 47 7 per cent to 54 7 per cent in the same period What is even more worthy of notice is that while the United Kingdom has been buying less from India than she sold to her all these years, (the balance against India amounting to Rs 36 crores and Rs 73 crores annually in the pre-war and post-war periods), the non-British countries have been buying more from India than selling to her, for instance, Japan's trade with India, since the Indo-Japanese Convention of 1905, has resulted year after year in a balance of trade in India's favour, the total of such favourable balances amounting to nearly Rs 450 crores since that year We have a favourable balance of trade in merchandise with the other countries like France, Belgium and Germany, such favourable balances with all the non-Empire countries amounted annually on an average to Rs 88 crores in each of the pre-war and post-war periods During the past three years, our average exports to Japan were 9 per cent of our total exports, while our average imports were 10 per cent of our total imports In the pre-depression year 1929-30, India's trade with all the countries of the British Empire (excluding the United Kingdom) was 11 6 per cent of her total trade, while it was 57 5 per cent with non-Empire countries

An increase of trade, however, between the United

Kingdom and India, which still amounts, as we have seen above, to a third of the total sea-borne trade of India, will be of mutual advantage to them As a predominantly agricultural country, India's exports consist largely of those very commodities which the United Kingdom, as an industrially developed country, needs India is still the biggest market for British goods, and therefore the interests of the two countries are interdependent The political relations subsisting between them and India's financial obligations are also factors that ought to swell their trade relations But it has not been to the interests of Great Britain to buy her raw materials solely or even largely from this country In 1932, the United Kingdom bought £ 32 million worth of merchandise from India, in the same year, she bought £13 million worth from Canada and £46 million from Australia and £84 million from the United States She, at the same time, sold to India £36 million of goods which is equal to what she was able to sell to Australia and Canada combined, and over twice what she sold to the United States of America

CHAPTER VIII

TRADE DEPRESSION AND TARIFFS

India and the Trade Depression—Trade Organization and Requirements—Need for a Network of Commercial Intelligence Offices Abroad—Chambers of Commerce and Trade Associations—Joint-Stock Companies—Exhibitions of Commercial Products, etc —Reshaping University Ideals—Importance of Statistics—Trade Agreements with Empire Countries

INDIA AND THE TRADE DEPRESSION

IN common with other countries of the world, India has suffered much from the trade depression and the resultant low prices India has also suffered because she does not enjoy true fiscal autonomy It is necessary to examine what the tariff policies should be, if the country were free to adopt the measures best suited to her own interests

In the United Kingdom, three out of every four persons live on imported food, and the country's factories have to be fed almost wholly by raw materials obtained from abroad As the two problems of ensuring continuous employment and a satisfactory standard of life are inextricably bound up with her export trade, Britain has got to maintain the productivity of her manufacturing industries at a high level and find a ready market for her manufactures to enable her to pay for imports Unless she is able to do both these and also continue her services to the Dominions, Dependencies and foreign countries in shipping, banking, insurance and administrative fields, her supply of essential articles of food as well as of raw materials to keep her people and factories engaged will be greatly at stake.

Her present tariff and protectionist policies are all directed to safeguard these ends

The United States of America also has raised a high tariff wall to protect local production, particularly from industries Unlike the United Kingdom, she is both an agricultural and industrial country and the high standard of living of her people is partly maintained by the export of her surplus products to foreign markets She has, however, a large domestic market, and external markets are not to her such a great necessity as they are to the United Kingdom Assiduous devotion to commerce and industry, which are responsible for her prosperity, has metamorphosed her from a debtor country before the War to a creditor country after its close

Conditions in India are different in their entirety from those of the United Kingdom and, in some degree, from those of the United States India, being subordinate to the United Kingdom, her interests with regard to finance and trade are finally settled by the Secretary of State for India, who has instinctively to view things from the standpoint of the needs of Great Britain Speaking about *India's Foreign Trade Since 1870*,[10] Sir Josiah Stamp, the eminent economist, has said —"If an ordinary Englishman thinking on India thinks about trade and commerce , he . does so in terms of famine or irrigation, or the currency value of the rupee, or else on India as a market for British goods and the growing menace of Indian industrialization or Japanese competition to the vested capital and labour interests of British foreign trade "

Import duties are levied more for revenue purposes than for the protection of Indian industries The policy

---

[10] Published in 1934

of discriminating protection, which has been operating since 1923, has been of limited value to industry and trade The existence of a "convention" which is supposed to allow India to follow trade policies best suited to herself is often mentioned, but what is needed is a statutory recognition of this convention and a legislature having the power to implement sound tariff policies At present, only 5 per cent of the customs revenue is derived from protective duties, and foreign countries find it easy to dump their goods into India

In other respects, India is in a strong position in that she has a large domestic market which none of the Dominions have By a system of effective tariffs, she should be able to protect her essential and key-industries from outside competition The country's production and exports should be sufficiently increased to enable her to meet her heavy foreign debt and other foreign obligations, to pay for the import of materials and machinery that are essential for her industries, and to secure a reasonable rise in the standard of living of her people

Trade Organization and Requirements

The organization in existence to safeguard India's trade is most inadequate There are at present only three Trade Commissioners outside India, one in London, another in Hamburg and a third in Milan to deal with India's trade with the rest of the world Within the country, the Department of Commerce and its Commercial Intelligence and Statistics Branch at the head-quarters of the Government are the official agencies, the former to foster trade and the latter to furnish statistical information to business men There are, in addition, unofficial agencies like the Chambers of Commerce in the provinces and in certain important centres and

States to look after local trade interests and needs, and separate European Chambers of Commerce to safeguard non-Indian commercial interests

The remarkable progress in industry and trade made in recent years by Japan, Canada and the United States of America is in no small measure due to their trade organizations within and without A small country like Canada has 34 Trade Commissioners in the principal centres of its foreign trade, including distant countries like South Africa, Peru, Hongkong, Brazil and Argentine The United States of America has, it is understood, 58 such foreign offices and over 300 representatives abroad, and the foreign field force is in the closest touch with the Washington Bureau by "letter, cable and radio"

Need for a Network of Commercial Intelligence Offices Abroad

If India is to keep pace with these countries, she must necessarily maintain a similar network of trained commercial intelligence officers throughout the world who should be Indians of sound commercial training and experience Each such officer posted to a foreign country should submit monthly reports to the Government Department of Commerce in India—as is being done by Trade Commissioners of Canada—containing information on every feature of India's trade with that country in which Indian business men may be interested He should, in particular, dwell on commodities which India can supply and on materials which she can advantageously import from that country He should further be a standing expert adviser to Indian business men residing in or visiting that country His monthly or other periodical reports should give a picture of the future trade possibilities for Indian firms, and suggestions for promoting the same

Within the country, the present Department of Commerce should be enlarged with a view to enable it to discharge functions similar to those of Boards of Trade in progressive countries The enlarged Department should, in general, be the central authority for the dissemination of all reliable information regarding both the internal and foreign trade of India , it should collect and analyse the reports of the Foreign Trade Commissioners and of the commercial organizations within the country, both official and unofficial, and issue a weekly Journal on the basis of such reports for circulation amongst industrialists and tradesmen in general Such a journal is being published weekly by the Canadian Department of Commerce *The Indian Trade Journal* does give some commercial intelligence, but its usefulness would be enhanced, if it assimilated more closely the features that are so prominent in the *British Board of Trade Journal*

Chambers of Commerce and Trade Associations

The number of business organizations like Chambers of Commerce and trade associations in the country should be substantially increased Trade in important commodities should, as far as possible, be represented by separate associations which should provide for inspection of export products, enforcement of trade ethics and the like At present, except in the case of cotton whose interests are cared for by the Indian Central Cotton Committee, there are no suitable organizations for looking after the trade in important crops like jute, rice and oil-seeds It may be necessary to institute permanent influential committees for these products also. Mixing up of different strains of food-grains and their marketing with no proper organization or supervision have, in several instances, resulted in failure in India's competition with the pure food-grains of other countries in foreign markets These defects would have to be attended to by the committees referred to, if they came into existence It is known that to an increasing extent trade associations, technical societies and organized consumer groups in the United States of America are co-operating not only in the establishment but also the maintenance of standards of quality in commodities in which they are particularly interested

All these organizations should work in close co-operation with the Government Departments of Commerce Such commercial bodies should ordinarily function as organizations parallel to those of the Government for collecting and publishing information in all matters relating to Indian trade and progress They should be given full access to information in the possession of Government relating to trade matters

Joint-Stock Companies

The bulk of the trade and industry in any country is nowadays in the hands of Joint-Stock Companies The Joint-Stock Company has, indeed, become the standard form of enterprise the world over As already mentioned in another part of this book, the number of these companies is very much smaller in India than in the leading countries of the world, their growth, both in numbers and importance, is of vital concern to the industrial and commercial interests of the country Every effort should be made to ensure that the defects peculiar to this country in the working of joint-stock companies, such as the evils of the managing agency system, absence of technical experts and advice, inefficient management, financial difficulties, etc, are speedily remedied

EXHIBITIONS OF COMMERCIAL PRODUCTS, ETC

Exhibitions of commercial products should be held in every important city, as frequently as possible,—taking advantage of public festivals and other occasions when people gather—in order to advertise the articles produced in the country and let people know where to find them Such exhibitions do not often get the support and guidance of Government in this country, no help is given to enable the exhibitors to find markets for their wares If local industries and internal trade are to flourish, Government departments should openly co-operate with the organizers of exhibitions and guarantee monetary contribution and other aids Commercial museums should contain samples of imported goods side by side with similar local products, with full comparative descriptions of quality and value, in order to stimulate local production of goods of the highest quality wherever practicable In this connection it may be mentioned that the practice of running exhibition trains from station to station advertising the wares of the local manufacturers and producers which has recently been introduced by the Great Indian Peninsular and other Railways, is in the right direction and may be considerably developed with advantage

Apart from these constitutional defects in the organization of the trade of the country, by far the greatest contributory cause of its unprogressive character is the want of technical and business knowledge in the majority of men placed at the helm of commercial enterprises In all big enterprises, the greatest difficulty is to get a good start Want of definite aims and absence of detailed plans and expert and skilled direction in the initial stages have brought ruin to many a concern Institutions giving commercial education in India are few and they are often looked upon with indifference by the people themselves

RESHAPING UNIVERSITY IDEALS

Even Universities fight shy of instituting degrees in commerce, because no openings for people possessing such degrees are readily available in Government offices or under unofficial agencies None of the existing commercial colleges in India give higher training in business organization, marketing, advertising, salesmanship and other allied subjects so as to qualify their graduates to become captains of industry and trade. A few of the Universities in the country might well concentrate their efforts on giving training to hundreds of young active graduates every year in methods of direction and control of modern business organizations. Some of them should be sent to foreign countries for completing their training by means of liberal scholarships This should be done in close collaboration with the Government and Commercial Associations It is undoubtedly true that India has produced some men of great directing talent without the groundwork of advanced university education, but that is largely accidental Progress in the large majority of cases can be assured only by the systematic training of large numbers of business leaders through higher education in Colleges and Universities of Commerce

We read in American publications of the great advance the United States has made in this respect. The Chamber of Commerce of the United States and its affiliated associations, for instance, have been reservoirs of illuminating business statistics The press in that country has amplified its facilities for spreading financial and commercial intelligence A new generation of trained business leaders, able to interpret the stream of statistical facts, has been developed The great Universities have opened schools of business, raising the art of barter to the dignity of a science or profession

Another contributory cause of stagnation in commercial activity in India is the lack of co-operation between economists and practical business men Men of learning in the Universities, who ought to give a lead to the country in these matters, are either too academic by reason of want of touch with business enterprises and practices, or are found to be reluctant to express opinions freely Such drawbacks are bound to disappear, if the people come to believe that the Government is really sympathetic towards the progress of local industry and trade and will welcome free expression of opinion by officials in its employ

Following the Fiscal Commission Report, the Government of India have adopted a policy of "protection with discrimination" for Indian industries and have instituted a Tariff Board to advise them in regard to measures of protection Judged from its work these ten years, the Board has established a reputation for loyalty to the objects for which it has been constituted and its usefulness will grow with the growth of the representative character of the Government

Importance of Statistics

None of the measures for progress will be correctly understood by the people, unless adequate statistics of industries and trade are periodically published Government should publish a *Year-Book*, dealing, as a statistical annual should, with the resources, history and institutions in the country and the social, economic and commercial conditions and life prevalent in it It should be designed, as is, for instance, the *Canada Year-*

Book, to bring out with the aid of statistics the salient features of the country's past progress and future needs.

The annual publication, *The Review of the Trade of India*, should be published soon after the close of the year, instead of long after the statistics to which it relates have become out of date For some years until private enterprise comes to the fore, the Commerce Department should publish an Annual Directory of the principal exporting and importing houses in India and their representatives abroad It should also undertake the publication of scientific and technical bulletins relating *inter alia* to research, economic production and prevention of waste The Department of Commerce in the United States of America issues such bulletins in very large numbers every year

Public institutions like the chambers of commerce and important joint-stock banks should also issue, as they do in countries like the United States of America, Sweden and others, annual reviews of their own on the commerce, trade and finances of India as a whole, and also in greater detail of the region in which their interests are centred

For the future progress of trade and industry, it is necessary that the country should have *real* fiscal autonomy not by convention but by statute

The present halting policy of discriminating protection should give place to sound tariff policies aiming at making the country as self-sufficient as may be economically practicable

Such articles, as are now being imported into the country but which are capable of being manufactured on a commercial scale locally, should be protected by adequate tariffs and bounties

Indians engaged in trade in foreign lands labour under disadvantages through lack of adequate banking facilities Branches of Indian joint-stock banks should be opened in all important foreign centres for exchange and remittance transactions through the offices of the Trade Commissioners and the Government Departments. The Yokohama Specie Bank, one-third of whose capital stock is subscribed by the Government of Japan, has 38 branches in all parts of the World and handles about 50 per cent of the country's foreign exchange and trade bills

Existing railroad and shipping services and the freight charges from ports into the interior and also from local industrial centres to the ports should be frequently examined, so that the Indian producer may get the prices and all reasonable facilities to which he is entitled The main reforms suggested by a survey of India's trade position will be found summarised under Scheme No IV in Chapter XV

TRADE AGREEMENTS WITH EMPIRE COUNTRIES

How important it is that the country's economic interests should be regulated by sound policies and long-range vision and controlled by an efficient business organization will be evident by a brief reference to the recent trade agreements entered into, on behalf of India, with the countries within the British Empire, and with Japan In order to offset the effects of contraction in world trade due to the upward movement of tariffs, the United Kingdom has been trying to cultivate closer trade relations with the British Dominions and Dependencies, and has arrived at an agreement with them for charging preferential tariff rates in future for products exchanged between any two Empire countries The first move in this direction was made by convening a conference of representatives of Empire countries at Ottawa in 1932 The Government of India was also represented and among the trade agreements entered into at that conference, there was one in respect of India which committed this country to certain reciprocal obligations with Great Britain and Empire countries for a period of three years The agreement is subject to reconsideration at the end of this period

As this book was passing through the press, the official report on the results of the year 1933-34 has been published and it is found that in respect of several important commodities included in the Ottawa scheme of preference the anticipated results to India have not materialized The share of the British Empire in India's foreign trade has steadily declined in recent years Taking imports and exports together, India's trade with Empire countries fell from 57 1 per cent during the War to 45 3 per cent in 1932-33 and with the United Kingdom from 41 2 per cent to 32 2 per cent It is evident that the bulk of India's foreign trade is with non-Empire countries and India cannot, therefore, be too careful that in accepting comparatively minor advantages from Empire countries she does not antagonize non-Empire countries and jeopardise the prospect of further expansion of her valuable trade with them

Indo-Lancashire Agreement—In recent months, preferential rates have been sanctioned separately for a short period for certain special classes of Lancashire goods imported into India on the understanding that the Lancashire manufacturers will buy more raw cotton from India and help to find markets for Indian products within the Empire countries

Indo-Japanese Agreement—A trade agreement has also been entered into between India and Japan which provides for admitting into India 400,000,000 yards of cotton piece-goods on the understanding that Japan will purchase 1,500,000 bales of raw cotton from India

Before the War, Japan's proportion of the total import trade of India was only 2 6 per cent , in the fiscal year (1932-33) it had risen to 15 4 per cent Japan has advanced relatively little in her share of the Indian export trade, which was 9 1 per cent in 1913-14 and 10 3 per cent in 1932-33 These figures show that the benefits accruing to Japan are far greater than those to be derived by India In the same year, Japan shipped into India nearly 600,000,000 yards of cotton piece-goods Under the new arrangements her maximum shipments—and these are dependent upon her consumption of Indian cotton—will be two-thirds of the amount The balance of 200,000,000 yards is to be divided between Lancashire and the Indian mills over and above their respective contributions in 1932-33

India is producing just about 500,000 tons of steel and is importing 1,000,000 tons more America with one-third of the population of India produced in the depression year, 1930, pig iron and steel together amounting to 74,000,000 tons There is great need for cheap steel in India, if the people can find the money to purchase it and there is also great scope for the expansion of the steel industry locally

It is contended by those opposed to these agreements that there are enough mills in India which, if worked full time, would be able to supply all the cotton cloth that the country needs, that many Bombay mills are closed down while some others are in a critical condition on account of foreign competition, and that if cotton imports were restricted, it would stimulate the production of indigenous hand-made cloth It is also contended that there was no reason or justification for showing preference to foreign imports at a time when the cotton mill industry is passing through a crisis and when the only steel company in India has not been giving a reasonable return on its share capital ever since its inception

The reader may be reminded that at one time India was exporting cotton cloth to the United Kingdom and Japan, the two countries which are now exporting the same commodity into India The import of cotton cloth is not really required by the people The money to be paid for this unnecessary foreign product has to be found from the scant income derived from agricultural pursuits, which are the only occupation left for the bulk of the people and which in these days, moreover, are poorly recompensed

India can be easily made to be self-sufficient in regard to both cotton textiles and iron and steel, if these industries are adequately protected by levying high enough tariff rates for a few years Commercial treaties are justifiable only, if they secure to the countries entering into them mutual economic advantage Political considerations should have no place in, and should not form the basis of, such treaties

The more general question, whether these new agreements are of economic advantage to India with regard to her external trade, and if so to what extent, requires close study by a Committee of the Central Legislature as well as by Indian economists and political thinkers, till a permanent economic organization on the lines suggested in these pages or on other similar lines is established to assist in the shaping of correct commercial policies in this respect and safeguard the country's interests, in future

CHAPTER IX
FINANCE

Dependency Status of India and its Effect on its Finances—Budgets and Financial Position—Revenue and Taxation—Public Debt—Foreign Investments in India—National Income, Wealth and Indebtedness—Future Federal Budget.

DEPENDENCY STATUS OF INDIA AND ITS EFFECT ON ITS FINANCES

A GENERAL indication whether or not the finances of a country are satisfactory is usually supplied by a balanced Government budget and the maintenance normally of a favourable yearly trade balance in relation to foreign imports and exports If there is any foreign debt, it must have been contracted for productive enterprises or for measures connected with the defence of the country

The budgets in India, both Central and Provincial, are usually fairly well-balanced, but the relation between the position of a budget and the general economic condition of the people is not what it usually is in modern progressive countries, nor are such relations bearing on the development of agriculture, industries and trade and commerce, taken into account by the Legislative bodies concerned, at the time of sanctioning the annual budgets

India being a Dependency, its financial policies are controlled by the Secretary of State, in whom is also vested the authority to borrow money on behalf of India without the sanction of the Indian Legislature. The Secretary of State, as a member of the British Cabinet, is interested in British imports into India and uses Indian money for adjustment of exchange relations between the two countries from time to time on behalf of British commercial and service interests

In regard to fiscal policies there is, as might be expected, a distinct conflict of interests between Great Britain and India Britain wants this country to be a market for her manufactures, India, on the other hand, wishes to be self-contained as far as possible and therefore wants protection for her manufactures against indiscriminate imports

British capital is largely invested in Indian industries, trade, tea gardens, coal mines, etc, very often along with Indian money The annual trade balance, which should give an indication of India's net financial transactions with the outer world, does not show it, because there are many imports of an invisible nature which have not been authoritatively examined, assessed and accounted for This mixing up of British and Indian investments and interests, particularly while the ultimate control is British, has all along proved prejudicial to the interests of India Adequate statistics are not maintained to distinguish the Indian share of the capital and income from the British, and one great disadvantage of this omission has been that this country is deprived of the only means of finding out whether economically it is progressing or losing ground

The country's administration, compared to the income of its population, is the costliest among civilized countries There is no manner of correspondence between the average income of the Indian and the salaries paid to the establishments of the Government he maintains The expenditure on defence, though India is only a Dependency, was till recently heavier than that incurred by a great military power like Japan

Considering the matter over a fairly long period of time, one indication of the progress of a country would be afforded by the growth of its public revenue and, therefore, of its public spending power From this point of view, the revenues of the Central and Provincial Governments and local bodies in India have been growing very slowly To-day they are wholly inadequate for the administrative wants of its huge population, and are a measure of the poverty of the nation and of its slow progress The administrative machinery, at the same time, is not designed to improve the production of wealth The official review, *India in 1922-23*, stated the bare truth when it said that "the country is not at present organized for the production of wealth" Speaking in 1833 in the British House of Commons, Lord Macaulay said that India was "a territory, the present clear revenue of which exceeded the present clear revenue of any State of the world, France excepted" India's revenue has at present deteriorated to about three-fifths of that of Japan and one-fifth of what it is in Great Britain

The public debt of India rose from Rs 307 crores in 1900 to Rs 1,210 crores in 1931, there was thus an increase of over Rs 900 crores during the period, while the productive expenditure on railways and irrigation works during the same period amounted to only Rs 560 crores

Budgets and Financial Position

The revised estimates of the Central Government for the year 1933-34 show a surplus of Rs 1 29 crores made up as shown on the next page

During the War and the years immediately preceding, Government budgets, both Central and Provincial, were fairly well balanced with generally a surplus of revenue over expenditure The three years immediately following were a period of unparalleled financial strain caused by the Afghan War, costly Frontier operations

Revenue	Rs (in crores)	*Expenditure*	Rs (in crores)
Customs	46 87	Defence	44 42
Taxes on Income	17 13	Civil Administration	9 58
Salt	8 55	Other direct demands	3 58
Opium	1 50	Civil Works	2 07
Railways	*Nil*	Interest on obligations	9 66
Currency and Mint	1 23	Other heads	7 28
Other heads	5 51		
		Total	76 59
		Reduction of debt	3 00
Total	80 88	Total	79 59

and other connected expenditure which resulted in a total deficit of about Rs 100 crores, the Afghan War alone accounting for Rs 34 crores On the introduction of the new Government of India Act in April 1921, the finances of the Central Government were separated from those of the Provincial Governments An examination of the budgets of the Central Government since the separation reveals the fact that there was an accumulated *surplus* of revenue over expenditure of Rs 10 crores, between the years 1921 and 1932, although the Government showed a total *deficit* of Rs 52½ crores in their budgets during the period This was mainly caused by the utilization of large sums annually for reduction of the public debt Even in the two years following 1930-31, when there was an excess of expenditure over receipts of about Rs 10 crores, nearly Rs 13 crores were spent on reduction of public debt

There was practically no increase worth recording in the central revenues in spite of steady increases in Tariff rates In 1914, the central revenues amounted to Rs 80 crores, in 1921-22, to Rs 115 21 crores, in 1929-30 (the pre-depression year) to Rs 132 69 crores;

and in 1933-34, they receded to Rs 119 31 crores The national (central) revenues of Japan rose from Rs 96 crores in 1914 to Rs 208 crores in 1930 The increase in India was thus small in spite of the fact that the Government of India have retained for the Central Government such growing sources of revenue as the Customs and Income-tax

The revenues of the Provincial Governments are made up chiefly of receipts under Land Revenue, Irrigation, Excise, Stamps, Forests and Registration The provinces which are confronted with increasing expenditure are thus left without resources capable of appreciable expansion In the case of Bombay and other industrial provinces, the increased revenues occasioned by their industrial activity are not credited to them but are appropriated by the Government of India

The combined provincial budget estimates for the year 1932-33 show a total revenue of Rs 84 67 crores, of which Rs 33 crores is Land Revenue, Rs 14 crores Excise and Rs 12 crores Stamps, while the total expenditure was Rs 86 65 crores, of which Rs 52 crores was for salaries, etc, of Civil Departments and Rs 8 crores for Civil Works The result expected was a deficit of Rs 1 98 crores for that year

During the twelve years since the introduction of the Montagu-Chelmsford Reforms in 1921, the provinces as a whole, had a total deficit of Rs 23 8 crores, which they have met from loans from the Provincial Loans Fund maintained by the Government of India Nearly Rs 10 crores of this was on account of provincial contributions to the Central Exchequer under the scheme known as the Meston Award Even after the extinction of these contributions in 1928, the financial position of the provinces has continued to be unsatisfactory This seems inevitable so long as the provinces have to depend for any appreciable increase of revenue mainly on agricultural development

The gross income of the Municipalities in British India in 1930-31 was nearly Rs 36 60 crores, as against Rs 11½ crores in 1919-20, their main sources of income consisting of octroi, taxes on houses, lands and vehicles and tolls There are 781 Municipalities in India, with an aggregate population of over 21 million residing within their limits

The total number of District and Taluk Boards and Union *Panchayets* is 1,246 Their income derived from sundry taxes and rates during 1930-31 was Rs 16 57 crores as against Rs 9 8 crores in 1919-20, and out of this meagre revenue these bodies have to maintain and finance some of the most important of rural needs like roads, schools, markets, public health and sanitation for a rural population aggregating 242 million This is why Local Self-Government has not had a fair trial and why it has failed to confer any appreciable benefit on the rural population so far

Between the years 1914 and 1930, local expenditure in Japan increased from Rs 41 crores to Rs 229 crores In India, with five times the population of Japan, local expenditure in the same period rose from Rs 26 crores to Rs 54 crores only In other words, the *per capita* expenditure of Local Bodies in India for 1930 was Rs 2, while the corresponding figure for Japan was Rs 36 or over eighteen times that in India The increase in this class of expenditure in India between the years 1914 and 1930 was 2 1 times, while in Japan, it was 5 6 times

In the United States of America also, the gross expenditure of Local Bodies in 1927-28 amounted to Rs 1,874 crores while the gross total expenditure of the

Federal, State and Local Bodies taken together for the same year was Rs 3,468 crores The local bodies in that country have, therefore, a spending power of about 54 per cent of the total expenditure of the Federal, State and Local Governments, while in India, the local bodies spend only 20 per cent of the corresponding total. The *per capita* expenditure of the local bodies in the United States of America for the year 1927-28 was over Rs 150, or 75 times the corresponding figure in India. The reason of this extraordinarily low expenditure by local bodies requires special investigation

Since 1924-25, the finances of the State Railways have been separated from those of the Central Government with the convention that the management of the railways should pay an annual contribution to the central revenues The railways contributed a total of Rs 42 crores during the seven years following the convention, but during the two years ended 1932-33, they were not only not able to make any contribution but had to utilize the whole of the balance of Rs 5 8 crores in their accumulated reserve funds, besides contracting temporary loans from the railway depreciation fund The heavy fall in railway revenues to which this is due was caused by the general trade depression and competition from motor traffic

The gross revenue derived from the State-owned Railways in India in 1930-31 was Rs 96 83 crores. During the pre-depression year 1929-30, it was Rs 103 crores, the amount spent on the purchase of stores for the State Railways in the same year was Rs 30 crores In an earlier chapter, attention has been drawn to these purchases, which were mostly from outside the country and which could have been dispensed with, if reasonable provision had been made to manufacture machinery and stores within the country

The railways are at present controlled by a Railway Board under the Government of India, but the powers to be delegated to the Board under the Federal Constitution are still undefined The working expenses of the Railway System amounted to over 75 per cent of the expenditure of the Central Government in 1929-30, and if the purchases of stores on capital account works are also taken into consideration, the aggregate expenditure in some years may even exceed the expenditure of the Central Government The importance of an effective control by the Central Legislature over such huge expenditure cannot, therefore, be over-estimated

The principal ports in India, of which there are six at present, *viz*, Calcutta, Bombay, Madras, Karachi, Rangoon and Chittagong, are managed by locally constituted Trusts In the year 1930-31, the revenue from such ports amounted to Rs 7½ crores and their total capital debt to Rs 59 crores The development and increase of revenue of these ports will depend on the growth of trade following the industrial and agricultural development of the country

There are about 563 Indian States comprising one-fifth of the population and two-fifths of the area of India taken as a whole The taxable capacity in certain of these States, like Mysore, where there are profitable public utility undertakings like railways and electric power, is relatively high, in certain others revenue sources are meagre and consist mostly of Land, Forest and Excise taxes Thirty of these States have Legislative Councils, to which State budgets are presented and 56 of them have a fixed privy purse There is no uniform basis of taxation in the States, and the *per capita* taxation of States' subjects is not readily comparable with that in British India

REVENUE AND TAXATION

The total revenue of British India in 1930-31 amounted to Rs 260 85 crores made up as follows —

Central Government	Rs	124 60	crores
Provincial Governments .	,,	83 08	,,
Local Bodies .	,,	53 17	,,
TOTAL	Rs	260 85	crores

This, for a population of 270 millions in British India, works out to a little less than Rs 10 per head The corresponding *per capita* revenues, as far as they could be ascertained in other countries, are —

Japan	Rs 76
The United States of America .	,, 222
Canada	,, 197
The United Kingdom	,, 290

If it is remembered that the *per capita* income of India, as explained in Chapter II, is about one-thirteenth of what it is in Great Britain and one-twentyfifth of that in the United States of America, the proportion which the revenue bears to income in British India cannot be considered low The masses of the Indian population are so very poor that any taxation in a good percentage of cases works as a hardship In prosperous countries, persons with so low an income would be placed below the taxable limit and escape direct taxation altogether

The following table, giving the national income, revenue and percentage of revenue to income of some of the progressive countries of the world will show that the percentage of revenue to income in India is heavier than in the United States of America, but lighter than in all the other countries named —

Country	Estimated National Income	Total Revenue	Percentage of Revenue to Income
	Rs (in crores)	Rs (in crores)	
The United States	21,5[illegible]3	2,315	10
British India	2,223	[illegible]	12
Canada	1,319	21[illegible]	16
France	2,618	[illegible]	18
Japan	1,471	24[illegible]	17
The United Kingdom	4,[illegible]5	1 752	35

(Reference is invited to Table III in the Appendix)

The State revenues of Japan (pertaining to General Account) have, in the period 1900 to 1930, increased from Rs 34 crores to Rs 241 crores, i e, seven times; but the revenues of India (Central and Provincial), have, even making some allowance for changes in the value of currency in the same period, increased from Rs 105 crores to Rs 227 crores only, or a little over twice The revenues of both the United States of America and the United Kingdom have, as in the case of Japan, also increased 7 times during this period These facts show that even after allowing for special post war taxation in some of the countries, the development of this country has been very slow as measured by the standards set in the progressive countries of the world

Public Debt

The total public debt of India on the 31st March 1934 was Rs 1,210 crores (compared to Rs 919 crores ten years ago), of which about Rs 500 crores is foreign and about Rs 700 crores domestic debt The volume of foreign debt, caused by sterling loans raised in England, has steadily increased in the past ten years Against the total debt of Rs 1,210 crores, there are interest-yielding assets of the total book-value of Rs 978 crores (compared to Rs 661 crores ten years ago), and cash and bullion valued at about Rs 40 crores The balance of about Rs 200 crores of public debt is not covered by interest-yielding assets or cash or bullion It would, however, be a mistake to regard this figure as the only unproductive debt of the country The reason is, not that some of the so-called "interest-yielding assets", the most important of them being the railways, have of late been yielding no return,—which may be termed a misfortune—but that some Rs 200 crores of these assets represent capital advanced to Provinces and Indian States This capital, although it may regularly yield interest to the Central Government, cannot be regarded, from the point of view of the nation as a whole, as productive unless it is shown that it is invested by the Provinces and the States concerned in interest-yielding or productive assets Recent years have also contributed to the increase in unproductive public debt Between the years 1928-29 and 1929-30, there was a total increase of public debt of Rs 62 crores, while the capital outlay during the period (including that in the Provinces) was only Rs 38 2 crores

For some years in the recent past, the day-to-day administration of the Government of India was carried on by the device of loans and short-term treasury bills carrying, till recently, high rates of interest This policy of the Government of India contributed largely to the increase of the unproductive burdens of this country The Japanese Government have rarely, if ever, resorted to such short-term borrowing

According to accepted principles of Public Finance, a public debt should be contracted only for the creation of productive assets, to develop the material resources of the country or to improve the economic condition of its people—an exception being made in the case of wars brought on by foreign aggression The increase in the public debt of India has not been mainly due to productive or national development schemes Since the close of the War, the accumulated budget deficits of the Government of India amounted to Rs 156 crores, these (as well as the other foreign obligations which will be referred to in the sequel) were met largely by loans incurred on behalf of India

The annual interest payments necessary to meet the external debt of Rs 500 crores will have to be made in the form of export of gold or goods, and to that extent represent a corresponding diminution of the income of the country, while the interest payments towards a domestic debt will remain in the country and circulate amongst its own people

The arbitrary exercise of authority by the Secretary of State in the matter of raising loans on behalf of India even with the support of the British Parliament has led to various transactions to India's disadvantage For example, the Government of India raised a £ 7½ million (Rs 7 5 crores) loan in 1921-22 at 7 per cent in England, while in the same year they were able to raise Rs 49 crores in India at 6 per cent At the same time, South Africa and Australia obtained loans in London at a lower rate, *viz*, 5 per cent On account of the dissatisfaction caused in Indian financial circles, the Secretary of State subsequently converted the 7 per cent loan into two scrips each of 3 per cent, but of double the former value This apparently diminished the interest rates slightly but the burden of debt remained the same

In Japan, loans raised for purposes which are directly or indirectly productive, such as encouragement of industries, education, water works, electric and gas works, etc, increased from Rs 52 crores in 1919 to Rs 272 crores in 1929 Similarly, the expenditure on social services in England increased from about Rs 95 crores in 1910-11 to nearly Rs 528 crores in 1928-29

In future years, it is essential that the power to raise loans debitable to Indian revenues should be vested in the Government of India All such loans should be classified under one or the other of the following heads —

(1) Productive—comprising those utilized for financing State Railways, Irrigation Works, State industrial undertakings, etc,

(2) Developmental—in the shape of National Government Bonds, for expenditure on social services like sanitation, education, financing Local Bodies, etc, and

(3) Unproductive—such as wars and civil commotions, meeting current budget deficits, compensations, etc

Foreign Investments in India

The actual figures relating to foreign investments in India and India's total liabilities are not available, only a guess or rough estimate is possible By 31st March 1933, India's liabilities on foreign account consisted of £379 million in the shape of sterling loans and other obligations incurred in England and a sum estimated to be in the neighbourhood of £500 million in the shape of investments of Companies operating in India but registered outside the country Inclusive of certain other miscellaneous investments, the total volume of British investments in India is estimated at £1,000 million or about Rs 1,300 crores, which is the figure put forward recently by the British Associated Chambers of Commerce in India As there has been no excess of imports over exports these many years, the fact that foreign investments in India still amount to a thousand million pounds is, it is believed, proof that a good portion of the capital was not imported into the country by the British investors but was earned and re-invested in the country itself This is borne out by a statement of the late Lord Inchcape in an address delivered by him at Calcutta in 1922

The total volume of Great Britain's foreign investments is estimated at about £4,000 million, so that the amount invested by Great Britain in India may be taken at about one-fourth of her total world investments. The obligations of this country to pay interest to Great Britain at the average rate of 5 per cent on the capital invested in Indian enterprises, would thus amount to about £50 million or roughly Rs 65 crores annually

The Macmillan Committee in Great Britain has reported that the net income of that country from foreign investments in 1930 was £ 235 million A quarter of that sum is £58¾ million, which is better by only £8¾ million than the figure arrived at above as India's annual payment to Great Britain towards interest on British investments in India

National Income, Wealth and Indebtedness

In 1924 a detailed estimate was made of the national income or dividend of India, which for the year 1922-23 was estimated at Rs 2,500 crores, giving a *per capita* figure of Rs 78 It was also estimated that the total drain from India from all sources was about Rs 220 crores in a normal year, which would leave the net annual income at Rs 71 per head In a year like the present (1934), the country's income cannot be more than Rs 50 per head of population The national wealth of British India is roughly computed at

Rs. 12,000 crores, giving a *per capita* wealth of Rs 441

The following comparison, with approximate corresponding figures for some of the progressive countries of the world, will prove instructive —

National Income and Wealth

Country	Population (Millions)	Income Per capita (Rs)	Wealth Per capita (Rs)
The United States of America	122 77	2,053	9,365
Canada	10 37	1,208	8,023
The United Kingdom	46 18	1,092	6,371
France	41 86	636	4,581
Japan	65 36	271	2,308
British India	271 53	82	441

In the above table, the wealth and income figures are taken from different sources, and are not all reckoned for the same year

Proper efforts are not made in India to assess the country's wealth and income, the figures for India given above being only a reasonable deduction from rough estimates made by different unofficial agencies and economists, mostly foreign It is time, that a National Finance Commission were entrusted with the work of estimating the wealth and income of India periodically and publishing the same for the information of the Indian public

The magnitude of rural indebtedness and its effect on the agricultural economy of India have been examined in recent years by several expert Committees

As seen in Chapter III, this debt may be taken at Rs 950 crores, or about Rs 50 per head of the agricultural population of British India The estimate was made three years ago, assuming that the debt has not grown in the meantime, the burden of that debt on the agriculturists at present, in view of the precipitous fall in the value of agricultural prices, would be one and a half times as heavy as it would be in a normal year This figure has only to be taken in connection with the *per capita* income of the agriculturists in India, which is estimated at Rs 50, in order fully to realize their difficulty in meeting the heavy burden of debt

It is further important, in order effectually to tackle the problem of rural indebtedness, to give a close study to the questions of interest rates charged to agriculturists, and of land alienation by agriculturists in favour of *soucars*, and to devise means to give to the agriculturists some relief against usurious loans and improvident mortgage transactions

An important factor that operates to drain the country's wealth and increase *its indebtedness* is the large volume of "invisible" imports into the country One estimate of the total annual charges payable to Great Britain and foreign countries amounts to about Rs 161 crores This is exclusive of official remittances to England for pensions and other Home charges and liabilities to non-Britishers who have trade relations with India It is made up as follows, it being assumed that Great Britain has one-quarter of her world's investments in India and that India, therefore, contributes the same proportion of her oversea receipts —

	Rs. Crores.
British and foreign Shipping Service .. .	35
Exchange and other commission payable to foreign banks	21
Business gains, salaries, etc , of persons of British nationality engaged in Indian industries, such as coal, jute, tea, etc . . .	40
Interest on British investments in India, at 5 per cent , as already mentioned	65
Total	161

As already remarked, this is a very rough estimate. There is no means of ascertaining the actual position of India's liabilities in this regard Official publications are silent A National Finance Commission, like the one suggested above, should be entrusted with the work of determining, as accurately as possible, the total volume of India's annual liabilities on this account

FUTURE FEDERAL BUDGET

A workable and enduring scheme of Federal Finance in the contemplated new Constitution can be evolved only after a careful study of the financial position of all the federating units The Committees that were recently appointed to examine the finances of the future Federal Government have reported that it would be possible to have a satisfactory financial forecast for the Federal Constitution, only after the country is rescued from its present abnormal economic depression

The fears that, without such recovery, the budgetary position of the future Federal Government would be unsatisfactory appear to follow from the presumption that the present high cost of military and civil services to India will have to be continued in future. Expenditure on the Indian Army was Rs 13 crores in the year before the Indian Mutiny, while the revised estimates for the year 1933-34, in spite of the heavy fall in prices, cuts in salaries and the great need for economy show Rs 44 crores The true burden of defence in this country is, however, much more, if we take into consideration the cost of construction of strategic railways, the loss on the working of strategic lines, and the interest charges on the heavy borrowings that have been necessitated by the Great War, or for the prosecution of hostilities along the Frontier, or for the execution of military works of various kinds These would easily account for Rs 20 to Rs 25 crores more We have also to take into consideration the fact that this figure of Rs 44 crores is reached because of the desperate financial conditions of the times and by means of the postponement of mechanization and re-equipment schemes, so that in a normal year the military budget would not be less than the figure mentioned by the Inchcape Committee, viz, Rs 50 crores

On a comparison of the defence burdens borne by the Dominions, it would be seen that India gets her protection from foreign invasion at a much bigger price than they In Canada, for instance, the total combined expenditure on national defence and on the Royal Canadian Navy was 13 43 million dollars, this was but 4 per cent of the total consolidated expenditure In India, defence expenditure was 37 per cent of the total central expenditure

Such high expenditure is caused by the maintenance of a huge British Army in India intended more for Imperial purposes than for India's defence Fairness demands that the revenues of India should bear only the cost of that part of the army in India which is meant for India's defence

Expenditure on the Civil establishments is also unduly high and should be cut down to a level appropriate to Indian conditions and standards Certain reductions in the salaries of future entrants to the services are now being made, but this could be more effectively dealt with when a reformed Government comes to power While expenditure on the regular military and civil establishments is unduly high compared with the needs and the financial condition of the country, the expenditure on moral and material development is disproportionately low Education, sanitation and medical relief, scientific research into the problems of agriculture and industries, the development of communications, the supply of power on a large scale—these and many such other things (except perhaps railways and irrigation works) are provided for by the Governments in India, Central and Provincial, on an extremely inadequate scale A radical change of view as to the functions and objective of State action in India is the need of the moment

Another essential change that should be made in the future Federal Budget is in the matter of control over Federal Expenditure by the Legislature According to the proposals of the Committees that have examined Federal Finances, referred to above, the charges for defence, debt services, etc, amounting to about 80 per cent of the net revenues of the Federal Government, are to be outside the purview of the Federal Legislature The railway budget, the revenues of which, as already seen, are nearly equal to three-fourths of those of the Central Government in a normal year, is to be left to a new Railway Authority, the measure of control over which by the Legislature may not, in actual practice, be effective These arrangements do not even carry a semblance of Federal responsibility, and if accepted, may result in continuous conflict with popular opinion An Indian Finance Minister and the Legislature should be entrusted with the responsibility for providing for the defence and financial stability of India

The other matters pertaining to the future Federal Budget, on which decisions have to be arrived at are the feasibility of fresh taxation in Indian provinces to meet the increased expenditure entailed by the creation of new provinces, the right apportionment of surplus federal revenues among the industrial provinces, the federal taxes payable by Indian States, and the problem of Burma's separation from India and its true bearing on federal finances Changes of policy are also needed in regard to exchange and other financial matters already referred to A change of policy, as suggested previously, under the Federal System of Government, may help to expand industry and revive trade, permit of increase of taxation and bring in larger revenues The budgetary position of the proposed Federal Government would, therefore, depend on how many of these matters are satisfactorily settled

Some of the principal conclusions suggested by the above survey of Indian finance and banking will be found summarised under Scheme No V outlined in Chapter XV

CHAPTER X

CURRENCY, BANKING, ETC

Exchange and Currency Policies—The 18*d* Ratio—Pegging the Rupee to Sterling and Its Results—Currency Reserves—Gold Imports, Exports, Stocks and Production—World Monetary Conference—Banking—The Imperial Bank of India—The Exchange Banks in India—The Reserve Bank Scheme—Indigenous Banks—Co-operative Banking—Insurance—Competition of Foreign Companies—Importance of Insurance—Joint-Stock Companies—British Companies Operating in the Country

EXCHANGE AND CURRENCY POLICIES

THE policy of the Government of India in exchange and currency matters all these years has been not only at variance with the expressed views of Indian experts and business men but also in essential particulars opposed to the recommendations of the Commissions and Committees set up by the Government themselves to examine the specific problems that arose from time to time The refusal to set up a gold mint in India, the offer of unlimited council bills for sale by the Secretary of State to restrict gold imports into India, and the location of the currency reserves in England, were some of the early features of such policy

The exchange value of 16*d* to the rupee was regarded as permanent before the War During the War, the Government followed a cautious policy in Indian monetary affairs and allowed the rupee exchange to go up as demanded by the conditions at the time But, instead of permitting silver to follow its natural downward trend and return to its pre-war 16*d*, as one would expect, the Government fixed the rate at 2 shillings in February 1920 and stuck to it by artificial means, until difficulties gathered when it had to be given up as an altogether impossible arrangement This measure of Government resulted in a loss of Rs 32 crores to the Indian Treasury

The 18*d* Ratio

The fixing of the exchange again at an intermediate rate of 18*d* was in contravention of Indian opinion, though recommended by a majority of the members of the Hilton Young Commission of 1925-26 This has no doubt adversely affected the agricultural population of this country, and particularly those who produce commercial crops for export The artificial maintenance of this ratio has led to the over-valuation of the rupee, a shrinkage of India's export trade, and a further depression in rupee-prices of agricultural produce Critics are saying that a high exchange is persisted in to help foreign capitalists, importers of British goods, the British officers, British shipping and British insurance interests that send remittances to Great Britain from India The slight increase in the burden of foreign financial obligations that will follow, if the rupee exchange returned to its true rate, could be more than off-set by the advantages that would accrue to the country by the stimulus of increased export of goods, higher prices and a better trade balance

Pegging the Rupee to Sterling and Its Results

Apart from such heavy losses to India incurred by the fixing of a higher rate of exchange for the rupee, the Government have ignored, during the years following 1926, the definite recommendation of the Currency Commission that "no favourable opportunity of fortifying the gold holding in the Reserve should be allowed to escape" The policy of pegging the rupee to sterling, after Great Britain went off the Gold Standard in September 1931, prompted an exodus of gold from India, which has since that date and up to beginning of June 1934 amounted to Rs 187 crores At least a portion of this gold should have been purchased and conserved by the Government as a backing for its currency The export of gold from the country, on the other hand, has been encouraged by the Government's exchange policy and by official declarations extolling the immediate advantages to exporters of the metal on the present occasion It is worthy of note in this connection that the Central Bank of France, had, on behalf of the Government of that country, during the four years immediately preceding 1930, bought Rs 49 crores worth of gold coins from its public Another lost opportunity for increasing India's stock of gold occurred in 1927, when America sold 93 million dollars worth of gold to various European countries India was not permitted to buy that gold in spite of the patent need for the accumulation of gold reserves for the Reserve Bank then under contemplation.

CURRENCY RESERVES

After years of reverses in the management of India's finances, the Government decided that the future control of Indian currency and the maintenance of the exchange value of the rupee should be entrusted to a Central Reserve Bank in India free from all political influences, and that its establishment and successful working should precede the transfer of responsibility in fiscal matters to the Indian Legislature

In the peculiar circumstances of India where huge sums should be found annually to meet payments on account of "invisible" imports which, in the light of experience gained from the trade position of India in recent years, cannot always be covered by export of Indian merchandise, it is essential that a much greater percentage of gold than the minimum recommended by expert Commissions should be kept in the currency reserves The gold and sterling securities (taking gold at the old parity) in the Paper Currency and Gold Standard reserves amounted on September 21, 1931 to Rs 57 81 crores against a note issue of Rs 146 crores, or a proportion of 40 per cent In his last budget speech in February 1934 the Finance Member of the Government of India estimated that on 31st March 1934 the position would be gold and sterling securities Rs 106 crores, note issue Rs 178 crores, proportion 60 per cent This seems to be too high a percentage, but anything less than 40 per cent should not be considered as satisfactory In the Reserve Bank Act, passed in March 1934, it is provided that 40 per cent of the liabilities of the Note Issue Department of the Bank should be covered by assets consisting of gold coin, gold bullion or *sterling securities*, with a minimum of Rs 40 crores of gold coin and gold bullion If the whole of the 40 per cent mentioned were to consist of full gold backing, this (as things stand at present) would mean a requirement of Rs 70 crores of gold coin and bullion To replace this extra amount of Rs 30 crores gold by *sterling securities* can hardly be called satisfactory, considering that sterling is not at present linked to gold

There are inherent defects in linking the currency of one country to that of another, when the political and economic aims and interests of the two countries are so divergent The sterling exchange system in India is an adjunct of a Dependency form of Government and no proposals for a sound financial structure for India would stand any chance of success without the backing of political power If the British financiers have considered it prudent to let the sterling find its own level, it is difficult to understand why it should be considered ill-advised to do a similar thing for the rupee in India The price of sterling will depend on the balance of trade in the United Kingdom from year to year. The fortunes of the rupee will depend not only on India's foreign trade but also on that of the United Kingdom The rupee is tied to sterling, but the sterling is not tied to the rupee The obligation is not mutual An immediate readjustment of India's monetary policy and the fixing of the rupee exchange at rates suitable to India's international trade requirements, seem necessary to prevent further disastrous results to this country India should not wait, as she is in certain quarters pertinaciously advised to do, for world conditions to improve, in order to determine the monetary standard best suited to her No other country in the world has so waited to reorganize its finances Great Britain, herself, has not done so President Roosevelt's recent action in the United States of America in the field of exchange and finance and his forming the newly constituted National Reconstruction Administration to raise the level of prices in that country should serve as an object lesson to India

Gold Imports, Exports, Stocks and Production

The world's total stock of gold in 1932 was estimated at Rs 3,100 crores,[11] of which about Rs 2,000 crores or two-thirds, was held by the United States of America and France

India's stock of gold in 1931 was valued at about

[11] On May 17, 1934, the Bank of England had £192 million, France, Fr 78,000 million, and on May 10, 1934, the United States of America had $ 4,830 million

Rs 695 crores, and her total stock of gold and silver at Rs 780 crores

The world's total annual production of gold has been computed at Rs 107 crores,[12] about half of which is utilized for monetary purposes and the other half used for industrial and other purposes

Imports of gold and silver into India, both coin and bullion, for the ten years ended 1931 were appraised at Rs 466 crores or Rs 46 6 crores per annum These consisted of Rs 280 crores of gold and Rs 186 crores of silver The net imports of gold into India during the last 30 years have amounted to about Rs 530 crores

World Monetary Conference

The reparations and debts following the Versailles Treaty made the United States of America the chief creditor nation of the world The same country has also become the principal manufacturing and exporting country These two developments have tended to make it impossible for the United States to receive payments in kind, and so, gold from other countries has been flowing in one continuous stream into the United States This has disorganized the currency and trade conditions of the world and is perhaps the principal cause of the present world trade depression The European debtor nations have been, as a rule, unable to meet the obligations of the Versailles Treaty and to pay their debt instalments on the due dates Public confidence has been shaken, credit curtailed, currencies have depreciated and trade has become precarious A World Economic Conference was recently held in London to discuss the position in all its bearings and provide remedies, but the conflict of interests between the participating nations was so great that no decision or understanding was arrived at India, though not a debtor country, could not escape the repercussions of the trade depression and financial crisis brought about by these world changes

The traditional Indian habit of making use of gold for purposes of jewellery has, in a sense, been helpful, for, as seen during the past two years, it has enabled the people to get substantial prices in local currency for their gold and gold ornaments and tide over a difficult period Still the excessive use of gold ornaments is undesirable as it means so much dead capital, and the people should be taught in schools and by public propaganda the productive uses to which gold could be put

Banking

Banking institutions in India may be divided into six classes as under —

(1) The Imperial Bank of India with a paid-up capital of Rs 5 63 crores and reserves of Rs 5 20 crores

(2) Foreign Exchange Banks doing business in India with an aggregate capital and reserves of £188 million

(3) Indian Joint-Stock Banks, (i e, those having a paid-up capital and resources of Rs 5 lakhs and over) having a paid-up capital and reserves of Rs 11 84 crores

(4) Indian Co-operative Banks with a working capital of Rs 35 94 crores

(5) Indigenous banks, mostly unregistered but doing banking work on lines approximately modern, their capital and reserves being unknown

(6) Post Office Savings Banks

In the United States of America there were over 22,071 banking institutions in 1931 with capital and reserves amounting to Rs 3,541 crores and deposits of Rs 13,788 crores Canada had in the same year 4,176 banking institutions with capital resources of about Rs 114 crores and deposits of Rs 836 crores The corresponding figures for the United Kingdom for 1932 were—12,557 institutions, Rs 316 5 crores capital resources and Rs 3,226 5 crores deposits, in Japan there were, in 1930, 8,676 banking institutions (including branches) with paid-up capital and reserves amounting to Rs 362 crores, the deposits in 1929 being Rs 1,407 5 crores Whereas in India, in the year 1930, there were about 880 banking institutions with Rs 23 45 crores of capital (the capital and reserves of Exchange Banks being excluded) and Rs 227 66 crores of total deposits Of the latter Rs 68 crores were deposits in Exchange Banks in India

The average *per capita* banking deposits were in the United States of America Rs 1,123, in Canada Rs 804, in the United Kingdom Rs 698, in Japan Rs 215, and in India Rs 6 4

The total amount of bank clearings in the United States of America ran up to Rs 149,000 crores and that of Japan to Rs 6,838 crores in the year 1930, in India, it was only Rs 1,634 crores in the year 1931

THE IMPERIAL BANK OF INDIA.

The Imperial Bank of India had, in 1931, 172 branches in different parts of the country, it had Government deposits free of interest amounting to Rs 19 08 crores and other deposits amounting to Rs 61 49 crores It has been declaring a dividend of 16 per cent on its paid-up capital every year since its constitution in 1921, except during the last two years when it declared 14 and 12 per cent respectively.

Hitherto it was both a trade and general banking institution with a privileged position and governed by a special Act of the Indian Legislature On the passing of the Indian Reserve Bank Act this year, it has been divested of the purely central banking powers it possessed under the old law The Act regulating its affairs has also been amended Under the law now brought into force, the control of Government over it has been modified It is authorized to enter into an agreement with the Reserve Bank of India to conduct government business as the latter's agent It can now open branches outside India in London and elsewhere The restrictions laid on it, in regard to the foreign business it could do, have been done away with Certain extended powers in regard to its internal business have also been conferred on it It can now deal in foreign exchange business. Though powers are vested in the Governor-General in Council to examine its affairs in case of necessity, the privileged position assigned to it is still open to criticism, especially in the interests of the development of indigenous banking in India

THE EXCHANGE BANKS IN INDIA

The exchange banks, which originally confined their business to the financing of foreign trade, have, in recent years, been also taking an active part in regular banking work connected with the internal trade of the country To continue to call them "exchange" banks is, therefore, somewhat of a misnomer A large proportion, the figures for which are not available, of the financing done by these banks (which was originally accomplished by means of deposits from countries of their registration) is now carried on by means of money received as deposits from India itself These deposits increased from Rs 10 5 crores in 1900 to Rs 68 11 crores in 1930 They are mostly utilized for the financing of foreign trade and commerce in India In the case of Indian Joint-Stock Banks, the volume of deposits increased from Rs 8.07 crores in 1900 to Rs 63 21 crores in 1930

The total deposits in the first three classes of banks amounted to Rs 212 crores in the year 1929. Of this amount, the Imperial Bank held 38 per cent, exchange banks 31 per cent, and Indian Joint-Stock banks 31 per cent

Foreign banks are of much greater importance and wield a much larger power in the trade and commerce of India, than they do in other countries None of the Indian joint-stock banks has a branch in any of the Continental centres, and so the foreign trade of India has to pass mostly through non-indigenous banks The share of the Indian banks in the foreign trade of India is estimated roughly at 15 per cent of the total. The Imperial Bank, as already remarked, has the privilege of holding about Rs 19 crores of public funds free of interest, but it has often been the complaint of indigenous and joint-stock banks that it is too conservative in its policies and that Indian trade and business do not get the credit to which they are entitled

The general financial policy in exchange and currency matters, already adverted to, has, on several recent occasions, forced the Government to borrow at high rates of interest This has led the public to withdraw their holdings in banks and invest the same in the larger interest-bearing Government securities, thus interfering with the normal banking business of the country

The Reserve Bank Scheme

In the projected Reserve Bank of India, to which reference has been made, there will be a Central Board of 16 Directors of whom 8 will be elected by shareholders and 8 (including a Governor and two Deputy-Governors) will be nominated by Government As two of the latter group are not to be entitled to vote, the elected directors would be in a majority There is, however, no provision that any particular percentage of directors should be Indians The Bank is to be a shareholders' Bank, free from any "political" influence Not only Indian and State subjects can be shareholders in it but also Co-operative Societies, Scheduled Banks—certain Banks scheduled under the Act—and Corporations and Companies, incorporated under the Act of Parliament or any law in force in the British Empire, the Government of which does not discriminate in any way against Indian subjects, and possessing Branches in India, can also be shareholders in it Directors of the Bank and members of the five Local Boards composing it cannot serve on the Indian or local legislatures Its chief functions will be to act as the note-issuing authority, to control credit in the country's interest and to maintain the stability of the currency It will act as Banker to the Government and the commercial banks It is not so much intended to produce dividends to its shareholders or to collect deposits for loaning out money to its customers as to prove useful to trade and commercial banks by centralizing the surplus cash reserves of the Indian Banking System as a whole, so that it can be put to use when required Besides discharging these functions, it has to buy and sell sterling for immediate delivery on London at specified rates Scheduled Banks are bound to maintain with it a balance which at the close of business on any day must not be less than 5 per cent of the demand liabilities and 2 per cent of the time liabilities In return for this condition, the Reserve Bank is to discount their paper This provision has been described as of the greatest importance for the development of indigenous banks in this country, since it is capable of being used to advantage for affording cheap credit in rural areas The reserve provisions indicate the establishment of India on a Sterling Standard, a very different proposal from the plan for a Gold Bullion Standard put forward in 1926 This is fully confirmed by the obligation put on the Bank to buy and sell Sterling on demand at prices close to the parity of 1s 6d between the rupee and sterling

The Act perpetuates the linking of the Rupee to the Sterling No steps have been taken to incorporate in it the results of the Geneva Conference of 1922, which mark an epoch in the evolution of the art of Central Banking, *viz*, the responsibility of the Central Banks for the value of gold The framers of the Act have not laid to heart either the teaching of the Geneva Conference or the meaning of the resolutions adopted at the London Monetary and Economic Conference in 1933 bearing on the general principles of the Central Banking policy One of these, subscribed to by all the Governments represented on the Sub-Committee on Technical Monetary Problems except that of the U S A, which considered discussion of the question premature, stressed not only the maintenance of gold standard by each country and its proper functioning but also the securing to its Central Bank discretion in regulating the working of the gold standard in its own country "unimpaired" This principle has been departed from in fixing up the duties and functions of the Indian Reserve Bank Then, again, the constitution of the Bank—the Central Board is to be made up of members partly elected and partly nominated—is open to criticism from the point of view of its competence to handle the credit question of the country—especially of a country like India, long yearning for development Further, though there is provision in it for meeting a domestic crisis, it is to be feared that it is secured at too heavy a cost from the point of view of the scheduled Banks and the Banking organization of the country generally The powers of the Local Boards are purely advisory and non-executive in character Their relationship to the scheduled Banks—who are also shareholders of the Reserve Bank—is not well defined The latter may play an important part in the scrutiny of commercial paper—practically acting as discount committees—but there is no indication that they can exercise any control over the lending policy of member banks This is exactly what the United States Banking Act of 1933 has effected It is, indeed, a grave defect of the Indian enactment that it contains no provision to check the vagaries of the scheduled Banks, whose paper it is, under the Act, to discount The discount policy may affect the country's credit, the gold reserve and the general purchasing power It may be remarked generally that the Indian Reserve Bank Act does not appear to have been inspired by any logical philosophy, nor can it be said that it is a clearly worked-out scheme for the distribution of credit power as between the Reserve Bank Central Board and the Local Boards or as between the Reserve Bank itself and the Government

INDIGENOUS BANKS

In any consideration of the banking system of India, the importance of the smaller indigenous banks (from which category the mere money-lender operating on his own resources may be excluded) situated in smaller towns and important village centres has not been as widely realized as it deserves These banks have been rendering, in the absence of regular banking facilities in rural parts, a real service to the rural population. Most of these concerns are carrying on their work in areas which cannot be tapped by the agencies of joint-stock banks and they do so by methods which will not easily permit of direct imitation by registered bodies Their success depends upon the honesty and integrity of their principals, the wide and intimate knowledge of local conditions and local credit possessed by them, the rigorous cutting down of service charges and the efficiency of management generally

The Central Banking Enquiry Committee has not estimated the total number of indigenous banks operating in the whole country, though some of the provincial committees have given the number in certain provinces as ranging to several thousands Of these, the banking system of the Nagarattar community of South India operating in Burma deserves special mention The indigenous banks have, of late, adopted modern banking methods and have proved their worth as useful financial institutions, having survived the serious crisis of recent times caused by the prevailing depression Any scheme for relief of agricultural indebtedness will have to take into account and enlist the practical knowledge and vision of these banks

It is the considered opinion of the Central Banking Committee that banks in India should aim at the efficiency of the European banking system and the economy of the indigenous bankers This will only come about, however, by working on a well-devised country-wide plan and programme aiming at definite results

The Central Banking Enquiry Committee has also accepted the plea that some action to improve the position of the indigenous banker and to increase his usefulness as a member of the banking system of India is called for It is estimated that out of a total of 2,500 towns in India (with a population of over 5,000), only 400 towns enjoy the advantages of joint-stock banks or their branches, and that agriculture, rural trade and small-scale industry in the other 2,100 towns (and in thousands of other important centres) depend almost exclusively upon the indigenous banker for financing them Even in those towns, where joint-stock banks exist, it is well known that large volumes of internal trade and remittance pass through the hands of the indigenous banker Detailed investigations made about 5 years ago by the Indian Central Cotton Committee into the financing of cultivators' cotton revealed the fact that 65 per cent of the cotton cultivators borrowed from *soucars* or indigenous bankers, 13 per cent from co-operative societies, and 15 per cent from their landlords who must have advanced their own capital for the most part

In order that their future usefulness may be harnessed to maximum advantage to themselves and minimum of risk to the investing public, efforts should be made to organize indigenous banks and to link them with the general banking system of the country, if they are enabled to get the facilities of such an organization, they will naturally be induced to reduce the rates of interest on their advances and plenty of cheap credit would thus be rendered available in the interior for arresting the growth of rural indebtedness and promoting the financing of internal trade with profit to the bankers and visible relief to the villagers

Co-operative Banking

The banking work done by the co-operative societies in the country, and the habits of thrift and saving they encourage amongst the members, have been already dealt with in the chapter on Agriculture

The Post Office Savings Banks in India play a useful, though a very small part, in affording banking facilities particularly in areas where no banks exist The Post Office Cash Certificates and Post Office Savings Bank Deposits which in the years 1928-32 averaged Rs 3 47 and Rs 1 38 crores, respectively, totalling Rs 4 85 crores, have during the last two years suddenly jumped up In 1932-33 they amounted to Rs 11 06 and Rs 5 20 crores, respectively, with a total of Rs 16 26 crores, while in 1933-34 even this total figure was surpassed, the figures being Rs 7 80 and Rs 9 10 crores, respectively, and the total Rs 16 90 crores This shows that with suitable encouragement the savings of the lower classes could be usefully collected and applied for the industrial needs of the country

INSURANCE

The total number of Insurance Companies operating in India in 1931 was 282 of which 135 were Indian and 147 foreign The total number of policyholders in round figures was about 714,000 of which 502,000 were Indians The total amount assured was Rs 168 crores; they give an annual premium to the Companies of Rs 8½ crores, out of which the share of the Indian companies is about Rs 4½ crores on their policies of the value of Rs 94 crores

The life insurance business of Indian companies has been of late showing gradual progress, in the year 1920 the new business written and the total assurances in force were Rs 5 17 crores and Rs 31 crores while in 1931 they rose to Rs 17 crores and Rs 94 crores, respectively

The amount of life insurance in force about the year 1930 in the United States of America was Rs 24,000 crores, in Great Britain Rs 3,000 crores, in Canada

Rs 1,300 crores and in Japan Rs 1,019 crores This means an insurance per head of population of Rs 2,300 in the United States of America, Rs 1,760 in Canada, Rs 730 in Great Britain, Rs 157 in Japan and only Rs 5 5 in India [13]

In other forms of insurance, namely, Fire, Marine, Automobile, etc , the premium income of all companies, both Indian and foreign, amounts to Rs 3 crores of which Indian companies have secured only half a crore as their share of the total business effected

The total assets of all Indian Insurance Companies is Rs 27 crores, which are invested mostly in Government securities A sum of about Rs 3¾ crores is invested outside the country In Japan, the total amount of insurance contracts in force in 1914-15 was Rs 360 crores, which increased in 1921-22 to Rs 1,450 crores and in 1931-32 to Rs 3,658 crores Of this amount, about a third is contributed by insurances on life and the rest on accident, fire, marine, transport, fidelity, steam-boiler, automobile and burglary insurance

The Indian Postal Insurance Fund, admission to which is open to all Government servants engaged in civil duties, had over 79,000 policies in 1931, with assurances amounting to Rs 4 46 crores and an annual income of Rs ¾ of a crore

In the United States of America, one out of every 4 persons is insured, in England one out of every 10, in Japan one out of every 5 and in India one out of every 500 It is evident that the idea of life insurance has not yet become popular in this country

---

[13] According to the address of Mr Amritlal Ojha (President, Indian Chamber of Commerce, Calcutta) to the Rotary Club on the 19th June 1933, the *per capita* figures for other countries were —New Zealand Rs 984.5, Australia Rs 750.7, Sweden Rs 563 7, Italy Rs 418 0, Norway Rs 376 7 and Netherlands Rs 338.2

COMPETITION OF FOREIGN COMPANIES

The prosperity of Life Insurance Companies in India is hampered not only by ignorance of the benefits of insurance prevailing among the people but also by the competition of foreign companies operating in India. The complaint is often heard that the system of rebates allowed by the latter has proved prejudicial to Indian companies getting their normal share of business The attitude of banks in India in not giving the same accommodation to Indian Insurance Companies, as they do to foreign-managed ones, has also not a little to do with the slow growth of the indigenous enterprise One of the most important of the "invisible" losses to the country is the amount of insurance premia paid to foreign Insurance Companies working in India It is computed that taking all kinds of insurance into account, about Rs 10 crores go out of the country in this form If these facts are widely realized, and if Indian Insurance Companies concentrate their attention on accident insurance and plan a programme of development in this business for the next 5 years, it is believed that a substantial portion of these Rs 10 crores could be retained in India

IMPORTANCE OF INSURANCE

Insurance, apart from its intrinsic advantages to the insurer, accumulates huge sums of money in the hands of individual companies which can be made available for long-term credit in the country Life Insurance Companies can contribute their share to the accumulation of wealth for the country simultaneously with the encouragement of thrift amongst the population The growth of Insurance business is closely connected with the development of trade and commerce, for the assets created could be utilized on industries, railways, shipping enterprise, etc Unfortunately, owing to lack of direction and policy, most of the insurance funds are not so utilized in India In the United States of America, insurance funds are invested to the extent of 51 per cent in farm mortgages and industrial undertakings and only 9 per cent in Government securities, while in India 75 per cent of the funds are invested in Government securities, and Indian industries derive little or no benefit from them

Joint-Stock Companies

Businesses which are carried on by Joint-Stock Companies in British India numbered 6,675 for the year 1930-31 and those in Indian States, for which returns are available, numbered 653 The total number of companies in all India was thus 7,328 The total paid-up capital of Companies in British India to end of 1930-31 amounted to Rs 271 3 crores and in Indian States to Rs 11 4 crores, making a total of Rs 282 7 crores The average capital invested per company was thus Rs 3 9 lakhs

British Companies Operating in the Country

Besides these, there are British Companies registered outside the country but working in British India In 1930-31, they numbered 853 and their paid-up capital was £ 728 7 million Similar companies working in Indian States totalled 14 and their paid-up capital was £13 6 million The total number of British Companies working in India was thus 897 and their total capital £742 3 million, this was exclusive of debentures of the value of £134 million issued by them Of these, most of the Banking and Insurance Companies and some of the navigation and trading companies incorporated outside India had invested only a portion of their capital in India Exact information regarding the share of this capital invested in India is not available If the financial policies of the country are to be determined by the Government and the legislatures with full data before them, such information should be collected under the authority of legal enactments and duly accounted for in the estimates of imports and exports and the net results of the country's transactions

The annual profits of companies and registered firms in India were Rs 53 crores on an average of the eight years, 1922-1930 Owing to the depression after 1930 the profits have fallen heavily, and in 1932-33 they were only Rs 29 crores

An attempt has been made to ascertain the number of Joint-Stock Companies and the capital invested in them in the leading industrial countries in order to get a comparative view of India's position in this respect The result is shown in the following table —

Joint-Stock Companies Compared

Country	Year	Number	Capital paid-up
			Rs (in crores)
The United States of America	1927	175,031	22 810
Great Britain	1929	110,139	4 330
Japan	1931	57,226	1 860
Canada	1931	18 576	3,142
India	1930	7 328	282 7

The above table shows that Joint-Stock enterprise has made very little progress in this country This is due to the lack of a policy of encouragement on the part of the Government and the absence of systematic training for co-operative action among the people The growth of joint-stock enterprise is essential for economic progress Urgent investigation and measures are necessary to remove difficulties and give every encouragement to business people to promote this class of enterprise

PART II
RECONSTRUCTION

CHAPTER XI
DEFICIENCIES AND REMEDIES

Effects of Dependency Rule—The Country's Economic Plight—Some Urgent Needs—Lines of Future Advance—Planned Economy.

EFFECTS OF DEPENDENCY RULE

INDIA being a Dependency of Great Britain there has been no plan, no scheme, no provision in the country's legislative or executive measures on an adequate scale for helping the people to increase their production or income, or raise their economic standing in the international sphere The elementary needs in nation-building are *education*, *industries* and *defence* and these have suffered most under Dependency rule The people's creative energy has been starved at its source

Owing to inattention to education, the effective working power of the people has been greatly reduced and it is high time that the mind of the country is definitely set in the direction of abolition of illiteracy The Universities should be induced to realize that the instruction they are giving in practical and mechanical subjects is wholly inadequate compared to that imparted in liberal arts and culture They should be made to realize also that a radical change is urgently called for in the higher educational policies to-day They should so regulate their affairs that, till a proper balance is established between cultural and practical subjects, greater attention is paid by them, than is done at present, to preparing in large numbers men of directing ability and recruits who can enrich the industrial and commercial life of the country

The survey in Part I has revealed many deficiencies

in the economic life of India but none so grave as those attributable to the neglect of industries One of these is the incredibly low *per capita* income from industries which, as we have seen, works out to about one-fortieth of what it is in the United Kingdom or one-sixtieth of that of the United States of America As a result, the occupational structure has long been out of balance and while every self-governing country is developing its industries and encouraging the growth of urban life, India has been steadily drifting towards increasing dependence on land and progressive ruralization

Some publicists and even high officials in this country discourage industrial progress and give expression to the misleading idea that India is essentially an agricultural country and that her future is entirely dependent upon agriculture Why India's future should depend entirely upon agriculture, while all the evidence available points to the fact that the wealth and prosperity of modern progressive countries have been built up on industry and trade, is not made clear This is in marked contrast to the views expressed by President Roosevelt of America in his book *Looking Forward*, published at the beginning of 1933, wherein he says —

"We know from figures of a century ago that seventy-five per cent of the population lived on farms and twenty-five per cent in cities To-day the figures are exactly reversed A generation ago there was much talk of a back-to-the-farm movement It is my thought that this slogan is outrun "

Since 1901, the rural population of India has increased by nearly 50 million and the addition to the urban population in the same period has been less than 10 million While the American President welcomes the reduction of rural population in his country from

75 per cent a hundred years ago to 25 per cent at the present time as a satisfactory development, the advocates of Dependency rule in India have no word of disapproval for the growth of our farm population from 61 per cent in 1881 to 73 per cent at the present time

The following extract is taken from a recent English publication —

"*Back* to the land for the people of British Isles is difficult to reconcile with the general movement *away* from the land in all advanced countries Had agriculture remained the dominant industry (in Britain), the country could have supported only a fraction of the present population and that under rather precarious conditions as to food supply from year to year "[14]

Although only 14 per cent of the population of the United Kingdom is dependent upon agriculture, the authors of the above publication are disinclined to advocate greater attention to agriculture in their own country They recognize that "non-industrialization and poverty go together and excessive dependence on land is a phenomenon noticed only in the poverty-stricken countries of the East "

By the omission of military training, the potential capacity of the people to help Government to resist foreign invasion or to defend their hearths and homes remains wholly undeveloped The Indian Arms Act in operation since 1860 has weakened the country and caused loss of self-confidence in the people It is high time that India followed the example of the energetic nations of Europe and Japan, and adopted some form of conscription, at least in respect of families whose earnings are above the subsistence line Conscription will help to

[14] L W White and E W Shanahan, *The Industrial Revolution and the Economic World To-day*, 1932, pp 346, 347.

introduce the much-needed elements of regularity, method, and discipline into the daily life of the Indian population

The best test of the economic efficiency of a nation is its yearly income According to the expert opinion appended to the Simon Commission Report, the average yearly income of an Indian is Rs 110 In the Indian view, this estimate is too liberal, the income does not exceed Rs 75 If the normal yearly income of India's population is reckoned at Rs 2,500 crores, the same in the present trade depression may be taken at Rs 1,750 crores This is equivalent to about Rs 50 per annum, or 6 shillings per month per head of population

According to the figures revealed by the Income-Tax Returns for 1932-33, the individual earnings of only about 564,134 persons out of a total population of 272 million in British India amounted to Rs 1,000 or more a year Out of this number, 271,171 had incomes under Rs 2,000 and 293,263 of Rs 2,000 and over Of these latter again, only 355 had incomes of Rs 1 lakh and over Indians have no foreign investments worth mentioning, and even taking the average income at Rs 7 per head per month, the great bulk of the population must be eking out their existence on Rs 5 or less It is apparent that on such a low income, no saving is possible

The Statistical Tables will show at a glance the wide gulf which separates India in economic achievements from some of the prosperous countries of the world A few essential figures taken from the Tables will illustrate the point

The recorded death-rate in India is 24 5 per thousand of population, as against 10 7 in Canada. The average duration of life of the people of India is 26 7 years, while that in England is 57 6 Only 8 per cent of the population of India is literate, whereas in every progressive country the literacy is over 80 per cent or ten times as high The working population employed in agriculture, pasture, etc, is more than 67 per cent in India and only 7 per cent in Great Britain, that employed in industries, trade and transport is as low as 17 per cent in this country, while the same in Great Britain is 68 per cent

The *per capita* production in India from agriculture in normal times is Rs 59, whereas that in Canada is Rs 213 Production from industries is only Rs 12 per head in this country, while in the United States of America it is as high as Rs 721

The *per capita* trade of India during 1932-33 was less than Rs 8, and that of the United Kingdom was Rs 324

The *per capita* bank deposits in India come to Rs 6 4, while those in the United States of America are as high as Rs 1,123

These comparisons show that Indians come nowhere near progressive nations in economic strength and have much leeway to make up The chief aim of any future economic development scheme should be to secure a rise in the average income and standard of living of the Indian population

The public debt of the country is, as we have seen, Rs 1,212 crores, of which the foreign loans amount to Rs 500 crores Other foreign liabilities involve an annual drain, both visible and invisible, of about Rs 200 crores, in a normal year Some of these liabilities are the direct result of Dependency rule Some, again, are due to the fact that British investors do not settle down in India and identify themselves with the people of the soil, as they do in Canada or Australia Others are incurred because there has been no will or policy in the Government of the country to train the people in shipping, banking and other forms of self-help

The Country's Economic Plight

There was some sort of self-sufficiency in rural life at the time the British took over the country But the policy of the new rulers to utilize and retain India as a market for the manufactures of Great Britain gradually deprived the Indian rural population of its old-time advantage of self-sufficiency and safety Owing to the unequal competition between the products of hand labour and those made by machinery and power and imported from the West, the Indian craftsman, particularly in the rural tracts, lost one occupation after another, and the Government, though conscious of his decadence, made no attempt, largely under the influence of *laissez faire*, to provide him with substitutes for the occupations which he had lost Thus, during a period when many of the countries of Europe, England herself leading, were being rapidly industrialized, the Indian population was allowed to become increasingly rural Mr Lloyd George once said that the United Kingdom was four-fifths industrial and commercial and one-fifth agricultural The reverse is approximately the position in India at the present time, that is, nearly four-sixths agricultural and one-sixth industrial and commercial

The survey of the local conditions so far made plainly shows that there have been no recognized policies in the Government of the country to combat the many and grievous deficiencies mentioned above The equipment and the constructive measures usually adopted in the Dominions and in countries having national governments are lacking in this country, and the people's fundamental economic interests are wholly unprotected.

The industrial and financial policies under Dependency rule, instead of increasing the wealth of the country, have had a contrary effect and helped to demoralize and impoverish the population

The vast bulk of Indian industry and trade has a wholly out-of-date organization and is carried on along traditional lines Except in a few large-scale industries, labourers are not even sufficiently disciplined to observe regular hours of work The agricultural population fail to get continuous employment for four to six months in the year and their working methods continue to be primitive and uneconomical They do not use time-saving machinery and motive power, partly through absence of training in mechanical arts and partly through want of capital to purchase modern tools and machinery The bulk of the business under transport and finance, save that associated with Government or non-Indian control, is managed according to practices and customs which are obsolete in civilized countries

Government publications fail to give the people a knowledge of their resources In the meagre statistics supplied in them, the information and data necessary for ascertaining such basic facts as income, wealth, unemployment, etc, are wanting, and official reviews are silent as regards the interpretation to be put upon such data as are published

Even a casual examination of the figures given in the Statistical Tables appended reveals a tragic state of affairs Eighty-nine per cent of the population is rural, of which over sixty per cent, it would be safe to say, live in mud hovels or under thatched roofs Owing to lack of diversity of occupations, the pressure of the population on land is very severe, the peasantry is heavily immersed in debt and the foreign debt of India is growing In times like the present, the ryot has no purchasing power, all occupations are starved During 1932-33, the unfavourable balance in foreign trade, amounting to Rs 40 crores, was made good by the export of distress gold

No count is kept of the unemployed in India, but unemployment and under-employment are the rule. Millions of people live in abject poverty

The main economic deficiencies enumerated above are the combined effect of historic traditions, political causes and social defects The chief cause is the Dependency form of Government under which people have been living, and according to which they are expected to live and work as a directed nation, all important policies and laws being promulgated practically without their full consent This in turn is due, as we have seen, to lack of definite objectives and policies on the part of those wielding political power to improve the condition of the people The people could not effect important developments unaided because, even if circumstances favoured such co-operation, radical reforms cannot be carried into effect without the support of political power and there can be no permanency or thoroughness in reforms not recognized or supported by the Government of the country

The social traditions of the people have also been unfavourable to progress Due to racial and religious differences, men live apart and fail to interest themselves sufficiently in each other's common welfare The Government policies are concerned only with political safety and have tended to perpetuate rather than minimise or erase differences The evils of caste and the low place given to women still remain as stumbling blocks to progress, especially in rural areas Mass education might have long ago corrected these deleterious influences, but lack of policies to reduce illiteracy has left the bulk of the population ignorant and poor

The organization of the country's defences is kept a sealed book to the people Without the ability to defend their lives and property, the present top-heavy defence expenditure can never be appreciably reduced. The economic departments of Government are inadequately equipped and it has been one constant struggle for the people to get any help from Government to increase the country's income from organized industries

The rôle of the State in every self-governing country is to help the people generally to build up wealth and increase their assets, to provide avenues of employment to the workless, to stimulate activities in the economic sphere and make the country as self-sufficient as possible In India, the very reverse tendency is noticeable in all these respects Great Britain has been insisting on doing for the Indian people what the latter should be encouraged to do for themselves, namely, provide their own supplies of clothing, steel, machinery and the numerous varieties of manufactured staple commodities required for their daily use The resulting enforced idleness has had the unfortunate effect of keeping the Indian people inefficient and has condemned them to a low and diminishing income

Some Urgent Needs

The problems which confront India are not quite the same as those which the countries of Europe, the United States of America and Japan have to contend against. In those countries, the masses of the population are educated, their business capacity and economic achievements are high and they have already built up a satisfactory standard of living for themselves This country, on the other hand, has a far larger population than any of them, and the average standard of living here, measured by the consumption of goods and services or the expenditure incurred, is only about one-fifth of the average in European States or one-twelfth in the best of them In dealing with Indian economic problems, this aspect should be constantly kept in view

No credence should be given to the theory that the Indian people would not be capable of rising to the level of their compeers in progressive countries in production, industry or trade, even if the training and opportunities afforded in those countries were available here and a responsible government existed to regulate and control their destinies

Next to the attainment of responsible government, the most important question which should engage the attention of the public in India is, as already explained, how to maintain the country's huge population at a level of income which would not fall below what civilized communities would regard as a bare subsistence wage

The number of the educated unemployed is very large Some professions like law are overcrowded, while in others like engineering, industry and trade, there has not been sufficient scope to absorb any appreciable number of trained people Generally, the education given for some of these professions within the country is very meagre, and many men who have qualified themselves and some who have spent money and made sacrifices to obtain high technical degrees in foreign countries, find it hard to obtain suitable employment Some idea may be formed also of the huge waste of man power going on in this country through lack of a policy to conserve it

The aim of any plan of reconstruction should be, first and foremost, to increase production and income, to bring into the country up-to-date machinery and render its use familiar to the people, to spread among them a knowledge of sound business policies, principles and practices, to extend mass education and to equip the leaders with technical skill and executive ability

If the methods for citizenship training recommended in Chapter XIII are undertaken vigorously as part of the Ten-Year Plan, we shall be building up an intelligent, wide-awake, self-reliant population, which will be approaching its task with a determination not only to mobilize all available human energy and material resources, but also to utilize all modern experience, inventions and discoveries from whatsoever source obtainable

Reference may be usefully made at this stage to certain fundamental economic truths that should be adopted, if occupations and income are to be speeded up and life quickened in this country

Every national Government, including the Dominion Governments, encourages the export of manufactured goods and surplus raw materials The export of manufactured goods is preferred because the local labour will have been employed in their production All exports tend to affect the trade balance in favour of the country and add to its assets The tendency of every country in the present trade depression is, therefore, in the direction of economic nationalism, that is, to restrict imports and encourage exports to the utmost extent considered reasonable and possible, and there is no reason why such a policy should not be pursued in India

We have seen that production and the standard of income will not appreciably increase without the use of modern tools and machinery As regards the impetus which machinery and motive power usually contribute to the economic strength of a people, this is what has been said by Mr Henry Ford —

"One has only to go to other lands to see that the only slave left on earth is man *minus* the machine We see men and women hauling wood and stone and water on their backs We see artisans clumsily spending long hours and incredible toil for a paltry result We see the tragic disproportion between laborious hand culture of the soil and the meagre fruits thereof We meet unbelievably narrow horizons, low standard of life, poverty always on the edge of disaster—these are the conditions where men have not learned the secrets of power and method—the secrets of the machine "[15]

Yet another need is the recognition by the people of India of the advantage of working in co-operation with their fellowmen and developing a spirit of team-work, oneness of view and nationalism in regard to their economic problems In these days, it is easier to secure opposition and resistance than agreement to constructive proposals This largely accounts for the lack of initiative and adventure noticed Differences there must be among thinking men and, if there be disagreement on some one or more points, that should not be a bar to unity of effort in the cause of the community or country in other directions Indians ought to make a special effort to get over this great weakness When one is faced with the necessity of a decision on a public question, what one should ask oneself is—Is there any good in it for the community or the country? If there is, sound patriotism dictates that every effort should be made to secure the greatest common measure of agreement for it

The people of India cannot be too earnestly warned

[15] *To-day and To-morrow*, 1926, pages 167-168.

against the various unsound economic and social theories that are spread among them by bigoted and interested persons A community should not be made to believe, as is often done in this country, that to be content with a low standard of living is a virtue, or that agriculture ought to be the principal, if not the only, occupation of the people It is hoped that the information and data placed before him or her in the previous chapters will readily convince every unprejudiced reader that for a community to be non-industrial is to dedicate itself to inefficiency and poverty Persons who advocate increased attention to agriculture, in preference to industries, will realize what a great disservice they are doing to the people of this country by their propaganda

Lines of Future Advance

Many of the economic policies followed in India at the present time are those deemed appropriate to a Dependency It we are to build up a sound economic structure for the future, these practices should be speedily replaced by others already well-established in self-governing Dominions and largely also followed in Great Britain itself

The lines of future advance should, therefore, be —

(1) to make a survey and prepare a list of deficiencies and wants,

(2) to compare Indian conditions with those in progressive foreign countries with a view to profiting by their experience and preparing new rules of conduct for India's benefit,

(3) to prepare a plan or comprehensive scheme for India embodying all reforms and developments needed to remove the deficiencies and wants disclosed by the survey, supply the characteristics, etc, as also all necessary

equipment, and to frame a programme which can be worked out with the resources at the country's disposal, in 5 to 10 years' time,

(4) to make provision for the funds needed for the capital as well as recurring expenditure on the scheme,

(5) to introduce a country-wide organization to give effect to the plan and programme; and

(6) to utilize the same organization to deal promptly with the reforms and developments needed in future to meet current deficiencies and wants and the changing conditions from time to time

Such, in substance, are the lines of reconstruction proposed in subsequent chapters

Planned Economy

Every modern national government is in possession of a vast amount of information of economic value, and whether it makes it public or not, it uses the information for building up sound policies and maturing schemes for the betterment of the condition of its people But India being a Dependency, such information is either not collected, or, if collected, is not always revealed to the public for political reasons

Every progressive country in these days maintains consistent, co-ordinated plans for economic betterment and, even where no regular plans are maintained, their objectives are not lost sight of Progress is maintained and the results are reflected in the daily transactions of its economic life Some backward countries have also begun to regulate their affairs by a planned economy and to develop production and resources to the highest level attainable in their individual circumstances It is known that some fifteen countries have already adopted well-thought-out plans of this character

Both the Government and the people in this country agree that a constructive plan is overdue A planned economy is required to ensure the rapid advance of industry, agriculture, commerce and finance and particularly for increasing production and earning power, reducing unemployment, and encouraging greater self-sufficiency and closer inter-dependence between the various parts of India It should provide for the profitable utilization of the material resources and man power of the country and the application of the latest inventions and discoveries to economic interests to the fullest extent. It should provide for securing a proper balance of occupations, for the abolition of illiteracy and for giving the educated section of the population training in the practical arts of business and administration

Each region and unit area, separately demarcated as such, should be entrusted with the responsibility of fulfilling its due share of this national task and its progress watched by a central agency by stock-taking from year to year With a planned economy, a rapid growth of economic activities and achievements will be assured, enthusiasm will be stimulated and full play given to the creative impulses of a vast majority of the population

In what follows, it is proposed to gather all the various suggestions and recommendations made in Part I into appropriate groups or concrete schemes and to outline a provisional Ten-Year Plan for the whole country. The Plan will give specific estimates of the developments to be achieved in production from industries and agriculture and the advance needed in other directions to secure progress at the rapid pace demanded by the conditions of the country For the satisfactory execution of a sound plan, the enthusiastic support of both the Government and the people will be necessary When such a Plan is prepared and successfully brought into operation, the people will have a guarantee that their future is being sufficiently safeguarded and a new economic order is really being brought to birth

The Plan needs a country-wide organization and the enlistment of the shrewdest brains in its service to work it to the best advantage The rules of the organization should provide for the selection of the most competent persons available in each region, with the approval of business men in the country or locality concerned Provision should also be made for changing the men as soon as there is loss of efficiency or vigour on their part The Soviet first Five-Year Plan, if all report says of it is true, may not have been an unqualified success, but it has some remarkable achievements to its credit, attributable chiefly to the enthusiasm roused in the people and to the discipline to which they subjected themselves

At present, while some few of the Government policies and measures in the economic field are of a progressive character, there are a great many which encourage stagnation and are having a prejudicial effect, and provision is necessary for organization and rules to inaugurate and enforce sound administrative and business policies for the future

Before giving an outline of a Ten-Year Plan, it is proposed to devote two chapters to these objects, namely, one to indicate the administrative and business policies which the public should be advised to follow in the economic sphere in future and the other to define the training to be given to the average Indian in business life and citizenship in order to improve his knowledge and capacity, and indirectly the efficiency of the nation as a whole

CHAPTER XII.

ADMINISTRATIVE AND BUSINESS POLICIES

Administrative Policies—Industrialism and Nationalism—The State and Industries—Conflict between British and Indian Interests—Constitutional Reforms—Need for Political Compromise—Business Policies—Forms of Business Functioning—Capitalism and Socialism—Capital and Labour—Mechanization and Mass Production

ADMINISTRATIVE POLICIES

THE Government of India is treated as a subordinate branch of the Government of Great Britain and the higher administrative policies are laid down under the orders of the Secretary of State for India in London The Secretary of State in Council controls the expenditure of the revenues of India and retains the power to borrow money on behalf of the people of India without reference to the Indian Legislature The administration is practically conducted according to the will of a handful of Englishmen in power for the time being in the Government of India, the India Office and the British Cabinet Not more than half a dozen Englishmen, perhaps, are concerned at any given time in the formulation and final control of the larger policies, which govern the fortunes of the 350 million people of this country Minor administrative policies are sometimes modified in accordance with Indian opinion and the wishes of the Central Legislature The complaint is that, in the determination of policies, the men in control are guided first, by the powerful trade and financial interests of Great Britain and next, by the consideration that India's political and economic status should undergo as little change as possible

Changes have been going on in the Constitution of India, as the result of political agitation, the general trend of which has been or is intended to be in the direction of responsible government on the Dominion model But such changes are taking place at an unconscionably slow pace The people are growing increasingly restive, there is growing disparity between India and progressive nations in economic efficiency and earning power, and the distress caused by unemployment and under-employment is becoming more and more acute Except under severe political pressure, the Government rarely go out of their way to initiate improvements They put forth no active effort even to keep the people correctly posted, by means of statistics and otherwise, with the true state of the country's affairs. Central policies have remained substantially unchanged for fifty years or more The only hope of redress for the people lies in a radical change in the administrative and economic policies of the country after an exhaustive survey of existing conditions by the chosen representatives of the people themselves

INDUSTRIALISM AND NATIONALISM

Industries and manufactures supply the elements needed to make a people self-sufficient and self-reliant and develop their organic life as a nation They quicken and stimulate business and add to man's executive capacity and efficiency Industrial life connotes production, wealth, power and modernity

Some ninety or hundred years ago, Great Britain had attained a leading position in industrial pursuits and production, chiefly by the use of steam as a motive power and by enterprise in navigation and overseas trade Seeing how rapidly Great Britain was building up wealth, Continental nations like the Germans, French,

Belgians and Swedes began to emulate her example and to industrialize themselves The United States of America followed next, then came Canada and Japan All these have shown considerable enterprise and progress in building up industries and thereby made substantial additions to their income and wealth Within recent years, the principal nations of the world have all been concentrating on industries and manufactures with a view to strengthening their economic position

Such in brief has been the origin and development of industrialism It has rapidly advanced with every development of new machinery and motive power. Its chief result has been to multiply human power, quicken and increase production, accelerate communications and raise wages and standard of living

Closely associated in its political and economic aspects with industrialism is nationalism, a force tending to make the country that has developed it an independent economic unit Since the close of the War, economic nationalism has been gaining rapid recognition both among the nations of Europe and in Japan No modern nation whose national policies are not guided by the two forces of industrialism and nationalism has gained military power or become rich and prosperous No nation which desires to be economically and politically self-sufficient can ignore industrialism

THE STATE AND INDUSTRIES

Industrialism thrives under a Government which encourages both corporate and individual enterprise, and this usually happens only where there is a *national* government There is in every progressive country close relation between its political and economic policies Industries flourish under any civilized *national* government, whether that government is semi-autocratic like that of Germany before the War, or oligarchic like that of Soviet Russia since, or under one-man dictatorship, as Italy is to-day But India, through lack of identity of interests between her people and her rulers, has not been able to make any headway

In the matter of industries, production, wealth or military power, experience shows that one nation rarely helps another No government treats a people controlled or directed by it on a level of equality with its own subjects Great Britain is now obliged to treat her Dominions more or less as her compeers because they would not submit to the commercial and political domination of the mother country In the case of Canada, the fear that she might break away from Great Britain and seek the protection of the United States of America, induced the British Government to grant her full responsible government This concession in its turn paved the way to the other colonies one by one claiming and attaining the status of a Dominion and becoming a partner in the British Commonwealth

It may not be inappropriate to invite attention, in this connection, to the views expressed by certain recognized British and foreign writers on the subject

Mr J Taylor Peddie, writing about Ireland in his book *Economic Reconstruction*, published in 1918, states "The successful development of a nation wholly depends upon the favourable conditions which Government may create within it for productive industry, wherein men can use their minds, body, health and intelligence with every freedom, each individual rising to his maximum power in the accomplishment of which he will derive his greatest happiness "

The following statement occurs in a book entitled *Industry and the State—A Conservative View*, written by Four M P 's of Great Britain —"Few people nowadays seriously suggest that the State should conduct the industry of the nation But it is the duty of any Government to create and to sustain conditions under which it is possible for other people to conduct them Captains of industry must look at the industrial activity of the country primarily from the viewpoint of their own undertakings The Government alone is in a position to survey the whole field of industry impartially, to judge each industry not only from the economic standpoint but from the point of view of its national utility, to apply remedial measures to the black spots in the national interest, and, above all, to safeguard the interests of the consumer as well as those of the producer "[16]

Speaking at a Royal Empire Society luncheon in January 1933, Sir Alfred Watson, a former editor of *The Statesman* (Calcutta), said "Industrially India was a land of missed opportunities, the blame for it resting heavily on Britain The mischief had been that Britain did not seriously tackle the problem of developing India's industrial potentialities "

A Report of the Liberal Party of Great Britain entitled *Britain's Industrial Future*, published in 1928, admits "No matter how firm the determination of any government to avoid interference with industry, it finds itself called upon to remove difficulties from its path or to assist it In any case, it is driven to recognize that in modern conditions its policies necessarily affect industry "

President Roosevelt has said in his recent book *Looking Forward* "It has been traditional for business to urgently ask the government to put at private disposal all kinds of governmental assistance.... Our Government, formal and informal, political and

---

[16] Published in 1927.

economic, owes to every man *an avenue to possess himself of sufficient*[17] for his needs through his own work .. The task of government in its relation to business is to assist the development of an economic declaration of rights, an economic constitutional order This is the common task of statesmen and business men It is the minimum requirement of a more permanently safe order of society Happily, the times indicate that to create such an order is not only the proper policy of government, but is the only line of safety for our economic structure as well "

The foregoing quotations serve to show the importance their authors attach to the need of a government formulating sound economic policies and associating itself closely with their execution The people should have the power of self-direction, they should be at liberty to combine for all practical purposes to build up wealth and prosperity, in other words, responsible government is an indispensable prerequisite for the development of industrialism and economic independence

Conflict between British and Indian Interests

A new constitution is at present being framed under which India is expected to be raised to the status of a Dominion, save for certain safeguards and reservations said to be necessary to protect British interests vested in this country The safeguards proposed are intended to be in force only for a very limited time, yet the representatives of the British Government are unwilling to face the issue and agree to a time limit

The difficulties alleged to exist in the way of the grant of full Dominion autonomy are —

The italics are by the author.

(1) That the Indian States will not immediately consent to join the Federal Union and that the evolution should, therefore, be slow and gradual ;

(2) That the Muslim and other minorities want special protection ; and

(3) That, on account of illiteracy and other causes the Indian people are unprepared for an immediate rapid advance

The most formidable obstacle, however, to the concession of Responsible Government arises from the disinclination of the British statesmen and British public to part with the powers and privileges which they have for so long enjoyed in this country and which practically fall under four heads —

(*a*) Defence ;

(*b*) Civil Services ;

(*c*) India's Debt in Great Britain and British Investments in India ; and

(*d*) British Trade and Commerce

Taking Defence first, it is stated that India cannot have Responsible Government, unless without external aid she can maintain internal order and defend herself against foreign aggression For this purpose, she should have an effective Dominion Army manned and officered by Indians There is no objection to an understanding being arrived at to treat defence as a reserved subject and to give a fixed grant for defence purposes for a period of, say, five years But the new Government should, simultaneously with the commencement of the Central Responsible Government, appoint a Committee of Defence and take vigorous measures to build up its defence policies and to provide the requisite number of Indians with training for all arms within ten years, or fifteen years at the outside, so that

India may have all her defence arrangements ready by then

The Civil Services are a body of officers who are very valuable when the business is to enforce discipline and maintain law and order But generally the British element are not in sympathy with the progress of education and the economic and nation-building activities of the country Their predilections and training tend to suppress rather than stimulate co-operation and enterprise in the people The existing services should be treated generously so far as their pay, prospects and pensions are concerned, but future recruitment from outside should be strictly limited

The third obstacle to progress is the fear entertained in some quarters that the foreign debt and British investments in the country might be placed in jeopardy at the hands of an Indian executive There should be no difficulty to give reasonable guarantees that all legitimate rights in this direction will be respected in the same way that they are in the Dominions of the British Commonwealth

The fourth obstacle is the apprehension felt that British trade might suffer Trade should be as free in India for the British merchants and firms, as it is in Canada or Australia But all existing monopolies and preferences exclusively enjoyed by them in any shape or form, the like of which are not acquiesced in in other Dominions, should be eliminated

The reason why administrative policies, equipment and measures in India are not always such as to benefit the people is the existence of conflict of interests in some essential direction or other between Great Britain and this country According to the recorded opinion of eminent Englishmen and English officials themselves, the past policies and acts of the British Government in this country have often been injurious to the true interests of the people There have developed certain monopolies and privileges for the British community in the Indian economic order, which are detrimental to the advancement of Indians in their own country This diversity of interests is distinctly noticeable in the controversies that have taken place over the constitution of the Reserve Bank, Exchange Ratio, the Statutory Railway Board, Protection to Indigenous Industries, Coastal Shipping Reservation, etc It should, if possible, be removed because with such removal will disappear the demoralization that has overtaken the Indian people on account of lack of exercise of their natural gifts in the service of their own country

By arriving at an understanding with the British Government and British trade interests, a way might be found to the mutual advantage of the two countries, whereby the interests referred to may be suitably compensated, and the way left free for India to advance with the rapidity with which the Dominions under similar freedom have been forging ahead The present Dependency form of government will have to give place without delay to a responsible government

Constitutional Reforms

The British Government in consultation with the delegates invited by them from India have proposed certain constitutional reforms which are embodied in a White Paper, and the proposals are at the present time undergoing further scrutiny in London at the hands of a Select Joint Parliamentary Committee It is important that, when it comes into operation, the new constitution should be able to remedy the many disabilities in the economic sphere under which this country has so long been labouring It is not proposed to make more than a passing reference to the draft constitution, because the scheme may undergo further change before it is actually accepted by the Parliament and the Government of Great Britain But there are certain features in it, which are so unfavourable to Indian aspirations and so opposed to the aims set forth in this book, that no patriotic Indian can reconcile himself to them

The proposed scheme makes provision for leaving the control of about 80 per cent of the revenues of the Central Government with the Viceroy or in non-Indian hands It is only when India gets full financial responsibility, that is, the power to borrow money, levy and spend taxes, initiate new enterprises, and grant financial help or subsidies and subventions to such enterprises as require them that its government can launch reconstruction plans and start with sufficient confidence in its power to build up new assets and wealth Unless the reconstituted Government is armed with these powers, the prospects of any real economic advance seem very remote

The control of the proposed Federal Reserve Bank is sought to be placed in the hands of the Viceroy, who will appoint its Governor and his Deputy In other words, the policies of the Bank will be controlled in the ultimate analysis by the exigencies of the London Money Market

According to the White Paper scheme, the future responsible government will not have full control over the Railways, the gross revenues of which amounted in 1930-31 to over two-thirds of those of the Central Government Railways require machinery, plant and stores, which, being standardized products, can be easily manufactured locally But the major portion of these at present continues to be imported from abroad Provision is required for giving adequate training to Indians to qualify for the manufacture of machinery and for employment in all departments of railway traffic and administration The railway workshops should be thrown open to persons who require training or instruction, so long as it can be done without interfering with the routine requirements of traffic Apparently all this will continue to be impossible under the proposed scheme

In order to develop the country's foreign trade, the new Government will need full control over its fiscal policies, and power to depute its own men as Trade Commissioners to foreign countries

One extraordinary feature of the scheme is the omission of any reference to the political entranchisement of the people of Indian States The States subjects will be represented in the Federal Legislature, but in their own States they are to remain under their age-long autocratic rule The British Government do not hesitate to interfere with the States peoples' rights when, for instance, there are disturbances, but they do not seem inclined to adopt constitutional means for preventing such disturbances The Central Government should be strong enough to protect and supervise the economic interests of the people of the States, but the proposed scheme leaves the Princes as autocratic and unhelpful to their subjects as ever before

The aim of the scheme, briefly stated, seems to be to place the greater part of the finances, a portion of trade control, the Railway Administration, the entire Army and Foreign Affairs outside the purview of the future Responsible Government

Since the beginning of the Montagu-Chelmsford Reforms, several innovations have crept into administrative policies, some of which have lowered the morale of the public services and are indefensible One of these is recruitment to the services on communal considerations and another is the policy openly avowed by the Secretary of State of favouring particular communities, some of whom are not advanced enough to demand a national form of government and not sufficiently progressive to place the interests of the country as a whole above the temporary benefits to themselves or their own communities

What the Indians want are policies, equipment and measures in the administration similar to those which have enabled the Dominions to improve their finances and national income By providing these at this juncture, the British government and people will derive considerable moral support which, in the long run, will be the truest safeguard for the maintenance of their connection with India

Need for Political Compromise

The safeguards and the reservations contemplated in the White Paper are clearly inconsistent with the needs of the political and economic progress of the country They do not lead to the creation of a strong Federal Government, capable of dealing impartially with all the races and communities coming under its sway during the transition period The duration of that period is also left in uncertainty

The safest course for Great Britain, in her own interest, is to grant to India without further loss of time, and without equivocation, a satisfactory form of Federal Dominion Government which will give it full control over its financial and fiscal policies

The feeling of estrangement and distrust between the two races has deepened on the one side by the excessive dilatoriness displayed by the British Government in framing a new constitution and by the attempt of the British authorities to force imports on the country and to rule by repression and, on the other, by the claim to independence advanced by certain representatives of the people and the demand for an independent scrutiny of India's debt to Great Britain

The Indian leaders have been anxious to see the industries of the country protected against foreign competition and indigenous business enterprises encouraged whenever possible, by subsidies, subventions and other special measures But this cannot be done by routine methods On the other hand, it is quite reasonable for British traders and business men to demand special protection for their investments and business enterprises started in this country to the same extent that they receive in the Dominions But in respect of the special privileges enjoyed by the British, which interfere with the rapid growth of Indian enterprise, and the like of which are not to be found in a Dominion like Canada, it should be possible to provide for their termination in the course of 10 or 15 years In the case of all interests injuriously affected thereby money grants might be made to compensate the owners for minimising the immediate hardships caused to them Such compensation for the abolition of all forms of existing monopolies and privileges which interfere with the expansion of Indian business may not exceed Rs 10 crores per annum to begin with and the payment need not extend beyond 20 years If India regains her freedom to develop as she chooses, the growth of income and wealth will be so rapid and enormous that this payment of Rs 10 crores per annum will remain insignificant by comparison This measure is suggested with a view to prevent any interference with the smooth progress of business enterprise and good relations between the two countries

It is believed that, if half a dozen trusted

representatives of each of the two countries could sit at a table and discuss these questions, a reasonable compromise and a fair award of compensation to injuries likely to be caused can be easily arrived at After such a compromise is duly ratified by the reformed Central Legislature, Indian industries should have the same full scope for development and expansion that corresponding industries enjoy in the Dominions Tariffs should be controlled entirely by the new responsible government

BUSINESS POLICIES

Having considered at some length the administrative policies suited to a future Responsible Government for India in relation to those practised abroad, we shall proceed to explain what the proper business policies should be in a national government

At the present time the most dominant type of organization for conducting industries or business enterprises of any appreciable size is the joint-stock company Since the capital invested in joint-stock companies is known to the public, the total amount so invested may be taken as a measure of the country's industrial prosperity or standing

FORMS OF BUSINESS FUNCTIONING

Individual Ownership—In the early stages, each business man tried to do things for himself and even now many a large business enterprise and innumerable small ones are owned and operated by individual entrepreneurs In the domestic system of industry, the individual ownership has been the rule In the case of large enterprises owned by private persons, the management, both in Great Britain and the United States of America, is conducted, save that portion bearing on ownership of capital, on the same sound business lines as those of joint-stock companies

Partnership —The partnership type represents the association of two or more persons to carry on business enterprises for profit as co-owners This type came into use with the growth of the size of the business unit and is still largely in vogue in the business world

The advantages of this type are that the organization itself is simple, the expense is small, activities are comparatively unrestricted, quick decisions can be taken in regard to day-to-day transactions and also in emergencies, and the association can be easily terminated by mutual consent

The disadvantages, however, are more pronounced First, there is the risk of disagreement between the partners Each partner will have to be personally responsible for any debts or commitments prejudicial to the success of the concern contracted or made by a single managing partner Much depends on the capacity of the partners to share and exercise managerial power, while always maintaining amicable personal relations among themselves Grave difficulties are also experienced, when one or more partners decide to withdraw from a concern The capital invested cannot be quickly turned into liquid assets, but in a joint-stock concern it is possible to do this by selling the shares or by issuing debentures, whenever the shareholders are so inclined

Joint-Stock Companies —With the growth in the size of business enterprises, the company or corporation form of management came into vogue in Great Britain about the year 1862 and within the last 25 years it has developed very rapidly In a joint-stock concern, capital is hired from the public in small sums in the shape of shares, and business is started and operated by paid managers under the supervision of a board of management, the members of which are understood to be elected by the general body of shareholders At the present time, the joint-stock company is the most popular form in use for promoting and conducting business enterprises of various kinds, particularly in trade, manufactures, mining and transport

Besides the joint-stock company, there are two other types of company organization, namely, the private company and the trust company According to the English Companies Act, a private company is defined as a company having not more than 50 shares The transfer of shares is restricted and the publication of accounts is not obligatory

Trust Companies—A recent development of joint-stock organization is the trust company for the interlocking of business A trust company is often formed to bring under a unified financial control a number of different productive concerns in order to secure the resources of all for the good of the entire combination Such combinations are usually of two kinds, vertical and horizontal, as explained in Chapter V These combinations have grown to gigantic sizes, particularly in America, as a result of the experience that production and operation in large-scale businesses are usually more economical

Trusts and combinations in Soviet Russia stand on an unique footing by themselves Under the first Five-Year Plan, productive industry is said to have developed extraordinarily fast, mainly through a series of combinations, each covering a particular branch of production The basic unit is the factory which is controlled by an individual manager The manager is in turn elected by representatives of the employees Groups of factories in the same branch of production in a given region are controlled by bodies known as *trusts* and the trusts are supervised and controlled by a combination which is responsible to, and forms a section of, the Supreme Economic Council of the nation

Management of Business Concerns—In capitalist countries like the United States of America and Great Britain, the management of business enterprises, large and small, is usually left to private agencies In almost all modern countries, the government takes an abiding interest in the progress of industries, trade and agriculture It is very much alive to the fact that its own resources and power depend on the improvement in the wealth and tax-paying capacity of its people It is always ready to render certain recognized services in the interests of the nation as a whole

The persons connected with business enterprises form themselves into chambers of commerce, trade associations, etc , and in these bodies the business men pool their intelligence and resources for the benefit of the entire community or class represented by them

Hitherto, business interests in America were very jealous of the interference of their government and the common slogan till recently was "less Government in business and more business in Government" But on account of the trade depression prevailing for a few years now and the dislocation of normal banking and financial arrangements, the Government of the United States has been using its resources to support industry and has secured extraordinary regulatory powers in that regard for the ultimate good of the nation Under the control now exercised by the Government, an endeavour is being made to create an economic balance as regards profits and wages in the various industries including agriculture Production and prices are controlled, working of railway companies is supervised—all on the basis of a planned economy, devised on a gigantic scale to tide over the present crisis

There are also, at the same time, a number of national and local undertakings administered in one of three ways, namely, (1) by the Government itself, (2) by local bodies, and (3) by some sort of *ad hoc* authority or corporation appointed by the State

The form of administration of industries has already been described in Chapter V Every large business has under the Indian Companies Act a board of management for the control of its operations As in America it should, in addition, have a committee of internal management, consisting of the principal heads of departments and experts Every phase of the operation on the work, and also on similar works outside, should be under the constant study of the members of this committee By this means, a large number of officials will be kept interested in the progress of the business And when doubts, disputes or controversies arise, there will be enough knowledge and experience at the service of the management to come to quick decisions Committees should be appointed also to advise important individual departments in all large business enterprises

Attention has already been drawn to the urgent need for revision of the Indian Companies Act If industrial concerns are to function properly and benefit the country, the Managing Agency system should be suitably modified without delay, and some superior agency like the Tariff Board created with a staff of business and accounts experts, who would be available and ready for inspection of concerns, which are from any cause in a weak condition, and for rendering technical and financial advice to them The agency referred to should be able to carry out speedily an "efficiency audit" and an "accounts audit" either at the request of the management or of a considerable body of shareholders.

The authority should be so constituted as to inspire confidence and to have its decisions readily accepted

Capitalism and Socialism

Capitalism is the name given to a system of production under which producers carry on industry and business solely for profit, and not for rendering service Monopolies are a characteristic of capitalism, and their general tendency is towards a continuous expansion of business and the concentration of financial power

"Out of a population of 124 millions in the United States of America," says President Roosevelt, "American economic life was dominated by some 600 odd corporations, who controlled two-thirds of American industries and 10 million small business men divided the other third"[18]

Capitalism has helped to promote science and develop industries Without concentration on capitalist lines, many a country which is now wealthy and prosperous compared to its condition in the last century, would have remained poor At the same time, there is a growing distrust of capitalism because its tendency is to distribute unequally the profits of industries and production and to concentrate wealth in the hands of a few individuals, the bulk of the population remaining poor and unprotected

Capitalism has done much to facilitate the productive use of money It has helped to concentrate capital particularly by investment in machinery and to cheapen production It has been instrumental in developing technical progress and in the practical utilization of a vast amount of scientific knowledge It is responsible

Looking Forward, 1933, p 31.

for increased production, efficiency, enterprise and in a large measure also for increase of employment

In a book published in 1933 under the title *Moscow Dialogues*,[19] it is stated that more than half the wealth of the capitalist countries is held by less than 2 per cent of the population The middle class, which forms about 8 per cent of the population, owns at least a third of the wealth, so that under the capitalist system 10 per cent of the population owns more than 80 per cent of the wealth On account of this inequality of distribution of the profits of industries and production generally, the people in many a democratic State are encouraging State management of large enterprises This has led to the system known as State Socialism

Quoting the well-known publicist, Stephen Graham, on the tendencies of the inner development of the United States, a Russian author V M Molotov wrote in 1931 "For many years the tendency has been for America to become the land of a hundred thousand very rich people and a hundred million poor The fundamental tendency consists in the increasing poverty and misery of the broad masses and in the growing wealth and luxury of the ruling, privileged capitalist groups "[20]

In the struggle between Capitalism and Socialism, some people have come to regard the present as an age of ascending socialism and declining capitalism There is no doubt that the question of equitable distribution of the profits of industries is receiving increasing attention and therefore, socialism is gaining ground

An extreme form of Socialism is what is known as Communism, which has developed in Soviet Russia and under which the instruments of production, distribution and transport are operated directly by the State or

[19] By Julius H. Hecker.

[20] *The Success of the Five-Year Plan*, pp. 71, 72.

by trusts or combinations created by the State In Russia, it is understood, there is a minimum wage and a maximum salary and there is legislative provision to prevent the concentration of wealth above a declared amount in an individual

Mrs Sidney Webb in a broadcast talk published in 1933 said "Two great nations, on opposite sides of the world,—each comprising over a hundred million people, each having almost unlimited resources, each virtually protected by its magnitude against foreign intervention—are trying out the relative efficacy of an almost unbridled Capitalism on the one hand, and on the other, an almost complete State Socialism. The relative success of American Capitalism and Russian Communism is yielding a good life for the whole population, whether this be measured by material prosperity or by the development of human personality, it will, I think, largely influence, I might almost say, determine, the social and industrial organizations in Great Britain and throughout the civilized world Dean Inge, in his brilliant vision of himself as a world Dictator, emphatically endorsed the 'American way' as a 'marvellous achievement full of encouragement', whilst he condemned, dogmatically and without qualification, the social institutions of Russian Communism I am content to wait and see "[21]

Since the above statement was made, a new kind of State Socialism is, as mentioned above, being tried on a gigantic scale under Mr Roosevelt's National Recovery Act in the United States of America In that Act, provision is made for higher wages and shorter working hours The effect of these revolutionary measures is said to be to dethrone the unrestricted

The Modern State, 1933, pp. 211-212

individual *entrepreneur* and make the group the country's economic and social unit The object of the attempt at inflation of currency is to effect a reduction of the purchasing power of the people who have got money and increase the purchasing power of those who have got commodities

Having regard to the conditions prevailing in India, it is safe for this country to proceed along the lines practised in such capitalist countries as France and the United States of America India resembles France in the small size of the agricultural holdings and the United States in the large size of the country and the magnitude of its resources, particularly man power We have yet to build up some measure of moderate industrial prosperity, and for the present, capitalism is best suited for that purpose Only the monopolies incidental to capitalism should be minimised, and wherever they are inevitable, a watch should be maintained and special modifications made by legal enactments and otherwise, in the direction of service to the public It behoves the State to refrain from enacting any legislation to limit legitimate private enterprise and at the same time to ensure that large capitalist undertakings are carried on in harmony with the larger interests of the great mass of the people

The chief complaint against capitalism is that while it has successfully used the machine for mass production, it has not solved the problem of distribution of profits Even assuming that India henceforward concentrated on industrialism, it would take a couple of decades at least for her to build up a *per capita* income comparable to the least progressive of civilized countries. This measure of progress should be attempted first and by the time the country attains the same, it may be confidently predicted that Western nations, among whom the question of equitable distribution of profits has become an urgent issue, will have found some practical solution

CAPITAL AND LABOUR

As the size of industrial undertakings began to grow and large aggregations of labour became possible there have been frequent occasions for disputes and disagreement between capital and labour Wherever and whenever the disagreement became acute, it resulted in strikes These strikes are now threatening to become a feature also of Indian industrial life

In parts of Europe, the struggle between capital and labour is very keen Labour is stated to be in the grip of capitalists and that all the wealth of society goes to the latter It is said that "The farmer tills the soil, the miner digs in the earth, the weaver tends the loom, the mason carves the stone, the clever man invents, the shrewd man directs, the wise man studies, the inspired man sings and all the result, the products of the labour of brain and muscle, are gathered into one stupendous stream and poured into their laps" On account of the prevailing depression, however, even in Europe, this struggle is not much in evidence just at present In the United States of America, industries are carried on under more favourable conditions in this respect and labour is paid higher wages and enjoys greater amenities than in Europe The struggle between capital and labour was practically unknown in that country The following extract taken from a book written presumably by a Russian author shows that there is no rivalry between capital and labour in Soviet Russia because the ultimate control rests in the working classes themselves —

"With us every worker and peasant is a

stock-holder at par with every other He knows it is *his* factory, *his* farm and *his* railway which he operates He knows that every improvement, every labour-saving device and every other economy will benefit him directly, and this explains why in our country there is no opposition to rationalization, no strikes, but an unprecedented awakening of the creative participation of the masses "[22]

Labour in India has, by tedious steps, learnt the methods of collective bargaining and has organized trade unions as in Europe, and disputes between capital and labour are becoming common

One particular fact to be remembered in this connection is that hitherto strikes on a large scale have occurred, outside Railways, only in two important industries, namely, cotton textiles and iron and steel. A strike which showed its head some time ago in the jute industry which is under European management, was promptly suppressed

It should be remembered that in a country, where industries are undeveloped, it behoves labour to be more circumspect and not to assist, even involuntarily, in any revolt calculated to kill the goose that lays the golden eggs There is an immense body of unemployed labour which will gain with the growth of industries. It is true the standards of wages and of living of industrial labour are very low at present, but though low, the wages are appreciably higher than those earned in agricultural employment

The Government appointed a Royal Commission on Indian Labour in 1929, which issued its Report in 1931. Its recommendations included the constitution of an all-India Industrial Council, wage boards, encouragement of building societies for workmen, provision for

[22] Julius H. Hecker, *Moscow Dialogues*, 1933.

education and unemployment insurance and, last but not least, special representation of labour in the central and local legislatures An important recommendation provided that every employers' organization should set up a special committee for continuous consideration of the well-being and efficiency of the workers in establishments controlled by its members

When industries expand, wages and the standard of living are bound to go up automatically When an appreciable increase of wages takes place, say, even to the level of 25 per cent of the British standards, labour can assert itself and claim many of the privileges conceded in industrially developed countries But to do so, even before industries are properly started, seems suicidal in the interests of labour itself

Mechanization and Mass Production

By using machinery and mechanical power and by improving productive technique, that is, by utilizing many of the devices discovered by experience which enable operators to increase the output and reduce costs, America has been able with the aid of her enormous resources to develop methods of production which have vastly increased her prosperity The increase in output per individual is being brought about by shifting the task of production, as far as possible, from industries manipulated by human labour to industries operated by machinery, by standardizing commodities and by narrowing individual tastes to suit the methods of mass production Unlike its human counterpart, the business machine never gets tired until it gets out of repair It is said with truth that the mechanical method is automatic, error-proof, tireless, rapid, efficient In recent years, the daily output of work has been doubled or trebled and the number of persons employed has been reduced to half, or less than what it was before the new mechanical methods were perfected As a result, according to Dr T T Read of the Columbia School of Mines, the comparative output of work per person is nearly twice as great in the United States as in Great Britain and more than three times as great as in France These methods have rendered payment of high wages to labour possible and have enormously increased its purchasing power The wage rates in the United States are recognized to be about 75 per cent higher than in England, and the rates in England are double those paid in some of the States of Central Europe

The effect of all these developments is two-fold—one is to increase production and profits and the other to reduce the number of hands employed in production The profits chiefly go to the capitalists and, although such labour as may be employed may benefit from the higher wages paid to it, the reduction in the numbers employed affects the labour population as a whole This section of the population, therefore, looks upon the methods of mechanization and mass production with suspicion In some countries, the bulk of the labour population is positively prejudiced against them Efforts are being made to reconcile labour to those methods by reducing its hours of work, increasing its leisure time for recreation, etc , and by other means

India has not entered the machine age yet Any country which needlessly continues to use human labour, while machinery can do the same work at a much reduced cost, will be carrying on business at a great disadvantage compared with its competitors The neglect to use machinery till now has been extremely harmful to India The attitude of the people of India towards this new development should, therefore, be to accept unhesitatingly the principle that machinery and tools of the most modern type should be used in production Except in the case of the textile industry, the volume of production obtained from organized industries in this country, that is, industries which use machinery, is inappreciable As stated already, it may be a couple of decades before India can arrive at the stage when further use of machinery may reduce employment But in the earlier stages of their use, machinery and motive power are known to create new jobs rather than diminish employment Experience shows that although some one invention or other has thrown people out of work, scientific discoveries taken as a whole have provided work for millions The policy in India in the immediate future should therefore be to utilize up-to-date tools, machinery and power to the fullest extent permitted by its resources

CHAPTER XIII

TRAINING FOR BUSINESS LIFE AND CITIZENSHIP

The Building up of a Nation—Training for National Efficiency—Training for Individual Efficiency—Rules for Citizen Efficiency

THE BUILDING UP OF A NATION

HAVING regard to the great and rapid changes taking place in methods of production, means of locomotion and business practices, in the civilized world generally, the Indian has need to modify many of his traditional and obsolete ways of thinking and working Altogether a new outlook on life is demanded by the circumstances of the times If only the people are literate, active and efficient and are imbued with progressive ideals, the other conditions for them in their own country are so very favourable that they will soon be able to provide themselves with everything they may reasonably want

Enough has been said to bring to light the deficiencies of life in India The latest Census Report gives a gloomy picture of these deficiencies By far the saddest feature revealed in it is the fact that only 8 per cent of the total population is literate Even by excluding the population aged 5 years and under, the proportion does not rise higher than 9 5 per cent

As regards the economic aspects of village life, Major-General Sir J W D Megaw, the Director-General of the Indian Medical Service, who recently made a special enquiry, has recorded the following conclusions —

"Taking India as a whole, the doctors regard 39 per cent of the people as well nourished, 41 per cent. poorly nourished, and 20 per cent very badly nourished.

"The general conclusions derived from the survey are that (1) India has a poorly nourished population, (2) the average span of life is less than half of what it might be, (3) periods of famine and scarcity of food occur in one village out of every five during a ten-year period in which there has been no exceptional failure of the rains, (4) and in spite of the excessively high death rate, the population is increasing much more rapidly than the output of food and other commodities

"It is clear that the growth of population has already begun to outstrip the increase in the production of the necessities of life, so that even the existing low standards of economic life must inevitably become still lower, unless some radical change is brought about"

The lives of the bulk of our people are regulated by custom and tradition There is no appreciation of the precept that every person should prosper by his own effort, there is no agency responsible to watch whether people in any region or community are progressing or deteriorating, no organization to build up business, or to find employment for the workless The bulk of the rural population are deficient in discipline and sound working habits, they have no technical skill, no capacity for teamwork, no enterprise, they do not even observe regular hours of work

Action to eliminate these deficiencies is overdue. This duty will lie heavily on the new reformed Government, when one is established Till such a time arrives, the leaders owe it to themselves to do all they can, by suitable propaganda, to bring home to the people the realities of their position and induce them to educate and train themselves in all these respects Should, however, the present state of things continue and both Government and leaders remain indifferent, they will be leaving a heritage of growing inefficiency and poverty behind

A great danger to guard against is the spread of the doctrine that poverty is a thing to be tolerated At present an overwhelming proportion of the population is living below the poverty line It is necessary to fix a minimum standard of living, develop national policies and create occupations, so that no family or individual willing to work may be unable to attain that standard A minimum wage is fixed from time to time, particularly for industrial labour, in parts of Europe and America In Australia, a standard of living is recognized This is one of the reforms which Indian leaders in each district, city and village should take up and provide for with the aid of the proposed Economic Councils in the near future The most urgent training needed is to make the Indian a better worker and a better producer, so that he may earn enough to provide a decent standard of living for himself and those dependent upon him

In order to get the best out of the nation, the women-folk of the country should be put to work in increasing numbers and made to produce or do things for which they are best fitted Generally speaking, in Soviet Russia, women are not shut out from occupations in which men are engaged Women work alongside men in Japan, as also in many of the States of Europe If a woman in this country is enabled to do even two-thirds of the work of a man and if the work of both men and women is simultaneously regulated by local and national organizations, the capacity of the nation to build up prosperity will advance at a bound

It is necessary to develop an industrious, skilful and efficient type of citizen and workman The educational institutions should take the lead, by means of carefully prepared manuals, to instruct the youth of the country in regular working habits, character, discipline and co-operation, that is, all the essential qualities that go to build up an efficient and purposeful nation

There has been no definite policy or mechanism in the administration of the country to build up an efficient body of citizens in this way Provision should be made for it in future We shall explain in this chapter what should be done in this respect and deal with the measures necessary in two sections, namely, (1) *national efficiency* and (2) *individual efficiency*

TRAINING FOR NATIONAL EFFICIENCY

The principal measures needed to improve the capacity and quality of the average citizen and build up an efficient nation fall mainly under the following five heads —

(1) Education,

(2) Industrialization,

(3) Training for Defence,

(4) International business equipment, practices and habits, and

(5) Indianization

Education should be rapidly spread because the percentage of literate population with us is less than one-tenth, while universal mass education is the rule in all progressive countries Industrialization is suggested

Military training is required because the people should be ready to defend their hearths and homes at all times, both when civil peace is interrupted by local disturbances and national security is threatened by foreign invasion. It is unwise to postpone the training till an actual emergency arises If we are to keep in step with progressive nations, we should adopt many of the institutions and organizations which have helped to build up their power and prosperity Lastly, the importance and principles of Indianization should be brought home to every household by suitable propaganda, that is, the acquisition of new business practices and social habits and standards—based on approved foreign practices that may be needed to build up the future Indian nation

Education —The education imparted in India is inadequate, both in quantity and in quality, in *quantity* because only about 8 out of every hundred of the total population can read and write, less than 5 per cent is attending educational institutions and no attempt is made to increase this attendance, in *quality* because the education imparted is not sufficiently practical to prepare persons for the business of life

The greatest need of the day is mass elementary education which should be made both free and compulsory It is understood that in Soviet Russia even secondary education is imparted free The number of boys attending educational institutions in 1930-31 was 7 per cent of the total male population, the corresponding proportion for girls being 1 72 per cent The present average of 4 6 for both should be increased at least to 15 per cent within the next ten years In the United States of America, the number attending educational institutions was as high as 24 per cent of the total population in 1930 One of the speediest ways of extending mass education is by giving instruction to adults in their spare hours The adult population should be induced to submit to discipline and make the necessary sacrifices to learn to read and write, and where circumstances permit, also to improve its skill in practical arts

The desire to restrict education proceeds from a

fear of political democracy, because so long as the working classes are uneducated, the demand for free political institutions will be feeble There are persons who think that education should be withheld from the people in order to check such a desire "Increase of education," says Bertrand Russell, "may be taken as one of the inherent tendencies of industrialism With universal education come other things of great importance The first of these is political democracy which is scarcely possible where the working class is uneducated, and scarcely avoidable where it is educated "[23] There are also others who argue that practical or industrial education should not be spread as there are not enough openings and professions in the country for trained men, and in the absence of such openings the extension would lead to discontent On account of their unpopularity, however, such views are rarely openly declared

The greatest drawback in Indian education is the omission to give practical training to young and old in the use of modern tools and machinery, which is a part of the equipment needed for industrialism Mechanics and mechanical engineering should be taught at least to one-quarter of the total number of students in the various grades of educational institutions, as they are an essential equipment for practical work in agriculture, industries, transport, house-building and other occupations

In the present state of Indian education, the Universities should give special attention to courses in engineering and chemical technology, higher commerce and administrative and economic sciences A large number of business schools and colleges should be also

[23] *Prospects of Industrial Civilization*, 1925.

set up, as is done in America, to teach business administration, finance and accountancy It is a great and continued loss to the country that the provision for such classes of education should be kept down so low as at present In view of the inadequacy of technically trained men and skilled labourers required to man the very large number of factories, farms and shops to be started when the Ten-Year Plan is brought under operation, the instruction imparted in Indian schools should be given a distinctly technical and professional bias Polytechnization of schools must be the watchword for some years to come

The records of engineering and industrial education in Japan show that a large number of engineering graduates are turned out every year from the Universities There are higher *industrial* schools in that country with over 20,000 pupils, middle grade *industrial* schools with over 1,500,000 pupils and private *industrial* schools—higher and middle—with over 80,000 pupils In addition to all this, it is on record that every year 300 of the most brilliant graduates of the Universities are selected and sent abroad at the expense of the Government for foreign study, mainly to Germany, Great Britain, the United States of America and France in order that the nation may be constantly kept in close touch with the most recent advances in science and technology

In his new book, President Roosevelt has said: "In the State of New York, nearly *one-third* of all the expenditures of the State Government are going as aids to education Perhaps this is not the right policy, but it seems to be in line with modern thought and I do not believe there is anybody who can suggest any alternative that would not be reactionary "[24]

---

[24] *Looking Forward*, 1933, p 94.

In his book, *The Success of the Five-Year Plan*, in Soviet Russia, V M Molotov wrote in 1931 "In 1928, 14 8 million persons were embraced by all forms of schooling, whereas by 1931, the number had increased to 44 8 million " This shows how rapidly school-going population can be increased, if there is a will and a policy in the administration An intensive and persistent campaign is being carried on for the spread of education in Russia It is reported that more than 26 million children are receiving education at the present time and that more than 2 million students are attending technical schools

J Taylor Peddie in his book *Economic Reconstruction* (1918) has stated "Advanced education is of as much importance to the country as the building of railways, steamships and battleships " But, in India, the Universities, which are or ought to be administered by men of broad sympathies and culture, have failed to recognize that one of the main objects of education is to train the recipient for the battle of life The desire to equip people with capacity and skill and improve life exists in every community and country which has a national government including the Dominions, but there is no such pronounced move in India

We have about 100,000 students in our Universities, the largest number at the present time in any country, save in the United States of America and perhaps also Soviet Russia By changing the educational policies and enforcing a unity of purpose, this vast student force can be suitably distributed among all the professions and occupations for which trained men are wanted This will require careful planning If in this and other ways, the immense man power at our disposal is suitably mobilized, drilled and put to work, it may be the means of bringing an unprecedented harvest of wealth and power within a very short time

Industrialization.—The subject of industries and industrialization has been dealt with at great length in two previous chapters The organization to be set up, the developments to be attempted, the training to be given and the atmosphere to be created have been fully described We need only refer here to certain aspects of the training to be given to prepare young persons and adults for employment in industrial pursuits

A knowledge of mechanics, that is, of tools and machinery, is one of the indispensable preparations for industrial life By the use of machinery and motive power, human drudgery has been greatly lightened, hours of labour required to produce a given volume of goods or services have been shortened and the workers have been enabled to enjoy a higher standard of living It is known that the real wages of workers in Great Britain are about four times as great now as they were a century ago

One of the main drawbacks of the educational system in India is the neglect of instruction in mechanics and mechanical engineering In former times, every large village or group of small villages had its blacksmiths and carpenters Since the advent of British rule their number, instead of increasing, has been falling Provision should be made to give instruction in mechanical pursuits along with primary education This defect which existed also in Russia in the Czarist regime, is being removed by the establishment of factory schools and mechanical classes in large numbers In that country the primary schools are equipped with hand and machine tools and basic materials for wood, cloth and paper products Some of the secondary schools are combined with industrial and agricultural enterprises, and on account of the constant contact with industry throughout their school career, students become familiar with technical processes of the industry in which they may be specializing A carefully thought-out scheme to do the same thing in India is a desideratum The rural population will never improve unless an appreciable proportion of it is trained for mechanical pursuits and taught to manufacture for themselves agricultural implements, house-building materials and furniture, and other needs of efficient rural life

The well-to-do classes of the population who can afford to enter the Universities should receive training in higher mechanical arts and business, that is, in engineering—civil, mechanical and electrical—chemical technology and higher commerce Persons actually in business will profit if modern correspondence courses are introduced and made popular Where no regular training is available, apprentice courses should be resorted to There should be no large industry in any part of the country without special provision for giving such training

The University professors concerned with economic and business subjects should be in actual contact with industrial enterprises in which their theoretical or technical knowledge would be useful both to business and to their students

The Russians have realized that in all constructional work, a knowledge of technique is indispensable and in regard to technical matters, they have decided not to depend on outside experts in future but to train specialists among their own people so as to become absolute masters of their work In their second Five-Year Plan provision is made for about 200,000 specialists possessing University education (against 100,000 during the first Five-Year Plan), and 420,000 specialists from middle technical schools for the service of industry, transportation and rural economy

Training for Defence.—We next come to the question of defence. Although this is a subject which does not appropriately fall within the sphere of economics, training for defence is the first step in the building up of national life. The safety of individual communities and groups, their culture and civilization are often jeopardised or even destroyed, if they are not trained for self-defence. No nation can regard itself as safe that is not prepared to defend itself.

Most European countries, besides maintaining a regular army, give compulsory military training to young men from the civil population for a certain period of their life. Discipline is one of the characteristics in which the people of India are lacking, and military training through conscription or otherwise will have a salutary effect on the physique and character of the future citizen. For generations under Dependency rule, people have been taught merely to obey and this has naturally brought about a spirit of dependence leading to deterioration of character.

Along with any plan of Defence that may be decided on under Dominion rule, provision should be made to give military training to the civil population to the extent given in the Dominions of the British Commonwealth and in Japan. Till sufficient funds are available, the training may be limited to imparting the more essential knowledge connected with military technique and discipline, but, whatever training is decided on, a certain percentage of the entire population of each province should be allowed to share in it.

The training may be given in special military schools, military corps, University corps, territorial force and other organizations to prepare recruits for the second line forces for utilization in emergencies It may be mentioned that in countries like Italy, Germany and Russia instruction in military training forms part of the regular school curriculum

It is neither fair nor proper to confine military training to young men of the so-called martial races If military training is not given in every province, the omission may result eventually in the domination of the people of the trained provinces over those of the untrained If a nation wishes to be self-governing and reasonably self-sufficient in trade and industry, it should not be content to leave its freedom to be defended by outsiders

It cannot be too strongly emphasized in this connection that the supervision and ultimate control of the defence forces of the country should be completely Indianized within, say, fifteen years Capacity for defence is the *sine qua non* of nationhood

International Business Equipment—Every progressive country is changing its practices and habits according to the rapidly improving conditions of the world, and it is necessary that Indians should do likewise and assimilate the beneficial experiences of other countries in order to raise their own level of working capacity and material prosperity

It is the commonest thing for every civilized nation to-day to be constantly studying and adopting all new developments in other industrial and progressive countries likely to benefit its own working capacity, efficiency and earning power

Through lack of time-saving appliances, efficient business methods and practices, India's earning power and efficiency are very low There is much waste of power, energy and natural resources, due to lack of standardized practices, and indifference to or contempt for the wisdom and experience acquired by generations of practice in progressive countries.

There should be no hesitation on our part to adopt new policies, new institutions and equipment already in use in progressive countries and which are known to be of proved benefit to them Nor should there be any hesitation in adopting methods of mechanization and rationalization which are already benefiting industries in many a foreign country

Perhaps the greatest resource we have to-day is our man power This resource is nothing new, it has always been with us Had the Indian population known how to use it on the right lines and in the right spirit, this country of ours would to-day be the richest in the world, but man power can only be rendered effective by co-operation The capacity for co-operation is without question the most valuable virtue which Indians have to acquire from the example of progressive countries

Indianization —The Government of the United States of America took great care to spread the principles of economic nationalism among peoples of various European races, who migrated into that country, by giving them special training in the ideals of civilization, culture and enlightened living already prevalent among the older communities settled in the country The process was known as *Americanization* A somewhat similar process of *Indianization* is needed to make the various classes and creeds in India to coalesce for purposes of national development and improvement The Harijan movement inaugurated by Mahatma Gandhi is a courageous move in this direction Soviet Russia is attempting the creation of a classless society by more thorough-going methods. The permanent prosperity of individual communities and scattered groups, however well-off they may be for a time, depends ultimately upon the unity of aim and effort of the people as a whole The sooner the vast populations of this country realize that the spirit of division and disunion has been one of the chief causes of their backwardness and ruin, the more rapid will be their progress towards nationhood and the higher standards of living, self-respect and culture that it stands for

TRAINING FOR INDIVIDUAL EFFICIENCY

The second part of this chapter dealing with the training of the individual citizen falls under three heads, namely

(1) Home discipline,
(2) Creative spirit or initiative, and
(3) Co-operation or teamwork

We are dealing with characteristics, the lack of which is blocking the way to India's rapid progress

Home Discipline.—In the ultimate test, success is judged by the income derived from work Every adult member of a family should be made to put in normally seven to eight hours work every working day of the week,—six working days comprising the week The task given and the hours of work may be varied according to age, state of health, working capacity of the member and the time of the year When the work to be done is light, the working hours may be longer For both boys and adults in this country, a salutary division of time would be "eight hours work, eight hours sleep and eight hours given to culture, recreation and other amenities of life" This should be the normal distribution of the time for every working individual during the day

The value of the work is enhanced by a systematic arrangement of what a person has to do and by its methodical performance in close association with his fellow-men Many an American workman is able to live in comfort from his earnings of only five working days of the week, because he lives in an atmosphere of rapid methods and mass production, uses good tools and machinery, has learnt economic methods and is willing to work hard In England, too, a day and a half are utilized as a holiday out of every seven days in the week One holiday in a week for rest and recreation is a very desirable provision and this is given in most Government offices and business concerns in this country nowadays

In Italy, what are known as "leisure time" institutions have been organized on an extensive scale "These vast organizations promote schemes for the better enjoyment of the free time of workers of all classes with the object of raising their intellectual, moral, physical and social status in accordance with a policy of enhancing national values"[25]

India continues to be unprogressive and poor, because work in this country is generally unorganized and because on account of uncertainties of rainfall and the consequent precarious nature of agricultural occupations, the vast majority of the rural population have not formed regular working habits If only the farm population of this country acquires the habit of regularly putting in eight hours work a day by taking on some subsidiary occupation or other in the slack season, that single acquisition alone may prove the salvation of the community Measures to induce the rural population to acquire such a habit should form part of the proposed Ten-Year Plan and suitable subsidiary occupations should be provided for them

Every member of the family should be instructed

[25] Tomaso Sillani *What Is Fascism and Why*

to cultivate the saving habit, so that the family may as far as possible, not fall into debt by incurring unproductive expenditure It is easy to earn a rupee—but hard to save one The ignorant villager is badly in need of lessons in thrift, as he is often so improvident as to barter away even his land—his only source of livelihood—to meet the expenses of a social function, like a marriage or funeral

Success in life depends on work, on what a person does and on the profitable use he makes of his time and not on what he feels or thinks The price of success is hard work, preferably in an occupation congenial to his tastes To work, to initiate, to get results, and get results quickly, is the key-note of the age Industry, concentration, self-reliance and a resolute will added to integrity of character, are the chief passports to success, and these are within the reach of every healthy, active person, if only he makes the effort

Creative Spirit or Initiative—The heads of families should be advised not only to keep their family members regularly at work for a fixed number of hours daily but also to induce them to set apart some spare time for improving their knowledge or manual skill The habit should be inculcated in both young and old, not to be content with things as they are, but to seek always to do things better and better The spirit of investigation and research, the incentive to do things, the urge to be improving surroundings, in other words, the spirit of initiative should be instilled in the future citizen This is specially necessary because the Indian is born to unprogressive traditions and the present system of education does not provide the requisite corrective

The urban citizen has some opportunities of acquiring knowledge on account of the more active life led by the people around him In villages, however, where such facilities do not exist, provision should be made for giving manual and business training and instruction in some trade, occupation or profession both to young and old This need should be met through the agency of village improvement associations or committees similar to those common in the village life of Japan In Japanese villages night classes are held for agricultural courses and they are suspended only when unavoidably necessary in the busy season Subsidiary industries are encouraged in the villages by subventions given by the village councils and societies, by the district and prefectural authorities and occasionally by the Imperial Government

Co-operation or Teamwork.—These are days of co-operative effort A large measure of success attends the exertions of people who work in co-operation with others and who try to achieve results by joint or mass effort. If a number of people jointly engage themselves in gainful occupations, success will be greater and the results to individuals will be far more satisfactory than if each person worked by himself

The greater part of the world's business to-day in industry and trade is done by co-operative functioning, and by means of organizations known as joint-stock companies Under the old individualistic leadership of industry, each *entrepreneur* or business man tried to keep his secrets away from his competitors, but experience with modern trusts, mergers and co-operative enterprises has demonstrated that success now-a-days comes only to those who pool their resources and work together with large numbers of their fellow-men for common advantage

The habit of large numbers of persons working harmoniously in business, politics and social activities should be instilled into our people as a second nature. The qualities of frankness and trustfulness should be specially encouraged to remove distrust and promote brotherly co-operation among neighbours or among large numbers of citizens In village life, at harvest time and in emergencies, cultivators even now do help one another, but a closer and more deliberately planned co-operation is possible in many more fields of constructive endeavour, bringing manifold benefits with it In the execution of large measures of improvement or development, or where benefits or profits on a large-scale are aimed at, planned co-operation is indispensable, and it should be inculcated by special instruction, exhortation and example

We have seen in how many directions the people of India lack training As in the case of individuals, the difference between a forward and a backward nation consists in the greater knowledge, higher capacity for doing things and larger earning power possessed by the former

What has gone wrong with the Indian population is that their collective will power is feeble through want of practice, that is, the power to co-operate, to regulate their lives in small matters as well as large, by organization and deliberate planning

In countries like Germany and Japan and generally in most European States, a determined effort is made by the Governments concerned to promote the physical and economic efficiency of their citizens by education, by encouraging co-operation on a large scale and diverse other ways Our people should lay to heart the appeal which President Roosevelt of America made to his countrymen at the beginning of his term of office "If we are to go forward," said he, "we must move as a trained and loyal army willing to sacrifice for the good of a common discipline, because, without such discipline, no progress can be made, no leadership becomes effective "

RULES FOR CITIZEN EFFICIENCY

The Indian citizen will safeguard his future and, as far as in him lies, that of his country, by observing the following rules —

(1) *Practise Self-Help* —Work regularly a fixed minimum number of hours daily for six days in the week

(2) *Knowledge is Power* —Reduce illiteracy, encourage adult education and vocational training among members of your family and others over whom you have influence

(3) *Cultivate Teamwork* —Develop the habit of co-operation and be zealous of your integrity and promote mutual trust

(4) *Practise Thrift* —Put by at least one-twelfth of your earnings—(one month's earnings in a year)—to provide for sickness, unemployment and hard times generally

(5) *Increase Production and Service* —Use up-to-date equipment, working methods, tools and machinery and raise your own income and that of the country

(6) *Support Indian Industries* —Develop industries and manufactures, make the country self-sufficient and increase employment

(7) *Restrict Imports* —To keep money within the country, restrict imports and increase exports of manufactured goods and surplus raw materials, and build up credits abroad

(8) *Maintain Efficient Standards* —Standardize business practices, social habits and methods of discipline as far as possible to secure economy of time and effort Adopt efficient policies, equipment and practices from progressive countries

(9) *Think and Act Institutionally*—Maintain the work of associations, councils, committees, etc , with which you may be associated, or in which you may be interested, at a high level of efficiency

(10) *Think in Terms of the Nation*—Try to promote national efficiency to the limit of your power

CHAPTER XIV

A TEN-YEAR PLAN FOR INDIA · ORGANIZATION.

The Nature and Object of Plan—Economic Organization—Central Economic Council—Central Development Department—General Economic Staff—Provincial Economic Councils—Local Economic Councils—Responsibility for Execution of Work

THE NATURE AND OBJECT OF PLAN

WITH a view to increasing production and income rapidly and speeding up progress in other directions, a system of planned economy is being extensively resorted to in many parts of the world Planned economy is also found to be the most effective method for remedying many accumulated economic deficiencies and ills A survey of existing conditions is made first and then a plan of development and reconstruction drawn up, envisaging the main purpose and objectives aimed at The plan gives the conditions as found at the beginning, the improved conditions which it is its purpose to achieve, and the time or period within which the transformation is to take place Provision is made for the organization, equipment and funds needed, and the plan then given effect to

Planning like this is not altogether a new practice Every enterprising administration in the past has had to work on some sort of plan, but plans were usually kept secret in order that competing nations might not exploit any weaknesses in them or thwart them when brought into operation Plans of many European States, even at the present time, including the great powers, are a sealed book to the public

The first plan developed openly and put into execution on a nation-wide scale is the famous Five-Year Plan of Soviet Russia, which was in operation between the years 1928 and 1932 Russia has since embarked upon a second Five-Year Plan which she proposes to complete by 1937 Some particulars have been published of projected plans of this character for countries like Italy, Turkey, China and the newly constituted State of Manchukuo under Japanese suzerainty The latest country to embark upon a plan with a view to increasing production and employment in agriculture and industry is Denmark It is understood that Mexico, Germany, Sweden and the Irish Free State are contemplating the adoption of plans, either comprehensive for the whole State or partial, that is, intended to deal with specific local problems Planning in all these countries is confined to the economic sphere, while in Soviet Russia it embraces every phase of national life—political, economic, social and cultural

Side by side with an economic plan or without one, many a self-governing State has found it necessary to associate itself closely with the commercial and business interests of its people by establishing national economic councils for dealing with problems connected with their economic and social life The councils are usually composed of persons possessing knowledge and experience of agriculture, industries, trade, transport, finance and other connected activities The governments have in a manner entered into partnership with business by keeping themselves informed of its difficulties and wants and by doing everything in their power to advance its interests

Economic Councils have been established in leading countries like Great Britain, France, Italy, Germany and Belgium, mostly to work in an advisory capacity The functions of the councils vary from country to country In France, for instance, the object of the

National Economic Council is to study problems concerning the economic life of the country, find solutions and suggest their adoption by the public authorities The general object of all of them is the same, namely, to bring to bear the combined influence and resources of both the government and the people on augmenting the income and wealth of the country

In what follows it is proposed to describe how these two new measures or methods of development—economic planning and economic organization—may be applied to the conditions in India, and how the interest of the people in economic matters may be roused to promote their material well-being

The present state of production and economic activities, as far as it is revealed by Government publications, has been explained in Part I and the explanations are supported by the Statistical Tables given at the end of the book Many of the directions in which progress and expansion are possible or desirable have been already described It is now proposed to outline a suitable Ten-Year Plan for India The Plan will set forth the main objectives and forecasts of projected developments for a period of ten years Provision is made for bringing into existence an economic organization to co-operate with Government for giving effect to the Plan The work to be done in each province or region will be decided in consideration of its requirements and resources in raw materials, finance and human energy The average yearly rate of progress is determined beforehand, as are also the forms of local organizations to be set up, funds to be appropriated and staff to be employed for the purpose

A ten-year period is recommended for the plan and not a five-year or other shorter one, because the official statistics available are inadequate and there has been no survey of resources carried out, and no country-wide organization of any sort exists for the production of wealth. In these circumstances, an estimate for ten years would be more elastic and better adapted to the realization of the objectives of the plan. Once a ten-year plan is framed and approved, a detailed workable plan for the first year of operation is easily prepared. The choice of developments of unquestioned value and urgency for the first year's operation would for all practical purposes be unlimited. If a survey of resources is undertaken simultaneously with the commencement of operation of the plan, it would be possible to terminate the original plan at the end of five years, and frame for the second half of the ten-year period a separate five-year plan based on the results of the survey. The experience gained in working the larger plan in the first five years will also help to make the revised plan for the second half of the period more precise and reliable, and there will be greater certainty of achieving the results aimed at under the latter plan.

ECONOMIC ORGANIZATION

Central Economic Council.—The work of preparing detailed proposals for the Ten-Year Plan and for its subsequent operation has to be attended to by the Government in close co-operation with the people. This co-operation is best secured by a national economic organization with a Central Economic Council at its head, composed of about 50 members consisting mainly of expert economists and leading business men representing the various organizations and activities in all parts of the country in agriculture, industries, commerce, transport, banking and finance. This council may meet once in six months and at shorter intervals, when practicable. There should be a

Standing Committee of the Council stationed at Delhi, composed of 3 to 5 competent members chosen by the Council, with a person of outstanding ability as its chairman The chairman and members should be paid a fixed salary or allowance according to the time devoted and sacrifices made by them This Committee should have three or four experts to assist it in the discharge of its responsible duties The experts may be chosen for a year or six months or other short period at a time

Central Development Department—All operations connected with the Plan should be controlled by a Development Department at the Central Government under the supervision of a Cabinet Minister working in collaboration with the Central Economic Council The bulk of the work of the Ten-Year Plan will be attended to by a Development Committee working in close co-operation with the Standing Committee of the Economic Council These two Committees should between them constitute the *thinking section* associated with the administration, to supervise all development work in connection with the Ten-Year Plan, and also to advise Government on the policies they have to adopt on important questions like unemployment, tariffs, currency and exchange, export trade, production, distribution, price levels and other urgent problems which arise from time to time The Development Committee will be part of the Development Department of the Government and the Standing Committee, which will be appointed by the Economic Council, will be composed of members who will hold office for one to three years at a time The appointments to the Development Committee, even though made from officials, should be approved by the Economic Council and the Legislature Each of the two Committees, or both of them conjointly, may appoint *ad hoc* committees or sub-committees to work on special problems The latter may consist of experts, officials and non-official members of the public and may be dissolved after submission of their reports on the special questions referred to them

General Economic Staff—The Development Minister will have under him a General Economic Staff consisting of at least half-a-dozen officers and experts in economic science and practices This staff will be drawn from the various departments of government, large industrial establishments, merchants and bankers and, last but not least, from professors and lecturers employed in the various Universities of the country This body of trained experts and men of directing ability should in a manner correspond to the *brain trust* of President Roosevelt in the United States of America They will work in close co-operation with, or under the direction of, the Development Committee *and some of them will be also members of that Committee* The personnel of this staff should be changed frequently and, as far as possible, no one who is not conspicuous for his talents or rectitude of conduct should be retained on the staff

The first Ten-Year Plan may be prepared by a Special Planning Commission or Committee appointed by Government with the approval of the Economic Council The preparation of the detailed plans and their execution will have to be attended to, by the various Departments of the Central Government associated with economic activities, under the supervision of their respective Ministers, and in the Provinces by the corresponding Departments and Ministers in the local administration The Development Department including the Development Minister and the Development Committee will form a sort of *liaison* agency to co-ordinate the work of the various Departments of the Central Government and of the Central Economic Council and its Committee in regard to the business of the Plan and other economic problems that may arise from time to time These problems will include trade pacts, quota systems, production restrictions, tariffs, excise duties, etc The Development Committee will assist the executive staff of the Development Department in many of the duties assigned to it under the Plan, and one of its chief duties will be to bring to the notice of the Development Minister the more important economic deficiencies in all parts of the country for which remedies are required and to submit proposals and suggestions for the necessary remedial measures or new developments

The principal work of the Development Department of the Central Government will be to watch the progress of the Plan and the march of events both within and outside the country and put forward continuously, in collaboration with the Chairman and Standing Committee of the Central Economic Council, schemes and proposals, as required, for the satisfactory operation of the Ten-Year Plan and other developments needed for the main purposes of the Plan The Department will collect the information required for this purpose from foreign countries and place the same at the disposal of the Central, Provincial and other Economic Councils and also of the general public, whenever considered desirable.

Provincial Economic Councils—Each Provincial Government will have a similar organization at its headquarters and also a Provincial Economic Council consisting of about 30 members and a Standing Committee of the Council to do similar work in the Province The Provincial Economic Council and its Committee will be associated with the Provincial Development Department and its Committee, and will work in consonance with the general rules and regulations governing the Ten-Year

Plan laid down by the Central Government in consultation with the Central Economic Council

The Provincial Government will have a small General Economic Staff of its own, who will transact for the province duties similar to those performed by the General Economic Staff for the Central Government The Provincial Development Committee and General Economic Staff and the Provincial Economic Council and its Committee will between them attend to all the requirements of the Ten-Year Plan and all questions relating to the economic development of the province under the general supervision of the Provincial Minister of Development

Local Economic Councils—Then there should be Local Economic Councils, usually one in every district and city, to prepare plans and develop work assigned to them under the Ten-Year Plan and also to plan and bring into existence developments and improvements on their own initiative Any area smaller than a district may be constituted into a separate economic unit and have its own local council or committee, if the people of the area desire to have one and come forward to provide the funds and staff needed for its maintenance

The duties of the Local Councils will differ from those of the Central and Provincial Councils in that the latter will be advisory, charged with no executive duty, whereas the Local Councils should be both thinking and executive bodies for the work to be done in their respective unit areas The Councils which will normally consist of about a dozen persons will appoint an executive committee, usually of 3 persons, for one year at a time One of them will attend particularly to organization, another to finance, and all the three to the execution of the work entrusted to the committee under the Plan or the special work undertaken by the Local Council on its own initiative

The entire economic work of each unit area will be distributed in the form considered most suitable between the respective government officials under the various departments, employed for this work in the area, and the executive committee of the local council

The Local Economic Councils will raise their own funds, nominate their own staffs and carry on their appointed duties under general rules laid down for their guidance by the Provincial Government in consultation with the Provincial Economic Council Their work will be kept separate from that which the officials of the Government Departments may be doing under the direction of the Provincial Government in the same area.

Responsibility for Execution of Work —The responsibility for the execution of the work under the Ten-Year Plan, in each district and city, will primarily rest with the Departments of the Provincial Government concerned. Ordinarily, the work under the Plan will be executed by the staffs of the respective departments, although portions of it may be entrusted by mutual arrangement to Local Councils whenever circumstances admit of such a course The departmental officials, such as superintendents, inspectors, etc , employed in the districts may be required to attend the meetings of the Local Economic Councils and their Committees, supply statistical and other information that may be asked for by the latter and offer advice, when sought for

There will thus be two parallel organizations, between the Central Government at Delhi and the remotest district and city, functioning throughout the country, with the rural agencies as their base and the Development Department and associated agencies of the Central Government at the apex One will consist of representatives of business interests and the other of executive officials of the government departments, both working together for common objects The work of these two agencies should be carefully differentiated, but at the same time there should be close co-operation between them for the promotion of the general objects, policies and principles governing the execution of the Ten-Year Plan as well as all current economic developments generally

A rough programme of developments contemplated under the Plan has been given in the next chapter It may be taken as merely illustrative and not regarded as complete or final in any sense It gives the sum total of the detailed programmes of the provinces of British India and, in the case of a number of specific items like railways, shipping, air service, etc, it represents the requirements of the entire country including the Indian States There will thus be a horizontal distribution of the plan and programme by Provinces and States, and it will be the special responsibility of the latter to prepare their local plans in consonance with the all-India plan and execute their due share thereof The nature or volume of work assigned to each region will depend upon its population, resources and the status of the agency concerned, that is, whether it is provincial or local

There will be another system of classification according to the Government departments or agencies entrusted with the work of planning and execution The problems, for example, relating to industries will be dealt with by the Department of Industries of the Central Government and the Provincial Departments of Industries, those pertaining to agriculture similarly by the corresponding Departments of Agriculture This method of classification will constitute the vertical division of the programme In this vertical division, most of the work connected with the Plan will be attended to by the existing Departments of Government, both Central and Provincial

The economic councils may be assisted in their duties by other civic bodies, such as, economic conferences, chambers of commerce, industrial and trades associations and committees and by municipalities and district boards who may be willing and able to participate The Central and Provincial Economic Councils will collect information and data, independently of Government whenever required, and will also carry on propaganda on their own account to popularize sound business policies, standards and practices within their jurisdiction

The central idea running through the whole of this proposed national organization is that economic development is the work of the people and, to attain any measure of success, the working energy and enthusiasm of the public should be enlisted in its behalf All plans and schemes should be framed, generally, in consultation with the accredited representatives of business, so long as such framing does not conflict with other important public interests

The central responsibility will be with the Development Committee under the Development Minister and the Standing Committee of the Central Economic Council and its Chairman, both bodies being held jointly responsible to watch and see that each main scheme or measure is progressing at a satisfactory rate in every part of the country and that none of the developments under the Plan are lagging behind at any time without adequate reason The ultimate responsibility will be that of the Development Minister working in consultation with the Development Committee

The General Economic Staff in accordance with the duties assigned to it will help the Development Minister and the Development Committee in keeping a watch over the progress of the Ten-Year Plan in all parts of the country and bringing slow progress and deficiencies, wherever observed, to the notice of the governments and economic councils of the provinces and regions concerned The corresponding provincial staffs will, in their turn, watch progress in all district and city unit areas and do the needful for those areas The same staffs will maintain up-to-date information carefully watch tendencies and directions in which the general economic condition may be deteriorating and warn their respective governments whenever change of policies or timely action is necessary

One of the principal duties of the General Economic Staff, both at the Central Government and at the head-quarters of every Provincial Government, will be to render popular, by lectures and propaganda, the study of the fundamental economic problems of the country and the objects and details of the Ten-Year Plan Leading business men, experts, political leaders and University professors are all expected to take part in popularizing the movement, so that a volume of sound public opinion may be created to support at all times any reasonable policies or measures that may be undertaken for the benefit of the country

CHAPTER XV

A TEN-YEAR PLAN FOR INDIA PLAN AND PROGRAMME.

Criteria of Progress—Main Developments under the Plan—Seven Departmental Schemes—Schedule of Projected Developments—Finance—Statistics, Reviews and Record

CRITERIA OF PROGRESS

THE following are the main criteria by which the prosperity of a country is usually judged —

- Income and wealth,
- Production from industries,
- Production from agriculture,
- Number and variety of heavy industries and capital invested in them,
- Production of iron, steel, coal and machinery,
- Cotton mills,—numbers of looms and spindles,
- Character and value of exports and imports,
- Bank resources and deposits,
- Railways, public works and public utilities,
- Shipping employed in trade,
- Electric power plant capacity, and
- Size of population, state of its education and capacity for initiative and enterprise

The survey made in Part I and the Statistical Tables show that under all the above tests the position occupied by India is deplorably low Progress may be measured in terms of the commodities produced—like wheat, rice, cotton, tea and sugar, under agriculture, and steel, machinery, shipping, coal and textiles, under large-scale industries Part of the wealth created in this way is consumed, and what remains usually goes to increase the country's capital resources, some of which will be the source of non-tax revenues to Government It is authoritatively estimated that the United Kingdom was saving about £500 million a year, before the present depression set in In India we have no such balance sheet of resources Whatever public assets have been built up in the shape of railways, public works and irrigation works, are property created, not to any appreciable extent by money saved from the revenues of the country or by mobilizing Government resources and credit, but from loans floated both in India and in Great Britain Interest has to be paid on these loans and a good portion of it is remitted outside the country

Main Developments under the Plan

It is proposed under the Plan to double the income of the country within ten years The present yearly income is roughly estimated at Rs 2,500 crores for the entire country This will be increased approximately to Rs 5,000 crores by the end of the period The development works to be undertaken are classified under seven Departmental Heads or Schemes, as detailed below, and the department of Government or agency to be entrusted with their execution is indicated against each scheme —

		Department of Go or Agency to l Charge
I	Industrialization	Industries Department
II	Agriculture and Minor Industries	Department of Agriculture
III	Public Works, Public Utilities Transport and Power Supply	Departments connected with Public Works, Railways, Electrical Works, etc
IV	Commerce	Department of Commerce

No.	Scheme	Department of Government or Agency to be in Charge
V	Finance and Banking	Department of Finance
VI	Other Special Developments including— (i) Administrative and Business Policies, (ii) Training for Business Life and Citizenship, (iii) Education, Military Training and other Developments	A Special Commission or Board
VII	Unemployment .	A Bureau under the Development Department

Scheme No VI is for special or subsidiary developments which have to be carried out by various Departments of Government such as Education, Military, etc, not directly connected with the economic activities of the people As the work to be done under this Scheme will be of a novel character in this country, it is proposed to create a Special Commission or Board to study the problems, suggest policies, standards and executive measures needed, and watch progress in the Government Departments concerned and also in all the constituent provinces and regions

Scheme No VII will be dealt with likewise by the Departments concerned with the subjects coming under it, but the bulk of the work connected with unemployment, both in rural and urban areas, will fall on the Local Economic (or Development) Councils

What follows is a summary of the reforms and developments suggested in the previous chapters which bear on these seven Schemes

SEVEN DEPARTMENTAL SCHEMES

Industrialization (*Scheme No I*)—The low condition of Indian industries will be evident from Table VI and Chapter IV where the income per head of population (Rs 12) in this country is compared with corresponding incomes in several advanced countries

Since economic prosperity in these days mainly depends on industry and trade, many a backward country like Soviet Russia and Turkey is striving hard to develop industrially There is a limited demand for the products of agriculture, and in point of money value industries are any day more important In the United States of America, the prices of agricultural products have fallen by 60 per cent since 1929 when depression began, whereas those of industries and manufactures show a decline of only 24 per cent

In the schedule of developments given in this chapter, it is proposed to increase the indigenous capital invested in organized industries in British India from Rs 300 crores to Rs 1,000 crores and the value of yearly production from all classes of industries from Rs 100 crores to Rs 2,000 crores The detailed proposals may be worked out roughly on this basis The Proposals involve a combined outlay of about Rs 700 crores on all new industries over the entire period of ten years It may be of interest to note in this connection that the Central Executive Committee of Soviet Russia approved of an investment of about Rs 1,925 crores in large State and co-operative industries alone, in a single year (1933), the investment in the previous year having been close upon Rs 1,715 crores These investments were for a country of less than half the population of India

Of the three classes into which industries are divided, immediate attention is required to Class I or heavy industries The earliest investments should be on factories intended for producing machinery and supplies for Railways, the Army, Air Service, etc next, should follow industries connected with electrical machinery and apparatus, metal industries, chemical industries, tractors, automobiles, and the like The manner in which these basic industries might be financed and developed by the Provincial Governments by distributing them at the rate of two or three industries to each province has been fully described in Chapter IV already

The production of steel in the United States in 1928, before the commencement of the present trade depression, was 52,371,000 tons In Russia in 1924 the production was 1,408,000 tons, it rose to 6,852,000 tons by 1933 and in the second Five-Year Plan they are aiming at increasing it to 17,000,000 tons by 1937 The production in India in 1924 was 341,000 tons, by 1933 it rose to about 550,000 tons Steel is the basis of all other industries connected with transport, mining, agriculture, textiles, etc, and its importance to metal and machine industries cannot be over-emphasized Having regard to the magnitude of India's population compared with either of the above countries, it is disappointing to find that in recent proposals concerning tariff protection for steel, the Tariff Board has not stressed the need there is for a very considerable future increase in the production and use of steel in this country

Left to private enterprise, industries will not make satisfactory progress Government should take the lead, as every progressive government is doing now, bold policies should be laid down and adhered to, an official organization on the lines advocated in these pages or on other similar lines should be brought into existence, and correct comprehensive reports of progress supported by adequate statistics should be published yearly and at periodical intervals Statistics of capital invested, values of commodities produced, together with other necessary particulars should be given, along with the yearly reviews and reports of the

Industries Departments both of the Central Government and of Provincial Governments If this is not done, production will be uncertain, tariff protection may be insufficient, foreign competition may be let loose, and as a result on account of the risks involved, the public will not be willing to put money in new ventures

In Chapter IV, a dozen requirements needed to create a favourable atmosphere for the prosecution of industries have been described Every one of them should be adequately provided for, if even two or three of them be lacking, progress will be visibly checked Of these requirements, the most important for installing new industries and operating them are tariff protection and capital Unless the existing difficulties in these two respects are removed and the financial resources and credit of government are freely placed at the disposal of the public, rapid industrial progress will remain a dream

Agriculture and Minor Industries (Scheme No II) — Under the Ten-Year Plan, it is assumed that the dry crop area can be increased by 17 9 per cent, irrigated area by 20 7 per cent and income from agriculture by 25 per cent It is also proposed that the population employed in agriculture should be reduced by 20 per cent These results can only be realized, if there is an intense drive on a nation-wide scale to achieve them

The Indian cultivator, as we have seen, is very illiterate There is no agency to convey to him information and enlightenment concerning activities followed in other countries Nor is there any organization to teach him correct habits and the value of discipline, to stop wastes or to rectify the many defects noticed in rural life, such as irregular hours of labour, insufficient employment of women, primitive methods of cultivation, etc.

The agricultural practices followed in the country

are still in the main primitive Attention has already been drawn *inter alia* to the deficiencies under which agriculture labours, *viz*, lack of organization and scientific methods, want of modern tools and machinery, small size of holdings, lack of up-to-date marketing facilities, weakness of co-operative enterprise, feeble agricultural credit and heavy indebtedness of the ryot The principal measures necessary to remedy these and other deficiencies, and increase income both from agriculture and minor industries, will be briefly summed up here

Estimates of the annual value of food grains and other products of agriculture and of cottage industries should be prepared for each district and province, and compared with the expenditure required to maintain the population at a recognized minimum standard of subsistence

Steps should be taken by legislative enactments to place a limit on the fragmentation of holdings and at the same time to encourage their consolidation as far as possible

As farm operations give employment only for four to six months in the year, at least 20 per cent of the population now dependent upon them should be speedily transferred to industries and other associated occupations. A special agency or staff should be maintained under the Revenue or Agricultural Department to carry on propaganda and guide the people in starting and working cottage industries on a large scale, and make the region or district self-contained, as far as possible, in respect of its staple necessaries In the early steps of the Plan, this will be in addition to the work done by the Executive Committee of the Local Economic Council which will take time to gather sufficient momentum

A drastic attempt should be made to solve the problem of indebtedness of the rural population Suggestions have been put forward in some parts of the country to reduce this debt by legislation, by providing for a reduction of the creditor's claims by compromise The precise measures to be adopted in each province should be investigated by a committee of experts in agricultural finance, in the first instance, before the Development Committee and the Standing Committee of the Economic Council formulate final proposals for practical action In any measures to reduce the debt, care should be taken that no injury is caused to the credit of the ryot

Provision should be made through co-operative credit societies or otherwise for easy loans for current farm operations in order that the cultivator may procure good seed and manure and make his land yield better profits Capital for permanent improvement of agricultural land should be provided through Land Mortgage Banks

Agricultural engineering and technique should be taught in a more practical manner than at present in the colleges and schools of agriculture, and the number of these institutions should be also increased Also, an agricultural and industrial bias should be given to the education imparted in rural elementary schools

Every encouragement should be given to the use of modern tools and machinery Their use will help to increase production and wages of labour and reduce appreciably the hours of work and production costs Cost accounts should be maintained for all farms of any appreciable size

The greatest of all the facilities within easy reach of the farmer for bettering his condition is co-operation The cultivators should be instructed to work in associations and committees and to provide for their wants, as they do in Japan, in an ever-increasing degree by collective self-help and disciplined combination

Public Works, Public Utilities, Transport and Power Supply (*Scheme No III*)—In the ten-year period, it is proposed to extend the road mileage by 97 per cent and railway mileage by nearly 29 per cent, and to increase electric power plant to about twice its present capacity and electrical energy to over double its present output Provision is made for developing shipping up to 1,000,000 tons and for the production, for the first time, of nearly all the automobiles required in the country

Public works usually include large buildings, roads, bridges, railways, docks and harbours, irrigation works, navigation canals and the like Under public utilities come hydro-electric works, electric light and power supply, aeroplane service, radios, telegraphs and telephones, city and town water supplies, gas works, drainage and village roads Some of these will quicken communications, others directly or indirectly help to increase production and distribution, and all will add to public amenities In emergencies, some of these works will have to be undertaken to provide employment to labour

Railways have been a potent means of bringing together the people of all parts of this sub-continent and unifying their interests and aspirations They have helped to stimulate the industrial and commercial life of the people An indispensable preliminary for the rapid extension of railways is the establishment of factories and workshops for the manufacture of locomotives, machinery and stores required for future extensions

Shipping and commercial aviation should be encouraged, as is done in all modern countries, by special Government concessions and subsidies The grant of such subsidies is contemplated in Great Britain itself, where the shipping industry was till recently pre-eminently successful

Research is necessary in regard to the use, for purposes of transport, of powdered charcoal, wood alcohol and other local fuels for power generation so that the drain of money on imported fuel may be minimized

The use of electricity and electric power is nowadays a necessity There is in the United States of America a Central Power Commission for co-ordinating the use of power and power installations in the several States for the regulation and control of public utilities A Bureau or Committee of the Development Department of the Central Government might attend to similar work in this country to help in rapid extension of the use of motive power

Initiation of new enterprises of this class is at present done in a haphazard manner There should be some agency in future to study their relative value and select for execution new works from year to year according to their urgency and importance All these works will be under the supervision and control of Government Departments or of special Commissions or Boards created under the Plan

Commerce (Scheme No IV)—The development of commerce will automatically follow the growth of production under agriculture and industries The following are among the more important measures recommended for the rapid promotion of India's trade

The general guiding principle should be, as in all modern States, to encourage the export of manufactured articles, as far as possible, and to limit to an irreducible minimum the import of foreign manufactures There should be no objection to the import of machinery or special products not prepared or grown at present in India, or of raw materials needed for local manufactures

The country should be self-contained in respect of products for the manufacture of which greater facilities are available locally than, for instance, in Japan or Great Britain With an enormous population of over 40 million actually idle and 100 million only partly employed, the humiliation of supplying raw products to foreign countries and of purchasing finished commodities from them should not be perpetuated But foreign trade should continue to be encouraged, as it helps to maintain a high level of business activity and, in certain circumstances, also a higher standard of living

Adequate provision should be made, under the advice of a Committee of Indian business men, for the banking facilities needed for the country's internal as well as foreign trade Indian merchants in foreign countries keenly feel the lack of Indian branch banks to help their trade

Steps should be taken to reduce freight rates, both railway and shipping, on export trade In the case of imports, such rates should be suitably raised where they compete with local products

Industrial and commercial museums should be established in all large towns and cities Exhibitions should be held in many centres frequently all over the country and Government should begin to take an interest and lend its credit to make them a success

The appointment of Indian Trade Commissioners in the principal foreign countries to promote Indian trade with them is overdue The present arrangements in this respect are wholly inadequate and unsatisfactory It is understood that only 15 per cent of the foreign trade of the country is carried on by Indian merchants This should undergo rapid extension Statistics should be maintained of the growth of commerce handled by Indian firms and merchants at all the principal ports of the country An Indian Commerce Member should supervise measures for the extension of the country's foreign commerce and for its maintenance at the highest level of efficiency

Special expert staff is urgently needed in future to watch the trade with foreign countries and advise Government in regard to the exchange of products by special trade pacts on the quota system, by barter or in other ways For increasing production and internal trade, no appreciable increase of currency reserves or foreign capital will be needed

Finance and Banking (*Scheme No V*) —Every one of the developments under the Ten-Year Plan requires adequate finance for its execution It has been estimated that in the period covered by the Plan, Government will have to borrow at least Rs 500 crores direct for financing the many projects which find a place in the schedule and provide about Rs 10 crores annually for current expenditure connected with the operation of the Plan Government will also have to lend its credit to the future Indian Reserve Bank and other financial corporations so that they may obtain sufficient money for circulation in the country to help to increase production under industries and agriculture It may be stated in this connection that both the United States of America whose financial credit is very high and Soviet Russia whose credit with the capitalist world is very low, are carrying through their big Recovery and Reconstruction programmes without the aid of foreign money

The following are some of the urgent reforms needed under the head of Finance

The Indian rupee is at present pegged to the pound sterling at a fixed ratio of 18*d*, but the pound sterling itself is not linked to gold The rupee should be independent of sterling, as are the currencies of the Dominions, and allowed to find its natural level in international currency according to the strength of its gold reserves, trade balances and the general economic position of the country

Industries have suffered through lack of capital and insufficient tariff protection Sufficient money should be readily available for industries through an efficient organization such as is contemplated under the Ten-Year Plan Fiscal policies in future should be on a truly protectionist basis, sufficiently high import duties being levied against all forms of dumping that hamper Indian industry If capital is to be attracted to industries, Government should not change their tariff policies too frequently, as they have recently done in the case of sugar and match industries

It is hoped that the Reserve Bank recently approved by the Central Legislature will be speedily established and that it will operate the currency and credit systems of the country to its best advantage A sufficient number of commercial banks, industrial banks, agricultural or land mortgage banks and co-operative credit societies with their apex banks should be established and all of them should have cross connections with one another and be linked with the future Reserve Bank

The budget note presented to the Legislative Assembly should deal exhaustively with the economic condition of the country and should give a general idea of the invisible trade balance and also of the net gain or loss in transactions with foreign countries at the end of each year

As remarked in the Scheme for an Economic Census of India by Dr Bowley and Mr Robertson, practically no attempt has been made for several years to estimate the movement of private capital, even of that part of it which is represented by the issue of new securities

Until a project like the Ten-Year Plan is brought

into operation, there should be a Public Information Bureau under the direct control of the Central Legislature to collect and publish statistical and other reliable information concerning the finances, the effects of the trade policies of other countries on India and the economic condition of the country generally

Sufficient statistical data should be collected to indicate the extent of investments and income of British and Indian business men and shareholders separately in the various business enterprises in the country This will help the Indian public to find out whether they are progressing or losing ground in material prosperity

The All-India Economic Council should, as soon as it comes into existence, appoint a Committee to go into and suggest solutions from the Indian point of view—with as little injury to legitimate British interests as possible—for the many financial problems in regard to which there has been controversy between Indian public men and Government The report of the Committee should be the basis of Government policies in public finance when the new Government comes to power

It has been made clear that the money spent by Local Bodies on local improvements is incredibly low This has led to the starving of education, other nation-building activities and all productive enterprises in rural areas The Local Bodies should have the right to raise and use taxes for increasing production and for nation-building objects

Other Special Developments (*Scheme No VI*)—There are a number of subsidiary developments which are also of great importance As the money and staff required for them will be comparatively small, they are all grouped under one head The developments proposed to be dealt with by the Special Departments will be —

(i) To maintain sound administrative and business

policies, and suggest readjustment as conditions change from time to time,

(ii) To give training for business life and citizenship, and to develop standards in conformity with foreign experience,

(iii) To watch the progress of education,—University, higher, middle and elementary, including technical and professional education of all grades

(iv) To begin to train and equip people for self-defence and future control of the Defence Forces of the country,

(v) Reorganization of Government departments on the model of those of the Dominions,

(vi) Rural Reconstruction,

(vii) Urban Reconstruction,

(viii) Propaganda to spread correct information regarding the Ten-Year Plan and its working

The first two measures have been described in Chapters XII and XIII respectively Since there are separate departments for education and military training, the Development Department will have merely to see that a branch plan or scheme is prepared for each and approved by the Central Legislature and put into operation by the departments concerned

The Departmental Reorganization (Item No v) is intended to change the present unhelpful methods of the economic departments of Government under Dependency rule into the more modern methods in vogue in the Dominions, in order to help in the enthusiastic prosecution of the Ten-Year Plan

With reference to Urban Reconstruction and Rural Reconstruction schemes (Items Nos vi and vii), it is proposed that the inhabitants of each local area, whether city or district, should be encouraged to look after their own interests and held morally responsible for their own welfare They should be induced to take an interest in watching the growth of their area under the following tests of progress —

Average income per head of population ,

Production from industries and agriculture, capital invested in industries ,

Joint-stock Companies—number and capital issues ,

Bank clearances and deposits ,

Profits derived from trade, banking, transport and other activities within the area ,

Distribution of the working population under the principal gainful occupations ,

Number unemployed ,

Progress in education ,

Growth of public libraries

Results under these heads should be watched and recorded from year to year

Unemployment (*Scheme No VII*) —Among emergency measures which claim attention at the present time the most pressing one is unemployment relief, that is, finding occupations for educated men and the masses If work is found for educated men outside Government service, it will mean also additional employment for the workers. This subject, being very important, will be dealt with in a separate chapter by itself

SCHEDULE OF PROJECTED DEVELOPMENTS

Broadly stated, under the supervision of a genuine Responsible Government at the Centre, and with the aid of a Ten-Year Plan, it is considered possible to double production and income in the whole country and increase literacy in the population from the present level of 8 per cent to at least 50 per cent during the period

Everything depends upon the conditions under which the Plan is operated, the intensity of the effort which the Government and the people's agencies put forth and the financial support extended to the Plan. The following table gives a provisional list of the principal developments proposed under the Plan —

SCHEDULE OF DEVELOPMENTS UNDER THE TEN-YEAR PLAN

No	Item	Unit	From	To
1	National Income (Yearly)	Rs crores	2,500	5,000
2	Yearly production from industries—approximate net value	,,	100	2,000
3	Indigenous capital investments in large-scale industries	,,	300	1,000
4	Iron and steel	Tons	1,600,000	3,000,000
5	Coal mined	,,	24,000,000	40,000,000
6	Cotton mill industry—			
	Spindles	Number	9,500,000	12,000,000
	Looms	,,	200,000	300,000
7	Automobiles—to be manufactured per annum	,,		20,000
8	Yearly production from agriculture—approximate net value	Rs crores	2,000	2,500
9	Increase of cultivated area (British India only)—			
	(a) Dry crop area .	Million acres	212	250
	(b) Irrigated area	,,	49.7	60
10	Roads	Miles	253,125	500,000
11	Railways	,,	42,750	55,000
12	Electric power plant capacity	K W	1,000,000	2,200,000
	Electrical energy produced	Million K W Hrs	1,800	4,000
13	Shipping .	Tons	271,820	1,000,000
14	Population supported by agriculture.	Million	250	200
15	Population employed in organized industries	Number	1,500,000	10,000,000

No	Item	Unit	From	To
	Population employed in all industries	Number	15,361,000	50,000,000
	Population supported by all classes of industries	"	35,300,000	85,000,000
16	Scholars in Universities	"	92,000	200,000
17	Mass literacy .	Percentage of total population	8	50
18	Population under instruction	"	4.67	15

The principal items which should go into the Plan are given in the foregoing list Many other less important items will be included, when detailed schedules are drawn up In the ordinary course, the Central Ten-Year Plan will be compiled from detailed plans furnished by Provincial Governments, and the Provincial Plans in their turn will be mainly based on schemes received from the district and city authorities and councils The list, though provisional and illustrative, is sufficiently comprehensive to enable a working forecast and programme to be prepared for the first year's work, in less than three months, once a decision is taken to embark on planned economy

FINANCE

The cost of operation of the Ten-Year Plan on the scale suggested is estimated at Rs 10 crores per annum. Of this sum, Rs 2 crores will be required, and should be provided for, by the Central Government, and Rs 8 crores should be found by the various Provincial Governments roughly in proportion to their population For the first five years at least, the recurring expenditure will have to be met by loans, the annual debt charges being debited to the yearly budgets of the Governments concerned It may be reasonably expected that, from the sixth year onward, the industrial and other activities will have sufficiently advanced to bring enough additional revenues to enable the Governments to bear this recurring outlay We say this with all the greater confidence, because we have, as in the United States of America, but unlike other industrially developed countries, a home market to absorb the products of our new industries and manufactures

The expenditure to be borne by the Central Government will include the cost of the Development Department and its Committee, the Special Bureaux, the Expert and the General Economic Staff, and the Central Economic Council and its Standing Committee The Provincial Governments will make provision in their annual budgets for similar charges for the Provincial Development Department and its Committee, and the Provincial Economic Council and its Standing Committee, including the special staff employed by them and the subsidies to be paid to Local Economic Councils, when required The Local Councils in cities and districts should be normally self-supporting but they may be given small grants by the Provincial Governments in special cases to meet the expenses of work done in the area, under the Plan or otherwise, on behalf of Government A Local Economic or Development Council will only come into existence, as explained already, when the city, district or unit area concerned is able to meet from its own resources the expenditure necessary for carrying on its ordinary duties Every self-respecting city and district should come forward and express its readiness to make the small sacrifice required A tax or cess for the purpose may be levied by a resolution of the Local Council and the amount collected by the revenue officials in the district and made over to the Council

A large amount of capital will be required for starting and working new industries, new railways, public works, public utilities, shipping and other enterprises entered in the Schedule It is estimated that a loan of at least Rs 500 crores will be required, in the first instance, partly for productive public works, factories, etc , to be carried out or established under the direct supervision of Government, and partly for financing large-scale industries which may be started by joint-stock companies or private individuals with or without Government co-operation All advances made to companies, business enterprises and individuals would be through specialized financial institutions like Commercial Banks, Industrial Banks, Land Mortgage Banks and Investment Trusts If a Ten-Year Plan is approved and put into operation, sanction will have to be accorded simultaneously to the raising of loans by Government from time to time, as required, during the ten-year period

There should be a Development Budget in connection with the working of the Ten-Year Plan The management of the loans raised should be entrusted to a Central Finance Board, the members of which should be appointed with the consent of the Central Legislature and Economic Council Provision should be made for periodical inspection and audit of accounts of the works or concerns, to which advances are made, by a staff of experts working under the direction of the Central Finance Board, or independently under a body like the present Tariff Board The same staff may also give advice to business concerns when advice is sought

The capital issues required for this purpose might be obtained, partly from profits of existing industries and partly by raising loans to the extent necessary either from the local public or from foreign countries The frozen wealth of the country may be requisitioned for this purpose by suitable public propaganda If the policies of the new Government command public confidence, there will be no dearth of response from the public and there will be no need to borrow from abroad The volume of capital has to expand with the growth of business and production Government should use its credit, and by prudent borrowing keep sufficient money in circulation within the country so that the business public may obtain loans at reasonable rates of interest for assisting industry and trade and for promoting new enterprises

STATISTICS, REVIEWS AND RECORD

Reference has been made already to the preliminary economic survey and statistics needed for apprising the public of the present state of development After the Plan is put into operation, the work done, the additions and alterations made and the developments and improvements effected should be reviewed at least once a year, and the reviews together with related statistics compiled under well-understood rules Such statistics and reviews should be maintained for work done under the Plan for every department The reviews and essential records should be published from year to year with the same regularity, as the annual financial budgets of the Central and Provincial Governments are

CHAPTER XVI

FIVE-YEAR PLANS FOR PROVINCES AND STATES

Main Policy of an All-India Plan—A Provincial Plan for the Bombay Presidency—Special Characteristics of Bombay Presidency—Scope for Future Advance—Mechanism of Development—Schedule of Projected Developments—Economic Planning for Indian States—Political Conditions in States—Characteristics of States—Organization—Mechanism of Development—Conditions of Success

MAIN POLICY OF AN ALL-INDIA PLAN

THE provision made for developments in the All-India Ten-Year Plan represents generally the aggregate of the provisions for the individual plans of Provinces and States It may be assumed that the Indian States will also join the organization, if one is established, both in their own interest as well as in that of the economic strength of the country as a whole If they do not do so, they will come into the picture only in connection with a few all-India services and amenities such as railways, shipping, posts and telegraphs, which are common both to Provinces and States But if they do join, Provincial Plans and States Plans will together form constituent parts of the Central Ten-Year Plan

The main policy of the all-India economic organization should be to develop production and income, as far as possible, at the same pace in the larger, if not in all, Provinces and States, for, their fortunes are interdependent and interconnected If one province forges ahead and improves its occupations and income and its next-door neighbour remains unenterprising and poor, the people of the backward tract are likely to migrate to the more prosperous one and lower the wages of its labour and the average standard of living of its entire population

It is proposed that the working plans for Provinces and States be prepared on a five-year basis from the very start This is because the provinces have a far smaller area compared with the country as a whole, and their Governments are in possession of detailed information for preparing their Plans with greater exactitude than the Central Government can prepare the all-India Plan The provincial Five-Year Plan will start with a schedule of developments on the basis of the resources of the province concerned as well as of the provisions in the all-India Ten-Year Plan

A Provincial Plan for the Bombay Presidency

It is next proposed to consider how a Five-Year Plan may be prepared and operated in the smaller sphere of a Province or a State For illustrating a Provincial Plan, the Bombay Presidency has been chosen, particularly because it is an industrial province, and also because it is in the direction of industrial development that the progress of India in the immediate future will lie Bombay happens also to be the best equipped of provinces for further rapid advance in industries

Next to Bombay, Bengal is the only other province which is industrially minded It is believed that the combined value of production from industries in these two provinces is about Rs 200 crores, or one-half of that in the whole of British India The principal industries of Bengal are jute textiles, iron and steel and engineering Bombay has specialized in cotton textiles Out of 344 cotton mills in India in 1933, as many as 220 were located in this presidency and of these, 78 were in the Bombay Island, 82 in Ahmedabad and 7 in Sholapur The value of woven goods produced in the cotton mills of this province in 1925-26 was Rs 36 04 crores, the total for all-India being Rs 47 22 crores The publication of these figures has been stopped, but it is roughly computed that the corresponding values for 1933-34 show a decline, being Rs 19 crores and 32 crores respectively

There have been no attempts made at organizing occupations either in this Presidency or any other province of British India unlike in Japan, where adequate statistics of production are maintained, and some provinces are recognized as industrial and some as agricultural, according to whichever of the two occupations predominates

Special Characteristics of Bombay Presidency

The Bombay Presidency has a total area of 123,679 square miles and a population, according to the Census of 1931, of 21,930,601, representing an average density of 177 persons to the square mile Bombay accommodates 8 14 per cent of the total population of British India The urban population in the decade ended 1931 increased by 11 6 per cent and the rural by 13 9 per cent The urban population of Bombay is the highest in all India, being 22 6 per cent of its total But during the last decade a reaction set in and the tendency to ruralization, common throughout India, has begun to affect this province also

The percentage of literate population to population aged 5 years and over in the Bombay Presidency is 10 8 Some of the regions in India which have a higher percentage of literacy are Burma 36 8, Cochin, 33 7, Travancore 28 9 and Baroda 20 9 The total number of educational institutions in 1931-32 was 17,159 and the number of pupils attending them 1,332,693 or 6 per cent of the entire population Of the total male population, 9 96 per cent attended a school or college, and of the female population only 3 per cent The total number of scholars of both sexes in institutions of University grade in 1932 was 14,499

The *Census Report* for 1931 shows that the proportion of total population engaged in agriculture is 23 9 per cent and that in industry 4 6 per cent The figures show a decline in the population employed in industry and trade and an increase in that employed in agriculture and according to the *Report* this increase has probably been at the expense of industry and trade The decline referred to is attributed partly to world-wide trade depression and partly to the unsettlement caused by political troubles

Government have invested over Rs 9 86 crores on irrigation works in the Deccan and Gujarat, where the area irrigated is 1,035,000 acres, and on the Lloyd Barrage Works in Sind, the largest irrigation scheme in the world, a further sum of nearly Rs 20 crores has been invested up to date The latter scheme is yet young, the area irrigated under it in 1932-33 was 3,242,000 acres, the bulk of which was from the older canals now amalgamated with the Barrage Scheme The capital outlay on these older—the original Inundation—Canals was Rs 1 75 crores

Another advantage which this Presidency has over the other provinces of India is the proximity of its ports to Europe The city of Bombay owes its importance partly to its cotton mill industry and partly to its geographical position as the gateway of India

The educated and trading classes of this Presidency, though small in number, form an enterprising community Some of the trading classes of Gujarat have settled in parts of South Africa and many among them are carrying on profitable trade between India and the Arabian Coast The residents of towns, like Hyderabad and Shikarpur in Sind, have trade establishments in many foreign countries, and small colonies of members of the Sindhi trading community are to be found along all the principal trade routes of the world

No industrial or commercial survey of this Presidency has been carried out in the past and no adequate statistics of production or income are available The total yearly production from agriculture is estimated at Rs 112 crores and that from industries at Rs 67 crores This gives a *per capita* income of Rs 51 from agriculture and Rs 30 from industries, or a total of Rs 81 from both There is considerable scope for the development of both irrigation and industries in the Presidency If a development organization like that of a Five-Year Plan is brought into existence, there are enough men of energy and capacity and abundant resources to take advantage of it and to work for the rapid promotion of the prosperity of the province

SCOPE FOR FUTURE ADVANCE

The administration and operation of industries are well understood in this Presidency There are men of directing ability and also skilled workmen This is not an accomplishment of yesterday We have seen that thirty years ago Bombay used to supply cotton piece-goods and yarn to Japan

It seems a pity that the automobile industry, although practised in many a small State in Europe, has not found a place as yet in this Presidency or in any other Province or State in India Among industries already in operation, matches, aluminium, gold thread and a few others may be said to have reached the saturation point, so far as the local market is concerned Even these can be profitably developed, if foreign marketing facilities are improved Over Rs 2½ crores worth of metal products are yearly imported into India, though most of them can be produced in this country. Rayon or artificial silk can be manufactured in this Presidency up to the value of Rs 4 crores per annum and the whole of it sold within the country. Paper worth over Rs 9 lakhs was made in the Bombay Presidency in 1930, while its imports in 1932-33 amounted to Rs 2 86 crores Sugar worth Rs 4 23 crores was imported in 1932-33, while the newly projected factories are capable of producing this commodity up to the value of only half a crore If Indian boats are given facilities, the local shipping in the coastal trade can be increased from the present tonnage of 30,000 to over 100,000 The value of forest products in the Presidency, which at present amounts to about Rs 75 lakhs, can be easily doubled

Since the close of the War, the city of Bombay has been labouring under special difficulties and has received a set-back to its prosperity which, it is hoped, is only temporary This is partly due to the available capital in the city having been invested in municipal loans for road improvements, on the Back Bay Reclamation Scheme and also on the extension of mill industry The last two investments have proved unprofitable so far

Mechanism of Development

The mechanism and methods of operation of a Five-Year Plan with its attendant organization, may be considered under the following heads —

Provincial Economic Councils,
Local Economic Councils,
Survey and Statistics,
Analysis of deficiencies and resources,
Preparation of Plan,
Funds

Provincial Economic Organization —The provincial

economic organization has been explained already in Chapter XIV The apex of the organization in the province will be the Development Department and its Committee, both forming part of the Provincial Government and associated with the Provincial Economic Council and its Standing Committee There may be four to six experts, attached to the Development Department, and forming its General Economic Staff, drawn from the services, the Universities and the business and commercial life of the province Foreign experts should be employed also, as required, for short periods at a time At present some of the provinces have Development Departments but not Bombay

The first step to take in order to prepare a Five-Year Plan will be to convene a conference of about 50 representative persons, including political leaders, interested in industries, agriculture, commerce, transport, etc , in different parts of the province, to form decisions as to what reforms and developments are needed and should be carried out in the first five-year period

The developments entered in the schedule may be taken as representing the main lines on which the Provincial Plan and Programme should be drawn up. The details can be worked out by the Development Committee with the help of the Government staff and under the guidance of a competent organizer in about three months' time, or in the alternative, these should be prepared by a special committee appointed with the approval of the Provincial Economic Council In the ordinary course an economic survey of the Presidency would be necessary, before a satisfactory Five-Year Plan is prepared Simultaneously with the survey, an analysis of the deficiencies and wants will be made, the resources which can be mobilized selected one by one, and the manner in which similar deficiencies and wants have been met and resources utilized in advanced countries studied But it will not be difficult to prepare the first year's programme of the Plan without any survey at all, because there will be sufficient material for the purpose, there will be many long-neglected wants pressing for attention and many industries which, for lack of support, have hitherto lagged behind If time is not to be lost, it will be in the fitness of things to put the survey and the first year's programme of the Plan in hand simultaneously

The Central Government will expect the provincial organizations to carry out their share of the all-India programme in accordance with the rules and practices previously approved by them, but in other respects the discretion of the provinces will be unfettered For all practical purposes, the Central Government will be merely a co-ordinator

Local Economic Councils —The work of the Local Councils will be watched and stimulated both by the Development Committee and the Standing Committee of the province The Development Department will have the final word in dealing with all current questions, but always after calling for, and giving due consideration to, the opinion of the Standing Committee of the Provincial Economic Council

There should be a Local Economic Council for every rural district and for every city having a population of 30,000 or more As explained before, other smaller unit areas may also appoint local councils or committees, if they are sufficiently enterprising and can raise adequate funds for their maintenance It is proposed to make the local council an efficient working body both for deliberative and executive local work A high degree of discipline and operative efficiency should be insisted on from the very start In the early stages of operation, it will need supervision and guidance by experienced leaders and experts By the rules of their constitution, the local councils should be composed of the most competent persons to be had in the area—persons equipped with power of initiative and a high level of directing ability and integrity The opportunity will bring hundreds of competent men to the front

Schedule of Developments—In every programme of developments in British Indian provinces, those industries should be taken up first for the products of which there is a local or an Indian market Another aim should be to increase production from industries and to transfer some of the excess population from agriculture to industries The main aim of the Plan should be to increase the income of the province at least to double the present amount by the end of the ten-year period A tentative programme of developments is given in the following schedule arranged, for uniformity's sake, under the seven heads or schemes into which the Ten-Year Plan is divided The schedule given is worked out for ten years to harmonise with the suggested All-India Plan But it can be easily changed when required, into two plans of five years each This schedule will be serviceable for preparing the yearly programme for the first two or three years At the end of three years (*i e*, before the first five-year term is over), the provincial survey will have satisfactorily advanced to render the Ten-Year Plan out of date From the sixth year onwards, a more up-to-date Five-Year Plan, based on the results of the survey and the experience of the first few years of working, can be brought into operation Before such a programme is accepted and put through, it should be approved first by the Provincial Economic Council and sanctioned finally by the Legislative Council

TEN-YEAR PLAN FOR THE BOMBAY PRESIDENCY

Schedule of Projected Developments

Item	Unit	From	To
Income—			
Estimated total annual income from production	Rs. crores	179	329
Industries—			
Probable value of yearly production	,,	67	140
Capital invested in industries	,,	75	200
Cotton Mill Industry—			
Spindles .	Number	6,290,233	7,000,000
Looms .	,,	138,153	150,000
Agriculture—			
Probable value of yearly production	Rs crores	112	162
Cultivated Area—			
(*a*) Dry crop area .	Acres	31,018,840	38,000,000
(*b*) Irrigated area	,,	4,115,017	8,000,000
Value of Forest products	Rs crores	75	1 5
Roads—(both metalled and unmetalled)	Miles	30 303	40,000
Transport and Power—			
Railways ..	Miles	3 856	5,000
Automobiles	Number		20,000
Shipbuilding	Tons	30,000	200,000
Electric power plant capacity	K W	210,000	500,000
Electrical energy produced	Million K W Hrs	500	1,200
Occupations—			
Population employed in—			
Agriculture .	Percentage of total working population	65 9	50
Industries		11 9	25
Trade .		5 4	8
Literacy—			
Percentage of literate population to population aged 5 years and over	Per cent	10 8	40
Total population attending educational institutions	Number	1 287,246	3,000,000
Scholars attending educational institutions of University grade	,,	14,499	20,000

Funds—The yearly current expenditure on an All-India Ten-Year Plan, excluding the Central Government's share, has been estimated at Rs 8 crores The annual expenditure on the Plan in the Bombay Presidency in proportion to the population will be about Rs 65 lakhs As the province is partly industrial and the bulk of the future expenditure will be on industries and public works, the operation expenditure in this Presidency may be taken at Rs 90 lakhs or a crore

Towards the capital needed for developments, it has been stated that at least Rs 500 crores will have to be borrowed by the Central Government for expenditure on public works and for loans to banks, companies and private firms, to keep cheap money in circulation The share of the Bombay Presidency in the loan may be taken at about Rs 50 crores The Provincial Government should have power to borrow direct or through the Central Government, from time to time up to this limit during the ten-year period and invest in works and industries included in the provincial programme While the amount which the Government has to borrow may be restricted to Rs 50 crores, the total amount which can be profitably invested in new developments will be much larger The balance not covered by the proposed Rs 50 crores loans may be met from private resources and loans including, if necessary, foreign loans raised by private individuals or firms

In addition to subscribing capital towards industrial enterprises, Government should be ready to grant subsidies and subventions to suitable local works undertaken by District and City Economic Councils in order to assure the public of their real sympathy and support

For the first five years, Government may have to depend in some of the provinces on borrowed funds even for carrying on current operations connected with the

Plan but, as explained already, from the sixth year onwards it is reasonable to expect that at least the operation charges will be met from the earnings of the new enterprises themselves

A few enterprises may fail and cause disappointment, but, with proper care, the outlay as a whole is sure to repay itself many times over in the shape of taxable property built up, and new undertakings brought into existence, under the operation of the Plan

At the end of every year after the Plan comes into operation, the work done is examined and measured by means of statistics and a review placed on record At the end of the fifth year perhaps, if the public and the agencies appointed by them retain their enthusiasm for self-improvement, a second Five-Year Plan will automatically come into operation

Economic Planning for Indian States

Political Conditions in States—Economic progress will not be as easy in Indian States as in British India, because except in very few States where the administration is modernised, the Rulers exercise a patriarchal sway over their subjects though tempered by the legislative enactments and practices borrowed from British India Since the Viceroyalty of Lord Minto, about the year 1910, the hold of British authorities over the administration of the States has been perceptibly slackening Increased freedom was promised to the States by Lord Minto with the object of increasing the attachment of Princes to British rule as a counterpoise to the growing agitation for Home Rule then carried on by the people of British India The concessions to the States were readily availed of by the Princes, but the States' subjects do not seem to have derived any appreciable benefit from them Large sections of the States' peoples have advanced with the progress of the times and are demanding political institutions similar to those granted or promised, in British India

A common economic organization presumes that the Princes will enter an All-India Federation when established The Government of India have sufficient authority and influence over the Indian Princes to induce them to join the proposed Federation, to prepare budgets and statistical and other data on a uniform basis in conformity with the practices in British India and subject to the necessary reservations to participate in an All-India Ten-Year Plan

Characteristics of States—There are 560 States in India under the hereditary rule of Princes covering a total area of 712,508 square miles and containing a population of 81,310,845 souls The average area of a State is 1,272 square miles and the average population, 145,198 For the sake of comparison, it may be stated that the area and population of an average district in British India are 2,789 square miles and 690,908 persons, respectively

The aggregate revenue of all the States is about Rs 47 48 crores and the average per State Rs 8 66 lakhs The corresponding figures for the major States (119 in number) are Rs 45 45 crores and Rs 38 20 lakhs, and for the minor States (441) Rs 3 02 crores and Rs 0 68 lakhs, respectively Thirty-eight of the major States have a revenue ranging from Rs 20 lakhs to Rs 8 30 crores For the sake of comparison, it may be mentioned that the revenue of an average British district is Rs 23 lakhs

The people in the States are more self-contained in regard to their primary wants than in British India. The average standard of living is generally lower, and so also, except in a very few States, the general level of literacy In a few progressive States, however, as explained elsewhere, the standard of literacy is much higher than in any British Province save Burma In many of the States there has been no economic survey and there are no adequate statistics But there are a number of them, rich in agricultural, forest, industrial and mineral resources, and not a few among them are exceptionally well placed for raising better and more bountiful crops, and converting raw materials into finished commodities

Some of the Princes have large personal property and wealth Very good use can be made of the wealth by investing it in business enterprises for improving the economic well-being of their people By such use both the Princes and their subjects will be gainers and it will also have the moral effect of increasing the attachment of the people to their Rulers

Organization —The foremost need in a State, as in every other region, is to bring into existence some responsible agency to watch its economic interests In the States, as in the British Provinces, the development of economic interests should be attempted by the same two measures, namely, a Five-Year Plan and an organization of Economic Councils The organization required by some of the larger States will not be very different from that recommended for the British Provinces There should be a Supreme Economic Council in the State composed of representative business men numbering, say, between 12 and 30 according to the size of the State They should be representatives of all the principal business activities from which the State and its people derive their income

The smaller States, numbering 520 in all, have an area or population less than that of an average District in British India Each State need only have one Economic Council corresponding to a District Economic

Council in a British Province That Council will work in co-operation with a Development Committee or merely with a Department or Development Officer of the State

Mechanism of Development—The first step to take is to inaugurate a State Economic Council and place it in touch with the Development Department and Development Minister The Minister will discuss the deficiencies and wants of the State with outside experts when necessary and with the newly formed Economic Council, and will prepare a preliminary report defining the scope and magnitude of the operations contemplated For the British Provinces, it has been assumed that the income could be doubled in ten years For an average Indian State perhaps, a lower rate of development will have to be assumed The development will depend on several factors, namely, the freedom allowed for business combinations in the State, the funds available for the plan, the agency to be employed and the enthusiasm which the State authorities can bring to bear on the planning work In the general plan perhaps it would be safe to estimate that the increase in production and income would be only 50 per cent in ten years. There are some progressive States, however, in which it will be possible to advance faster in this respect than even in a British Province

The second step in this process of development will be to begin a survey and proceed with the collection of statistics and other necessary data This work should proceed simultaneously with the first year's operation of the Five-Year Plan

The third step will be the elaboration of the preliminary report referred to into a Five-Year Plan comprising schedules, estimates and a programme for the full period of 5 years

The fourth step will be to prepare a schedule of developments together with detailed estimates and a programme of work to be done in the first year of operation

The fifth step will be the arrangements to be made for the funds and staff needed for the execution of the Plan from year to year

The sixth or last step will be to prepare and publish a review, once a year, accompanied by statistics showing the progress made in each department of activity and on the Plan as a whole A clear record of progress in every department and on every item of development in the schedule should be maintained

In most other respects, the procedure will not be different from that laid down for the Provinces in British India

Conditions of Success —The credit facilities in many of the States are non-modern and defective The interest charged borders on usury It would be well if each State of any size starts a bank of its own and makes arrangements for its accounts to be audited by a recognized firm of qualified accountants The older credit systems existing in the State should be reformed as far as possible and linked with the new banks or branch banks when started

Some of the States at present levy their own import and export duties on certain classes of goods which pass in and out of their areas In the case of foreign goods the import duties charged will be in addition to those collected at the ports of entry into India There are no duties for inter-State commerce in the United States of America The retention of such duties in Indian States is inconsistent with rapid national progress The question should be investigated by a Commission or Committee with a view to induce the States to forego their income from this source

There are recognized money-lenders who enjoy a certain amount of credit, but it must be admitted that public credit in Indian States is not so high as in British India The facilities for co-operative effort are limited and in some of the States, individual liberty is liable to be interfered with in an arbitrary manner Business success depends upon credit and credit upon confidence And in order to inspire confidence the law pertaining to civil transactions should be strictly and justly enforced If the States' people have an ultimate right of appeal to a Federal Court, it will pave the way to the initiation of large-scale business enterprises on joint-stock principle and thereby help to raise public credit and also the level of income of the States' population

The people of the States should have scope to initiate new industries, new farms and new commercial organizations where required The power of initiative will be usually lacking where there is no satisfactory form of local self-government In Japan, which is under a constitutional monarchy, villages are self-governing and the village government is usually the place where people learn to get things done by teamwork If rapid progress of industries and wealth is desired in any area, a favourable atmosphere should be first created by granting the people, as in Japan, a genuine form of local self-government Under constitutional rule mutual trust is encouraged and people can co-operate freely and without risks in joint-stock and other forms of large-scale business enterprises No doubt progress on a plan can be more rapid under autocratic rule than in a democracy, but only if the people are blessed with a ruler who can be depended upon for practising constitutional methods in his business relations with them But, even then, progress will only last during such a ruler's lifetime and there is no guarantee that it will continue under his successor As the examples of the smaller States of Europe and of Japan show, freedom and discipline—that is, freedom under constitutional rule and business discipline among the people themselves—are both necessary factors to enable the people to rise above any mediocre level in wealth and prosperity.

CHAPTER XVII

CURE FOR UNEMPLOYMENT

Magnitude of the Problem—Government Attitude—True Causes of Unemployment—The Remedy—Organization—Funds—Need for Business Training—Two Examples—Concluding Remarks

MAGNITUDE OF THE PROBLEM

THE number of unemployed persons in the civilized countries of the world according to the statistics given in the League of Nations' Publications amounts to about 30 million There are no official statistics for India but the number in it is estimated by those competent to judge at between 10 and 50 million Of these, perhaps, the educated unemployed constitute a million and a half Government have not interested themselves in obtaining reliable figures, but as there is generally distress on a large scale and acute distress among some classes of the population, the public feel discouraged and anxious over the situation

GOVERNMENT ATTITUDE

The Government attitude towards the unemployment problem, shortly after this question was mooted in the Legislative Assembly in 1926, was studied by the present writer, and described in a public speech made by him on September 8, 1932 The following are extracts from that speech —

"The Legislative Assembly raised a debate on this subject in January 1926 The Government of India, in a Circular issued in the month of August of that year, forwarded a copy of the debate to the Provincial Governments and remarked that 'such remedies as might be found practicable were remedies which only Local Governments and, more particularly, the transferred sides of Local Governments, could apply ' At the same time, the Circular stated that the Central Government never intended to minimize the gravity of the problem which they believed to be one of increasing urgency and importance, but they did not consider there was any need then for a Central Committee which the Assembly had recommended and contented themselves by asking that the problem should receive most careful consideration of the Local Governments

"Some of the Local Governments went into the problem as a result of the above Circular and also in response to pressure from their local Legislatures Prior to this, the Government of Bengal had appointed a Committee which presented its report in 1924 After receipt of the Circular, the Government of Madras appointed a Committee which reported in 1927 A Committee appointed by the Punjab Government issued its report in 1928 In the year 1927, the Government of Bombay collected and published certain statistics about middle-class unemployment in that Presidency

"It may be of interest if I referred briefly to some of the recommendations made in these reports

"The . report of the Bengal Committee was strongly of opinion that the progress of the country depended on intensive industrial development They made several concrete recommendations of a practical nature, such as, the starting of farm colonies, industrial banks, and extension of technical and practical education They thought that in an ideally balanced development, technical training and economic progress should proceed forward together, each being stimulated in turn by the other They ended by saying that, though the question of the general economic development of the country was of the very highest importance, it was beyond the scope of their work

"The Committee of the Madras Government remarked that unemployment of whatever section or society was a complex evil which arose from many causes and the bringing about of a change lay in the hands of the public at large They suggested that steps should be taken to popularize agriculture as a means of livelihood, but they thought that there was no single panacea for the evil and that its remedy will have to be comprehensive and its scope all-embracing and will require a length of time to operate

"The Punjab Committee made several statements of a general nature, namely, that the present system of education produced men fit mostly for clerical occupations, that unemployment was due largely to extension of education in classes which previously did not aspire to Government service and that facilities for higher education should be provided only for the markedly able young persons, if poor, and for those who can pay its full cost, and so on And they concluded with the comforting observation that there was no unemployment worthy of mention except among the educated classes, whose education had been purely literary

"One Member of that Committee, however, recorded a note of dissent in these arresting words —

> 'It is in the matter of industries, however, that much can be accomplished by Government initiative The industries have not so far received the amount of attention which they should deserve Arrangements for imparting industrial and technical education are wholly inadequate '

"These reports dealt mainly with the question of middle-class unemployment Men of directing ability, men who can create employment come chiefly from the middle-class where they do not belong to the ruling classes, and the presumption is that if the problem as affecting the middle-classes is satisfactorily solved, the question of employment for the rest of the population, where it is not due to natural causes, will, to a great extent, solve itself

"The public have not heard so far that any practical action has been taken by any of the Provincial Governments on the reports submitted to them Had the Government of India collected these reports and referred them for consideration to a Central Committee, as they originally wished to do in certain eventualities, it might have done some good by keeping the subject alive or prominently before the public But they have chosen otherwise

"The Government of India Circular, referred to, draws attention to some of the root causes, but in other respects takes up a non-committal attitude It says —

> 'The root causes were far deeper and far more complex The educational system, the state of industrial development, the changes that are being slowly wrought in the social structure, such as, gradual disintegration of the caste system which at one time operated to prevent middle-class unemployment by restricting admission to clerical professions and, at bottom, the psychological factors inherent in the habits and customs of the people were all contributory causes for which, from the nature of the case, no Government can find a panacea'

"In the first place, the statement that there are deeper and more complex causes at the root of unemployment is, quite true, although not precisely in the sense intended by its authors There are root causes for which both Government and the people are responsible For example, the root cause of the economic backwardness of the country is illiteracy That a community could be prosperous, while over 90 per cent of its numbers are illiterate, is unthinkable Another root cause, according to Indian economists, is the neglect of industries to which much of the economic backwardness is due A third one is the lack of regular employment for the rural population for nearly half the year and the absence of any policy or organization to fill this vacant time of the cultivator People have had no guidance in creating or choosing occupations and the great majority of them have, in consequence, drifted to the least remunerative of them, namely, agriculture As stated before, the agricultural practices also are still for the most part primitive India in the last century used to export various staple products to foreign countries, but she lost one industry after another, because her people neglected the use of steam and machinery, and Government policies encouraged stagnation Free trade, for a long time, encouraged dumping of foreign goods to the prejudice of Indian industries The control of fiscal, financial and currency and exchange policies has also been operating against the interests of the country

"The next observation of the Government of India requiring comment is that people alone can produce a change in their habits and customs This is only partially true, because the controlling voice to effect any radical reforms is not wholly with the people A third statement made is that change must necessarily take time This is also only partially true, because the rapidity with which change can be effected in these days will depend upon the earnestness, energy and organization at the back of the attempt

"The causes mentioned by the Government of India

are thus, at bottom, defects and disabilities—economic, political and social—which demand drastic remedies on the part of both the Government and the people "

True Causes of Unemployment

An examination of Table II in the Appendix shows that the actual workers in India form nearly 44 per cent of the total population The workers employed in agriculture alone come to 28 8 per cent of the same total The highest proportion so employed in civilized countries for which statistics are available is in Japan, where it is 21 4 per cent, and the lowest proportion is in Great Britain, *viz*, 3 06 per cent The nations who desire to increase their wealth in these days look principally to income from industry, trade and transport The percentage of workers employed in these three classes of occupations in India, as well as in the leading countries of the world is given below —

Country	Percentage of total population employed in Industry, etc
India	7 3
Great Britain	30 5
The United States of America	22 3
Canada	16.2
Germany	29 2
France	26 4
Japan	18 0

Increase of numbers in agriculture above a fixed percentage leads to a lowering of the general level of income of the population Even a small increase in the number employed in industries is of much more value to a nation than a large increase in the less profitable occupation of agriculture

The above figures show that in occupations regarded as most remunerative in all advanced countries, India employs only 7 3 per cent of its population, while in industrially advanced Great Britain, the percentage is 30 5 There is a limit to the population which can be kept profitably employed on agriculture in any country; and if the number goes beyond that limit, the income falls rapidly and the average income of the population as a whole shows a decline Many countries which were formerly agricultural are now industrially developed and as a result have increased their income two, three or more times by investing more capital and employing more labour on industries The very low income of the Indian population is due to the fact that the price of agricultural products is generally low as compared with that from industries The total income from industries in undeveloped India is barely one-fifth of that from agriculture, whereas in a country like Great Britain it is about seven times the same These facts should be fully grasped by all persons who wish to understand the economic problem of India

The true cause of unemployment is that in an industrial and machine age, the country is becoming increasingly rural

On account of the abnormally excessive concentration of population on agriculture, holdings are small, income is low and poverty conditions are aggravated. It is this single circumstance that is responsible for the industrial inefficiency of India The proper course for the Government and the people to take is to check, and check at once, the present drift towards ruralization It will be easy to develop the country industrially at a very rapid rate, if the people have the assurance that their Government will do what all enlightened national governments are doing at present and will support a progressive policy

The Remedy

There should be some authority or agency to take

notice of the people's difficulties and sufferings caused by insufficient employment We have seen there is no such agency now, to all appearances the problem does not seem to exist so far as Government are concerned, and no count is kept of the unemployed

The first thing to do, therefore, is to prevail upon the Government speedily to set up an organization or agency to work on the problem and rapidly devise measures of relief and to get them to agree to deal with the problem in a comprehensive manner They should be induced to recognize that it is a problem of overwhelming importance at a time like this, when tens of millions of people are living below the poverty line To be really effective, the organization should be of an all-India character and, as the work to be done and results expected in connection with unemployment are in essentials similar to those aimed at under the "Ten-Year Plan"—though only more urgent—the same organization of Economic Councils—Central, Provincial and Local—already described, will answer this purpose

Under those proposals, the Development organization of the Central Government described in Chapter XIV will be concerned with large policies and unification of effort throughout the country, the district Government agencies and the district and city Economic Councils will be doing the actual constructive work, *i e*, building up farms, factories and shops, and the primary responsibility for results for giving effective relief should be entrusted to the Provincial Development Department and Provincial Economic Council

The source of all income is production and service—production from industries and agriculture and service through trade and other occupations In any measures to increase production, the preparation of commodities which command the highest prices, should be kept in view At the present time, industries and other subsidiary occupations give larger profits to the people engaged in them than agriculture, and people naturally choose those occupations which give the largest returns for the capital and labour employed on them Although they have vast areas fit for cultivation, Governments like those of the United States of America and Canada have limited the numbers employed in agriculture

Unemployment is caused through insufficient and unbalanced occupations, through deficiency, in number or strength or both, of *farms*, *factories*, *shops* and jobs in other subsidiary professions and occupations These units of business should be expanded and multiplied in order to increase work for the people and goods for consumption or export

A survey should be made of the wants and resources of each unit area and based on the results of the survey, a plan and programme of developments should be prepared for 3 to 5 years in advance From this, should be drawn up a detailed programme of work to be attempted in the first year of operations The classes of business, to which prominence should be given, may be decided after consulting the people of the area in conference once in six months or a year Business men, political leaders and experts should be invited to the Conference from outside for purposes of consultation

Unless the population specializes in any particular industry or occupation which gives higher rates of remuneration, the classes of business to be first selected should be such as to satisfy the primary needs of the people, *viz*, food, clothing, housing and household furniture and other consumption goods

Large Indian firms and corporations should be encouraged by Government and Local Bodies, who should assign to them contracts in connection with productive schemes, public works, public utilities, etc Such firms help to give continuous employment to large numbers of people and their very existence is an asset to the State, in that they will have resources in trained men and money which Government can use in emergencies to reduce unemployment or to do any kind of constructive work for the country

ORGANIZATION

The Local Economic (or Development) Council may consist of 12 persons elected on some reasonable basis by the inhabitants of the area From these, a working committee of 3 persons may be chosen, one of them to attend to the funds needed to carry on the work, the second to give technical help in organizing joint-stock companies, private companies, co-operative societies, etc , and the third to be in control of operations as President working in co-operation with the whole Council All the three should work shoulder to shoulder and help to increase business in the area They should make it clear to the public, by the publication of official statistics and otherwise, the precise amount of increase effected from year to year Only men of proved ability, integrity and spirit of service should be chosen for these three offices At the commencement of operations, it may be an advantage to borrow the services of trained officials from Government for this purpose to work under the Council for one year at a time

It has been stated that the Local (District or City) Economic Council, when established, will provide the organization needed for multiplying occupations, *i e*, increasing farms, factories, shops and other business units within the area At first, the General Economic Staff of the Provincial Government will provide the guidance needed by the District and City Economic Councils The members of the staff will visit the unit areas and give advice, as required, regarding organization, finance, design or technique They may be called upon to report on applications from Local Councils for subsidies or other financial help This sort of guidance will be needed for two or three years, after which, except for occasional advice, the Local Economic Councils may be expected to stand on their own legs In Japan, there have been notable instances of eminent city men taking part in Village Improvement work as advisers Such service may be confidently expected also in this country from patriotic men belonging to organizations like the Indian National Congress and the Servants of India Society of Poona

FUNDS

Money will be required to maintain the necessary staff under each Local Council and for various other purposes connected with the starting of new units of business Since they will be spent by the local representatives of the people themselves, it is believed there will be no difficulty in obtaining the necessary funds by levying a small tax or cess in each local area

But large sums of capital are required to start new business units and expand old ones Some of them will be found by the people themselves but, as rapid advance is desired under the scheme, a loan may be raised by the Provincial Government, if possible within the area itself, and made available through local banks, co-operative societies, trustworthy money-lenders, etc , to finance such new business enterprises as may require help A sum equivalent to half the gross revenue of the district should be raised in this way and treated as an Unemployment Relief Fund for the district The corresponding fund in an urban area may be equivalent to half the gross municipal revenue of the city In a district with a revenue from all sources of, say, Rs 40 lakhs, the loan raised for this purpose would be Rs 20 lakhs Similarly, in a city with a revenue of Rs 16 lakhs, the capital at first set apart for this purpose would be Rs 8 lakhs There is always an element of risk in investing money in a new business concern, of whatever character—a company, a partnership concern, a factory or a shop under an individual *entrepreneur* Money may be lost in some of these units, but such risks must be taken and development persevered in, because, in the long run, in a majority of cases, the profits will exceed the losses and the transactions, on the whole, result in adding to the income and assets of the area The Provincial Government should be prepared to share these risks along with District Boards and City Municipalities It is possible that after the first five years, the provincial loans in the aggregate will be yielding sufficient dividends to pay interest charges and also contribute to a sinking fund for the progressive liquidation of the debt

NEED FOR BUSINESS TRAINING

On each unit of business of any appreciable size,—a factory, farm or shop—an educated man, or a small group of educated men, will be required to look after the overhead work

A Business Training Institute is required in every large Indian city *to provide the final stages of instruction, chiefly practical,* needed by young persons who have passed through the ordinary educational institutions, before they take up or enter any particular calling or business Such an institute will be useful also to adult persons already in business who may wish to brush up, or bring up to date, their knowledge of technique, or rules and practices of sound management

A short course not exceeding six months is all that is usually intended to be given at these institutes. There should be, at the head of these, a manager of organizing ability, assisted by a staff of expert instructors, mechanics, farmers and accountants If a candidate wants information or instruction which is not available locally, the manager should be able to procure the same from wherever it could be had

A city may have a fully equipped Business Institute, a town may provide itself with a Business Training School, and a group of villages may jointly set up a Business Training Class There may be more than one institution of this class established in any given area, where there is sufficient demand A city *Business Institute* may provide practical instruction in half-a-dozen cottage industries, or in the management of a farm, or in the precise practical training needed by managers and accountants in the service of farming, industry or trade The town *Business Schools* will be doing similar work but of a lower grade The village *Business Classes* will give instruction of a primary standard required by farmers and artisans

The institution in each area will also serve as an Intelligence Bureau for collecting and distributing information for the benefit of persons engaged in agriculture, industry and trade in the local area

The training given in these institutions will fill the gap which at present exists between the instruction received by a young person in ordinary educational institutions and the full qualifications needed to manage, or to assist in the management of, a farm, factory or shop It will be of two classes —

(1) Factory training in one or more industries, and

(2) Training in management and accounts

A candidate may want to enrol himself for one or

both these classes of training The City Institute should be of the type of an "Experimental and Demonstration Station" in Japan described in Chapter V

Two Examples

When people in any advanced country desire to develop an area industrially, the usual practice should be to appoint a Council or Committee of persons in whom they have confidence and place the work of organizing and mobilizing local resources in its hands The principles followed by the agency so created are not materially different from those recommended in the Ten-Year Plan Two examples worthy of emulation may be cited

The present writer has visited several villages in Japan in which production had been increased four-fold or more in the course of about 20 years The methods recommended in this chapter for multiplying units of business are similar to those followed in the model villages of Japan, where Village Government is autonomous

One of the most successful industrial communities in Great Britain is reported to be that of the South Wales and Monmouthshire region, which has grown from an agricultural area into a hive of industry in recent years Realizing the urgency and importance of co-operative effort in this task, the Municipal authorities of the region acting in co-operation with Town Development Association, Banks, Chambers of Commerce, Chambers of Trade and with the support of railways, docks, electrical and gas undertakings, and industrial, labour and other organizations, have formed themselves into a Regional Council and embarked upon a well-considered programme to assist in the development of existing industries, starting of new industries and intensive cultivation It is said that the variety of products manufactured is large, covering a wide range of commodities from cosmetics to wire ropes and chains—from condiments to enamelware—and from asbestos sheets to hosiery The Development Council is able to render great assistance to firms contemplating the expansion of their business by furnishing full information and details of what the area can offer The Council has also set up various Technical and Research Committees, each composed of experts in their respective spheres, whose services are available without charge to any prospective industrialist

Concluding Remarks

There is much misconception among the public regarding the causes and cure of unemployment It is usual to state that no one has been able to devise a remedy, that there is no short cut to industrial progress, that the unemployment question has no connection with education, that intensive cultivation of land may bring relief and so on

There can be no mystery, as to the true cause of unemployment, at least in this country It arises from the pressure of population on the soil, there being twice the number of people employed in agriculture (*vide* Table II) that would be justified in a balanced occupational structure

European nations are willing to pay War Debts and Indemnities in commodities but the principal creditor, the United States of America, will not accept them because by doing so the people of that country would get a compulsory holiday, and thereby grow idle and become demoralized Only one per cent of the Indian workers in British India are employed on organized industries, and so India which at one time was skilled in industries, is in the above sense condemned to a perpetual holiday.

The average income and standard of living of the

people depend upon the aggregate production and income in the country

The greater the number of those employed on production, the larger will be the gross national income.

The percentage of producers to the total workers is a determining factor in the average income

The quality of the products grown or manufactured is another determining factor

Judged by these standpoints, the principal remedies are

- To multiply business units giving preference to the more profitable occupations,
- To develop industries,
- To arrest ruralization by transferring the population on agriculture to industries and other occupations,
- To industrialize agriculture, and
- To specialize in education, particularly, in technical and professional education of University grade

Above all it is necessary to drill and discipline the population so that it may put in skilled work and longer hours of it

It will be seen that the Government explanation, noticed at the beginning of this Chapter, namely, that unemployment is due to natural causes and not to omissions on their part, is not supported by the experience of civilized nations Nor is the statement borne out by the facts adduced above that the contributory causes are such that "no Government can find a panacea" for them

The plan of work for relief of unemployment suggested in this Chapter presumes that the Ten-Year Plan and the associated organization will have come into existence In fact, the most urgent scheme to begin after the Ten-Year Plan is introduced, would be Unemployment Relief But if it happens that Unemployment Relief is taken up immediately while the introduction of the Plan is delayed, some simpler form of organization on the same lines as those detailed for the Ten-Year Plan would be necessary

CHAPTER XVIII

REBUILDING THE ECONOMIC LIFE

The Fundamental Issue—Results of Dependency Rule—Solution of the Problem—True Responsible Government—Concessions to Great Britain—Organizing a Ten-Year Plan—Ten Urgent Requirements—Separate Appraisement of Indian Interests—Nation-Building

THE FUNDAMENTAL ISSUE

THE three nation-building activities, namely, (1) education, (2) industrialization, and (3) military training, are vital for the country's progress These activities are of necessity retarded under Dependency rule Taking mass education first, although over 90 per cent of the population is illiterate, we do not ordinarily hear of any one in authority or power drawing attention to this catastrophic omission in progressive rule

Recruitment to the Army is made from selected areas and the so-called martial races, instead of from all parts of the country and all classes of the population The fact should not be ignored that success in modern warfare depends more on brain power and machinery than on sheer physical strength

The training going on of cadets for the future Navy is as yet a mere plaything, and there is no institution started to give systematic training to youth in aerial warfare

The greatest obstacle to the progress of the country to-day is the lack of a sound industrial policy through the indifference or opposition of Government

In 1897, Sir Richard Temple in his book *Sixty Years of the Queen's Reign*, wrote "British manufacturers are as yet in sole possession of the Indian market. . Among the exports, cotton goods hold the first place, and iron and other metals, plant and machinery are considerable, amounting to one-fourth of the total export of these things "

The competition from England has laid a heavy hand particularly on these two industries To-day, after a lapse of 37 years, we find the cotton textile industry is still in a bad way, the steel industry is as yet in its infancy and machinery industries are not even started

We have seen that at one time India was exporting cotton piece-goods to England and until 25 or 30 years ago even to Japan To-day, both these countries are dumping cotton cloth into India and disputing over their respective shares of the Indian market Leading business men associated with the cotton trade are emphatically of opinion that it is not necessary to import a single yard of cotton cloth from outside But India is politically helpless to prevent this and to reserve the home market for home-made cloth A similar, though less unfair, situation exists with regard to iron and steel Attention has been drawn to the fact that at one time it was considered profitable to export steel from South India to Great Britain

With regard to the importance of steel for industrial progress and civilization, Stalin, the Russian authority, said in January 1934 "The main link of the Five-Year Plan was heavy industry, and its core, machine construction, because only heavy industry was capable of reconstructing industry, as a whole, and transport and agriculture, and of putting them on their feet " His predecessor, Lenin, has emphasized this in even stronger words "The salvation of Russia lies" said he, "not only in a good harvest in the peasant farms—that is not enough—and not only in the good state of the light industry which provides the peasantry with articles of consumption—that too is not enough—we must have also heavy industry Unless we have heavy industry, unless we restore it, we cannot build up any industry, and without it we shall perish as an independent country Heavy industry needs State subsidies If we are not able to find them, then we, as a civilized State will perish "

Heavy industries are a necessity to raise the people's standard of living and for many other important developments, for defence, for nation-building, for civilization itself If heavy industries are rapidly developed in India, railway locomotives, rolling stock and plant, army machinery, ordnance and stores may be easily manufactured locally instead of, as will be seen from an earlier chapter, the country having to import them from Great Britain or foreign countries to the extent of Rs 25 to 35 crores every year As in Russia, heavy industry affects national progress in many directions and therefore requires State subsidies to foster it If we are not able to find the subsidies, then, we too, as a civilized State, must perish

In the Chapter on *Finance*, attention has been drawn to a statement made by Lord Macaulay in the House of Commons in 1833, in the course of which, he said that India then had "a larger clear revenue than was under the direct management of the Executive Government of the United Kingdom,"—a clear revenue which exceeded the then "clear revenue of any State in the world, France excepted "

Again, in 1897-98, the revenue of British India was Rs 96 crores, the revenue of the United Kingdom £107 million, that of Canada $41 million, and of Japan 226 million Yen To-day, the figures for the respective countries are Rs 215 crores, £827 million, $516 million; and 1,944 million Yen The proportionate growths are respectively—less than 2½ times; about 8 times; nearly 13 times, and over 8½ times

These figures show how far India has lost its premier position in point of total revenue, notwithstanding growth of territory and population

The Governments of the countries named above, with the exception of India, have been developing their revenues and spending a good portion of them on nation-building activities Such expenditure is conspicuously lacking in India

India imports manufactured goods and exports raw materials, quite the reverse of what a progressive country should do We have seen that the past practice has been to buy manufactured goods chiefly from Great Britain and pay for them by selling raw materials to Great Britain and foreign countries In the relations between Great Britain and India, the trade balance is always of necessity in favour of Great Britain.

British shipping holds the monopoly for the carriage of Indian foreign trade and also Indian coastal trade At present, local boats can carry on coastal trade by sufferance on a minor scale Till very recently Indian enterprise in air service was not encouraged

One of the greatest losses to the country is that although India has the fourth largest railway mileage in the world, and double the mileage of Great Britain itself, all locomotives and railway stores are imported mainly from Great Britain and no encouragement has so far been given to their manufacture within the country This is because the purchases for the railways and the army are in British hands

Some of the Bombay cotton mills are not working full time and some are closed down The hand-loom industry is also languishing It is easy to stop the drain of money paid for cotton goods by raising a high enough tariff wall The mills in existence can fully meet the requirements of the country in this respect. There can be no complaint from the consumers; but, if there are any fastidious persons left who want foreign cotton goods, they may be supplied, as already suggested, by a special license under Government supervision

We have already seen that the freight rates on railways from the several ports are favourable for imported goods instead of being the reverse as is the case in countries like South Africa

It is the plain duty of the Government to hold a public enquiry and, if these statements are found to be valid and substantially just, the defects should be forthwith remedied in view of the low purchasing power and extreme poverty of the people

A gentleman, who has held two of the highest positions open to Indians and who is a business man himself, remarked to the writer recently that, if he had the control of protective tariffs and railway freight rates, he could bring fabulous wealth to India in the course of a decade

In a debate in the British Parliament in the year 1900, the then Secretary of State for India, Lord George Hamilton, said, "We must try to vary the occupations of the people, for so long as 80 per cent of the population is engaged in agriculture, the danger in the case of recurrence (of famine) is all the greater "

Mr Montagu and Lord Chelmsford wrote in 1918 in their Report on Indian Constitutional Reforms "On all grounds, a forward policy in industrial development is urgently called for .. in order to satisfy the aspirations of her (Indian) people, in order to provide an outlet for the energies of her young men . and in order that . the people may be better qualified to shoulder the new responsibilities which the new constitution will lay upon them "

And yet the danger against which the Secretary of State warned the country thirty-four years ago has been allowed to grow and no adequate remedies have been attempted or are within sight

RESULTS OF DEPENDENCY RULE

Great Britain wants India as a market for her manufactured products, so there is no incentive to the growth of industries in this country

Great Britain wants an investment market for her capital, so she feels she cannot let slip her financial control of India

Great Britain wants her market secured This security is assured by a huge army maintained at the cost of the Indian tax-payer but absolutely under British control

Relatively, very little property has been built up in India to yield non-tax revenues Against railways and irrigation works already constructed, a huge debt is piled up and over 40 per cent of this debt is held in England The country's debt in 1900 was Rs 307 crores, to-day it is in the neighbourhood of Rs 1,212 crores, of which Rs 500 crores are held in England.

As regards the extent to which technical education is encouraged, an idea may be formed from the fact that, in the two chief Government Engineering Colleges in Madras and Poona, admissions to the mechanical engineering courses are restricted to about 25 students, and this for a population aggregating not far short of 70 millions !

While industrialization is being discouraged in one direction, ruralization is growing without any attempt to arrest it in the other

When people clamour for developments, the smallest concession compatible with the immediate requirements of the situation is offered, but the grip of the fundamental obstacles to progress continues in full force

Is it any wonder in these circumstances, that the income of the average Indian should be the smallest among nations which have a civilized Government? Unemployment has grown to calamitous dimensions, death rate is the highest known, and Indians live to only about half the age up to which the people of England and other progressive countries live, production *per capita* from industries is the lowest, trade is the lowest, bank deposits are the lowest and literacy also is at the lowest level imaginable In every sphere of activity and prosperity, it looks as though India is competing for the lowest place among the nations of the world On whichever side of national activity one looks, the conditions appear extremely depressing

Solution of the Problem

This unhappy picture which is the outcome of Dependency rule leaves no room for doubt that the present system of administration is in need of a radical change

We have seen that the net effect of the rule has been to lower the country in almost every field of human activity, to foster special interests and to impede the well-being of the vast masses of the population A few people—an infinitesimal few—are well-off, but millions of human beings are living in distress, misery, poverty and destitution

To remedy this state of things, certain essential changes and reforms in the status and life of the Indian people are necessary and these may be classed under three heads:—

(1) A sound Federal Constitution which will give scope to all classes of people to work in unison, organize on modern lines and bring about order in the country by their own collective self-help,

(2) A planned economy setting out the conditions and mechanism needed for a rapid improvement in the economic position of the people, and

(3) A campaign or drive to change the outlook of the people, modernise their business practices and habits, prepare them for independent thinking and collective self-help and bring them into the company of the progressive nations of the world

It has been explained in Chapter XII that the conflict of interests that exists between the British rulers and the Indian population leads to clash of views on every important issue affecting the commercial and financial position of the country It is idle to deny the existence of this conflict

When any important question of reform or development comes up for consideration in these days, the solution reached is usually partial and unsatisfactory This is because the ultimate decision rests with one party only, namely, the British authorities

The present relations of India with Great Britain are clearly disadvantageous to the former Some way must be found to stop the great losses and sufferings, to which the people of this country are subjected

There are in India 7 or 8 times the number of people that there are in Great Britain, to be fed, clothed, housed and kept alive To be able to do this and to lift her submerged population, India wants freedom to practise whatever industries, occupations or professions her people find it to their advantage to do

Any reforms at this stage to be efficacious should be radical and comprehensive Piecemeal attempts can do no good, because by the time one good reform succeeds, others will have receded to the background or disappeared The disease in the body politic is in too advanced a stage to benefit by any such partial cures.

This country is in need of a sound political Constitution to enable her even to keep her people alive, and the British nation is unwilling to abandon the monopolistic position which it has so long enjoyed It is suggested that the sacrifice of interests involved in consenting to a right solution of the Indian problem should be met by reasonable money concessions in a spirit of compromise

An immediate solution is necessary, because the population of India is growing, and distress due to the country's inability to rapidly adjust itself to changing world conditions is deepening

True Responsible Government

It is to the interest of both countries that India should have a sound political Constitution without further loss of time

A sound Constitution for India will mean nothing less than a Dominion form of Government The right course to take at the present time is to fix the strength of the new Central Legislature and of each of the Provincial Legislatures and to grant a franchise based upon only two qualifications, namely, literacy and property, and to be in force for the first 10 years There should be no scope given to communal electorates as they are distinctly anti-national and will tend to retard progress Special representation, if any, provided during the transition period, should be strictly restricted to very exceptional cases and made subject to a time limit not exceeding 10 years in each case The country wants righteous policies and measures and not merely changes which have but the appearance of reform, sound political reform to-day should aim at self-development preferably without external permission or control

Nation-building would be impossible unless the control of finance is transferred to Indian hands from the very outset A time limit of 15 years should be fixed within which the entire Defence forces should be made over to Indian control The new Government should be free to take all the emergency measures that it might deem fit, to prepare the population and the defence structure for this new responsibility It should be at liberty to regulate customs tariffs, as it might find most appropriate in the country's interests, and should have full control over its Railways and over the purchases to be made for Railways and for the Army

CONCESSIONS TO GREAT BRITAIN

The White Paper, for some time now under the scrutiny of the Joint Parliamentary Committee, is contemplating a Constitution and Conventions which will not help India to build up her industries, or to remove the existing disequilibrium in the matter of occupations No one in authority in these circumstances need labour under the belief that the proposed new Constitution will satisfy public opinion and bring peace to the country

As regards the compromise considered necessary, the following tentative proposals are put forward —

(1) The British debt may be accepted in full

(2) The British interests in India which do not clash with the Indian may be secured

against any harmful interference by the new Government.

(3) All new enterprises and interests which are likely to result in the transfer of profits out of the country should be subject to the same restrictions, as are placed upon them in a Dominion like Canada

(4) The full control of Railways, purchases for the Railways and the Army, shipping, and similar national services and enterprises should be in the hands of the new Government as it is in the Dominions It is only when such control is secured that heavy industries will have scope for development

(5) The present tariff preferences, save in the case of steel products, machinery and cotton goods, may continue for a period not exceeding ten years in the case of imports which do not interfere with the expansion of local industries

(6) Immediate losses to British interests due to these and other changes may be compensated by a fixed annual contribution to be made by India This contribution may be taken provisionally at Rs 10 crores per annum for a period of 20 years

What India wants in return is political freedom—freedom to build up new industries and to employ her population in occupations expected to pay them best, so that they might be able to earn enough income to supply food and other primary wants for her enormous population

The extra money required for meeting the interest charges on imported capital and the loans raised in the country for heavy industries and other developments, should be found within the country itself partly by increased taxation The people should submit, as every progressive nation has done in similar circumstances in the past, to this additional taxation for a short period, in order to secure a permanent rise in the standard of living and also a prosperous future

ORGANIZING A TEN-YEAR PLAN

A sound economic order is unthinkable so long as a reasonably sound political constitution is lacking Many changes of a radical character are also required in the business structure of the country and it is for reconstructing that structure that the proposed economic councils and the Ten-Year Plan, combined with other attendant measures, are now suggested

The great value of the proposed new measures will be that they will bring into existence an agency which will promptly take note of the wants of the people and initiate measures to supply those wants to the limit of the country's resources

An agency which could take prompt notice of the needs of the people and is able to give effect to the remedial measures considered necessary is a desideratum. The proposed economic organization under the leadership of the committees of the Development Departments and Economic Councils combines both these functions The Economic Councils will be effective in voicing the business and popular interests, and the actual planning and executive work will be attended to by officials, engineers and others possessing technical skill and directing ability

The economic organization described will, in addition to giving its special attention to the execution of measures under the Plan, attend to new problems that arise from time to time and to the continuous development of sound economic policies and measures. When any deficiency or new want is noticed and action is desired by the public, the Government Development Department or the Economic Council or both will take cognizance The subject will be considered both by the Development Committee and the Standing Committee and, as a result of such consideration, a working plan or remedial scheme will emerge The scheme may be related to some item already included in the Ten-Year Plan, or it may be quite independent If the Government and the Legislature concerned approve and allot the necessary funds, the scheme will be carried into effect by the same agencies that attend to the work and propaganda under the Ten-Year Plan

There will thus be two agencies to take notice of any public want or grievance Each will be anxious to take the initiative as both will be competing for the appreciation and goodwill of the public

The same procedure will be followed when new business methods, practices, equipment or habits are required to replace traditional ones which are harmful or ineffective New standards will be formulated by the Development Committee with the help of experts and with the co-operation and consent of the Standing Committee of the Economic Council The special agencies responsible for propaganda work will spread a knowledge of the new standards and secure their rapid adoption by the communities or sections of the public concerned

The main aim of the Local Economic Councils should be to encourage initiative and co-operation as a habit among the local population for promoting their common economic interests The Councils should be a training ground for representatives and leaders for work to be done in the higher spheres in the years to come

If the developments proceed along the lines indicated, the great value of their work to the local community will become apparent after the Councils have been in effective operation for a period of three to five years

There will, no doubt, arise gifted popular leaders from time to time endowed with energy and public spirit and capable of achieving great things for their country Such men should be picked out, placed in positions of authority and entrusted with powers and responsibilities, for specific periods so long as they work unselfishly in the public interest If appointments to key positions in the economic organization are made on the basis of qualifications and character, confidence in the organization will grow and many men will aspire to those positions for the mere privilege of working for the public good

In this way, the proposed Ten-Year Plan and the economic organization, associated with it, will between them provide *a mechanism of development* through whose aid the country will be able to make rapid progress in reconstruction and recovery

If the people have enough to eat and maintain a fair standard of living, they will be healthy, long-lived and physically efficient and will also have sufficient leisure for improving their mental capacity, culture or manual skill Economic progress should, therefore, be held to be the pivot round which all other activities revolve

Ten Urgent Requirements

The most urgent reforms and facilities required by the people of India to ensure the country's economic safety in the immediate future are primarily the ten following —

(1) Elementary Mass Education ,

(2) Training in Defence ,

(3) Industrialization with special attention to Heavy Industries,

(4) A Comprehensive Survey of Resources and Collection of Statistics according to International Standards,

(5) Balancing Occupations and arresting the tendency to Ruralization,

(6) Indian control of Finance, Currency and Exchange, and of Reserve Bank and Gold Reserves,

(7) Indian control of Purchases for the Railways and the Army,

(8) Indian control of Railway Administration;

(9) Indian control of Protective Tariffs and Railway Freight, and

(10) Training in the highest branches of Administration, Commerce and Technology

People may ask whether there are not many other reforms and developments which should be pushed forward concurrently with those suggested here The answer is There are, but these are the most urgent ones and if a mechanism is created which takes care of these ten requirements, the other less important needs are not liable to be overlooked

SEPARATE APPRAISEMENT OF INDIAN INTERESTS

Clear accounts or estimates should be annually available of the investments and profits of Indian and non-Indian interests, respectively, in the business transacted in the country, so far as they may be necessary to measure the rate of progress of the indigenous interests from year to year The following five or six measures seem necessary to this end —

(1) The rupee which is now pegged to sterling should be separated and kept independent, otherwise,

the value of the rupee and of Indian assets generally will be affected by every fluctuation in British credit. There was never any necessity in India's interest to link the rupee to sterling and, since the relations are not reciprocal, but one-sided, *i e*, since sterling is not pegged to the rupee, it is positively harmful to maintain this relation in future

(2) In the meantime, should there be any delay in this separation, the exchange ratio should be lowered to the level that may be recommended by representative Indian business men, ascertained at an all-India conference to be convened for the purpose

(3) The credit mechanism of the Government should be freely utilized to support industries and business enterprises and particularly sound private enterprise in industry and trade

(4) The investments and yearly profits in the business transacted within the limits of India by Indian and non-Indian agencies, respectively, should be separately accounted for by maintaining the necessary statistics and estimates

(5) The fiscal policies of the country, such as the regulation of tariffs and decisions regarding the export of gold, should be under Indian control, *i e*, under the control of the future responsible government

(6) Statistics or estimates should be available to show separately the value of foreign trade conducted by Indian and non-Indian agencies, respectively

These measures are necessary, chiefly because, without them, the precise position of the Indian public in Indian business will not be known and there will be no means of measuring progress or regress from year to year They are not suggested with a view to place any restrictions, unknown in the Dominions, on British industry or trade in this country If India becomes free to develop her business interests in the way she thinks best, her advance will be so rapid that there will be no occasion to grudge any growth of British business At present, the business of both parties is on a low level The financial and fiscal policies followed are harmful to the business interests of both the political units

Nation-Building

The policies to be followed to lead the people into the company of progressive nations and the training to be given to the citizens for that purpose have been explained in Chapters XII and XIII Let it not be forgotten that prosperity and leadership will not come without planning, organization and effort To do all this satisfactorily, a section of the mechanism of the Ten-Year Plan should be charged with the duty of continuously studying the policies and training in advanced countries, with a view to advise and help the people of this country to adopt or assimilate from time to time whatever is good in the ideals and practices of those countries

The resources of India are great and particularly, the human energy, which, by suitable training, can be rendered fit and capable and put at the service of her people and of the world, is for all practical purposes illimitable If the statesmen and citizens of this great country plan and work with the ideals herein explained, if preparations for the new economic order are vigorously set on foot and if every Province or State does its share of work in a spirit of emulation and harmonious co-operation, the country will go on gathering momentum as a progressive State from year to year at a rate which will astonish the world

CHAPTER XIX

A NEW OUTLOOK

India's Problem Essentially Industrial—Government Still Hesitating—The Example of Other Countries—Fundamental Prerequisites of Plan—Financing the Ten-Year Plan—The Making of an Immediate Beginning

INDIA'S PROBLEM ESSENTIALLY INDUSTRIAL

BY neglecting industrial pursuits to the alarming extent revealed by the statistical information given in the Chapters on Industries, the Government and people of this country have been following a policy prejudicial to its national welfare Safety lies in immediately reversing this policy The Indian problem is fundamentally industrial and should be solved by the same methods as have proved efficacious in countries like the United States of America, Japan and Canada and latterly also with such startling success in Soviet Russia

In a speech made in the British House of Commons in 1833, Lord Macaulay, then Secretary to the Board of Control in Great Britain, said that it would be, on the most selfish view of the case, far better that the Indians "were ruled by their own kings, wearing our broadcloth, and working with our cutlery, than that they were performing their *salaams* to English collectors and English magistrates, but were too ignorant to value or too poor to buy English manufactures"

So recently as in 1928, Lord Snowden, who was Chancellor of the Exchequer in the Labour Government of Great Britain, stated in the course of a debate in the House of Commons that, if the purchasing power of the Indian peasant were raised by only 3 farthings a week, there would not be a spindle or loom idle in Lancashire. And he went on to add "If we wanted to restore the iron and steel trades and develop the great possibilities of the Indian Empire, let us send machinery to cultivate the land and money for manure and other necessaries"

It did not occur to either of these noble Lords that the true interests of the Indian people, whose custodians they were, demanded that India should be self-contained, as she once was, at least in the matter of her staple needs, such as steel and cotton piece-goods and yarn, if she was to escape poverty and ruin

Our association with Great Britain, instead of making us an industrially prosperous nation, has tended to keep us far away from that position The lack of balance between industries and agriculture in India has been allowed to grow to a degree disastrous to the country's material prosperity In the calculations of British statesmen, this country was to remain for all time a market for British manufactures and that position was to be maintained by political power The position is now rendered impossible by the great and rapid increase of population without a corresponding increase in production or income, while the recent tendency of all active nations is to become as self-contained as possible

The noted British economist, Mr G D H Cole, writes —

"There is no reason why industrialization in undeveloped parts of the world should not proceed at an extraordinarily rapid rate, or why those countries should not equip themselves within a small space of years with instruments of production fully equal to those now in use in the developed areas "[26]

[26] *The Intelligent Man's Guide through World Chaos*, 1932, p 47.

This prophecy should hold true of India, if only a proper organization and atmosphere such as are outlined in this book are brought into existence

India may be an industrially developed country, or it may be a market for manufactured goods from outside, but it can never be both The government of the country should make up its mind to do for its people in this respect what other national governments are doing for theirs Real economic progress is not possible with a non-modern organization such as we have, and with the ideas of the Manchester School, referred to by Sir Basil Blackett, still dominating the policies of the Secretary of State and the Central Government

Dependence on foreign manufactures for staple products, such as clothing, steel, sugar and salt, which the people of this country were at one time not only manufacturing for themselves but also exporting to foreign lands, would in any part of the world be regarded as a sign of grave national decay It purchases of clothing and such other primary necessaries have to be paid for from the meagre earnings from agriculture, as is done here, no country can escape impoverishment But if industrial development is undertaken on the lines urged, commodities produced locally will increase in volume, and the technical skill, working power and standard of living of the labour population will automatically improve

India cannot prosper except through rapid industrialization, and rapid industrialization is not possible with the sort of organization and policies pursued in this country Industrialization has to be organized, planned and worked for Left to the chances of unregulated growth under the existing unnatural limitations, it is impossible to expect any progress Not only can there be no progress, but there is a very real danger of a further set-back, a further drift towards ruralization, with consequences too dreadful to contemplate.

GOVERNMENT STILL HESITATING

One disappointing feature of the present Dependency rule is that there is no plan, no policy, to deal with the serious economic problems which confront this country and in the solution of which both the Government and the people can agree and act jointly

There is no organization either to initiate or carry out progressive measures Some one in authority should have the will to plan improvements and execute the same For a long time past this lack of will and organization has been the greatest handicap in the way of the country's progress

The people's representatives in the various legislatures have been drawing attention to the importance of planned economy as a panacea The Government of India, too, have been anxious to do something The present Viceroy referred to these topics in his addresses to the Legislative Assembly on two occasions In the second of these delivered in January 1934, Lord Willingdon drew attention to the fact that the international economic system of the world was becoming more and more affected by the deliberately planned economic policies of all countries

At the request of the Government of India, Sir Arthur Salter, K C B , Director of the Economic and Financial Section of the League of Nations Secretariat, prepared and submitted in February 1931 a scheme for an economic organization for India He suggested the constitution of a Central Economic Advisory Council consisting of persons possessing specialized knowledge in agriculture, industry, etc , representatives of various national economic bodies, officials and members of legislature, economists and others A similar council was suggested for each of the provinces The scheme drawn up by him was quite feasible for the limited purpose for which it was intended

Before an economic plan is prepared, the usual practice is to carry out an economic survey and for such a survey the collection of statistics is an essential preliminary The Government of India invited two distinguished experts in statistics from England to submit recommendations for an economic survey Three Indian economists were associated with them The Government of India have received a report from this Committee who have advised that a period of three years will be required for the preliminary survey and collection of the necessary statistical data

It may be relevant to state in this connection that in the year 1925 the Government of India appointed a Committee of which the present writer happened to be the Chairman for the preparation of a scheme of economic survey, but when the scheme was put forward, no action was taken and, so far as is known, no reason has been assigned why Government failed to act upon the proposals submitted

The report furnished by Sir Arthur Salter favoured a purely advisory agency, and even this has been dropped presumably because the element of popular voice in the scheme would be inconvenient The late Finance Member of the Government of India put it aside by stating that some of the provincial governments had set up local councils and that, for the time being, the Central Government might be content with a small organization of permanent officials till the result of the provincial experiments was known

So, the Government of India have been obtaining reports, considering, hesitating and laying them aside, and there is no serious move in the direction of a planned economy which might lead to results of practical value in the near future The economic survey is expected to take three years and till it is completed, there will be no organization and no plan and the country will be merely marking time

The truth seems to be that the present Government, by the very nature of its constitution, is unable to initiate economic planning or to make any courageous advance in this direction Besides, the present Members of the Viceroy's Council are admittedly too few for developing and working such schemes and they are over-weighted with routine duties Apparently the question must wait till a responsible government is installed at the Centre

In his report referred to above, Sir Arthur Salter has specifically recorded his view that "no great country can hope to solve problems of the complexity which face India in the near future, without being able to draw upon the resources of knowledge and experience possessed by private citizens of first-rate ability in economic activity and enterprise" Government seem to have objected to this aspect of Sir Arthur's report and preferred to set up a small organization of their own of permanent officials, of whose work, however, the public so far know nothing Apparently, the report of 1925 of the Economic Enquiry Committee shared the same fate and for the same reason

The situation calls for a comprehensive plan to be prepared with the co-operation of business men and experts, for the entire country, including the Indian States, to remove the many existing economic disabilities and deficiencies to which attention has been drawn A move is overdue on the part of the Indian Government for the preparation of a plan on the scale here recommended

Every prudent Indian who has his country's future at heart should give thought to the problems and proposals discussed in these pages The Ten-Year Plan here put forward is by its very nature tentative, but it is believed that it will be found to be sufficiently precise to form the basis for a working plan If Government fail to establish an economic organization and to prepare and put a plan in operation on the scale needed, the people of India should, through their chosen representatives, bring into existence a smaller National Economic Council of their own, to draw up a scheme comprising a Ten-Year Plan and an economic organization to execute the plan to the extent permitted by their political position The expenses of the scheme should be met by public subscriptions Such a scheme, if placed before the public with the authority of the leading political thinkers and business men, will have a preparatory and educative value and will help to bring the date of initiation of the desired developments sensibly nearer A sound plan will fill the minds of the public with definite objectives, put hope into them and stimulate collective self-help

THE EXAMPLE OF OTHER COUNTRIES

Attention has been drawn to most of the big issues of the day and if these have to be adequately met, the changes to be effected in the administration of the country and business life of the people will have to be of a drastic character, almost revolutionary

The Government of the country has till recently been content with merely maintaining law and order, *i e*, policing the country and gathering taxes, it has made no special effort to improve education and business efficiency, or build up the material prosperity of the people There has been one uniform code of policies and ethics observed in relation to this Dependency—no matter what political party wields power in Great Britain The country is ruled by the Secretary of State, who adds to the duties of his high office those of a banker to British trade with India Most questions affecting this country are decided by him, and, as must be expected, he has been doing this after giving priority to the immediate needs and permanent interests of Great Britain This is no criticism or characterization, but only a plain statement of fact

When other progressive countries found themselves in similar emergencies—though far less acute than what India is faced with to-day—their governments have had recourse to extraordinary measures For instance, when recently the world trade depression affected Great Britain and that country's financial structure was temporarily disorganized, the Government was changed and a new party—the National Party—came to power almost overnight with a fresh outlook and new policies There are always two or three parties in the British Parliament, and while one party is in office, the others watch and criticise its shortcomings If mistakes and defects accumulate, the party in control is dismissed and the strongest party in Opposition is called to office and given an opportunity to correct the deficiencies and omissions which it had helped to bring to notice. Similarly, when in the United States of America, the trade depression thickened, financial credit broke down, banks failed, panic seized business men and unemployment increased, a new President came to power in March 1933 and he has been making heroic efforts to reduce unemployment and restore prosperity The latest reports go to show that at the end of the first year of the new regime, business activities and labour conditions have improved, wasteful competition has been in part eliminated, profits have replaced losses in many an industry, and unemployment has ceased to be a menace for the time being The Fascist movement in Italy has resulted in power being vested in a Dictator, practically with the consent of the people, for the past eleven years and so far the new movement has resulted in great good In Soviet Russia, the Communist Government has been industrializing the country and spreading literacy and practical education among the people at a far faster rate than was ever thought possible The progress achieved by this nation particularly in industries and literacy in less than a decade is little short of marvellous

The people of India without the support of political power have been unable to put their house in order As a result of unfavourable administrative and fiscal policies, the country has lost much of its economic self-sufficiency and staying power The people are impatient for a change and if the change is to do any good, it has to come soon, and it has got to be of a radical nature involving a complete readjustment of the basic conditions of the country's political and business life

FUNDAMENTAL PREREQUISITES OF PLAN

Save in a few directions like Railways and Irrigation Works, there has been no plan, no scheme, no attempt to effect a progressive improvement in the condition of the people or to increase the country's wealth One of the unfortunate effects of Dependency rule has been that many a defect and weakness has persisted without enquiry or recognition, many a calamity or hardship which is causing suffering has failed even to attract notice

The control of developments in this country is in the hands of the Parliament and Government of Great

Britain, five thousand miles away If any substantial relief is to come to the Indian population, this control should be transferred to Indian hands and Responsible Government on the Dominion model established without delay

Various monopolistic and special interests have grown up in this country, the like of which do not exist in any British Dominion and, if India is to advance, these should be abolished Where such privileges conflict with the interests of the Indian people, the surrender of the former will become necessary Some measure of hardship may be caused and some losses incurred by the sudden call to the surrender of long-established privileges and monopolies In all such cases, the proper course is to minimize the hardship or suffering, as far as possible, as explained before (Chapters XII and XVIII) by payment of a reasonable money compensation Provision should be made for such compensation in the financial implications of the Ten-Year Plan

The key positions in the organization of the Plan should be held by Indians of capacity and merit, if the Plan is to be carried to a successful issue in the spirit in which similar programmes are executed in self-governing countries It would not be fair to say that competent men are not available in this country, when Indian Universities are turning out annually a larger number of graduates than in the United Kingdom itself Many of the educated men may not have the technical knowledge or the special experience for any particular office or job at the commencement, but there are hundreds and thousands of persons in our midst who, when they are put on a job, will with proper encouragement be able to acquire locally the special knowledge required, by research and study Some of the best men can do this in a few months and others in a few years But they will never acquire such knowledge or experience, if they do not get the opportunity to shoulder responsible duties Many of the business men, who had charge of large industrial and commercial enterprises in Japan till 15 or 20 years ago, were persons who were not trained in modern schools or colleges They nevertheless managed the concerns efficiently, some with the assistance of technically trained graduates from modern Universities

It is of some interest to quote the opinion of the American author, Mr Samuel Crowther, in this connection "At one time," he says, "the Americans thought that they alone could design labour-saving machinery just as Germans imagined that they had a monopoly of the world's chemical knowledge Now Great Britain and the United States are at least abreast of Germany in chemistry, while Japan in a space of twelve years has become self-contained as to chemical products and is on an export basis Our automobile companies by establishing American plants abroad, have learned that skill and adaptability are to be found almost anywhere *They destroyed the tradition that a few races were destined by nature to do the manufacturing of the world* "

We have got many competent, trained men in this country , we have got the money, too, though much of it is concentrated in the hands of a very small portion of the population Only a responsible government is needed to do the things the people want and in the manner they want done Nothing great or permanent is ever done without organization and, in the absence of responsible government, there will be no agency with the will to initiate or organize large enterprises The leaders who can do this will not take the risk without the assurance of Government support

The present Dependency rule is ill-adapted for the

execution of reforms on the lines and on the scale required It will not accept any initiative or suggestions coming from the people or their leaders for any large move or enterprise And since the rule has had the effect of encouraging the drain rather than the accumulation of wealth in the past, India's first duty is to secure a change in the system of administration and acquire the status of a Dominion Under a Dominion form of Government, the people will have the right to choose their avocations and, with it, the opportunity to build up a sound industrial and financial structure The people will be placed in a position to solve all their problems, as they think best and provide as many of their wants as possible by their own collective effort

Hence it is that the prime prerequisite of all economic progress in this country is the early establishment of Responsible Government at the Centre A responsible government and a suitable economic organization are both absolutely necessary to replace the present sterile economic order

Financing the Ten-Year Plan

It has been explained that the cost of operating the Plan is estimated to amount to Rs 10 crores per annum, of which Rs 2 crores should be met by the Central Government and Rs 8 crores, roughly in proportion to population, by the Provinces Similarly, the capital issues required for heavy industries, public works, public utilities, transport facilities, extensive banking operations, etc , should be met partly by local loans from the frozen wealth of the country, partly from the profits of industries and agriculture themselves and partly also, if necessary, from foreign loans There will be liberal response, if the constitution and policies of the new Government develop along lines which command public confidence, i e, if the new Government gives its whole-hearted support to the economic reforms and measures desired by the people, most of which are included in the developments suggested under the Ten-Year Plan and subsidiary requirements already described

The Government can greatly influence business by placing its money and credit facilities in a large measure at the service of the people Opinions of British officials themselves are on record, which go to show that it was not the lack of money but the lack of policy to create wealth that has prevented the growth of large industries and public enterprises in this country

Modern governments, as a rule, help to build up industrial and commercial enterprises, even though they may be in debt It is not that production is increased or wealth created only, when Government has large balances of liquid capital in its hands Government may lend money to banks for financing agriculture and industries—small industries require financial aid in this way—or it may contribute to the share capital of companies as the British Government did in the case of the Oil Mines in Persia, the Cunard Liner Shipping Company, the Sugar Development Scheme, the Manufacture of Liquid Fuel from Coal, etc As these words are being written, they are considering the question of subsidizing the shipping industry From all this, it is clear that wealth creation activities in this country will not be advanced, unless the future Responsible Government is given control of the public purse and the public credit is fully utilized for the purpose

THE MAKING OF AN IMMEDIATE BEGINNING

If the Government of India are really serious about having a planned economy, there is no need to wait till elaborate surveys are carried out The country has hitherto been so starved of practical reforms that there is abundant material waiting to be utilized, and a constructive scheme of great economic value can be prepared and put into operation within six months of the Government's decision to act A Ten-Year Plan and a plan for the first year of operation may both be easily developed with all the requisite detail and put into operation in the whole of British India within these six months For practical purposes, the result will, in the peculiar circumstances of India, be just as good as if the reforms were undertaken after years of elaborate enquiry and preparation There is no uncertainty about the immediate wants of the people It is practical action that has been lacking and every one has been vainly looking for. Simultaneously with the commencement of the operation of the plan, surveys may be undertaken and further details collected with a view to making the plan more and more precise and thorough from year to year In this way, planning and operation can proceed hand in hand with improved efficiency from stage to stage The surveys can in any case be satisfactorily finished in the first five-year period

The best way to make a beginning would be for the Government of India to convene an All-India Economic Conference of about 60 members composed of officials, political leaders, economists and business men for discussing the broad requirements of the country and initiating a plan The executive work to be transacted between the sittings of the conference may be entrusted to a Planning Commission of 5 to 7 members Such a conference will help the future Development Department of the Government of India to put the first Ten-Year Plan into shape and draw up a detailed scheme and budget for the first year's operations The Provincial Economic Councils may be constituted shortly after this, the members being partly nominated by the Provincial Governments with the approval of their respective Legislatures, partly elected by the various chambers of commerce and business associations in the provinces and partly also co-opted, so as to be representative of all fields of economic thought and work

The Plan outlined here has been carefully thought out and prepared after more than one visit to, and years of study of the economic activities in, the progressive countries of the West and Japan It is believed that for a provisional outline picture, the Plan set forth in these pages is as complete and practical as any such Plan can be

The Ten-Year Plan is intended to remove, in the shortest possible time, the more glaring disabilities and deficiencies inherited from the past and to introduce reforms and developments considered indispensable for a rapid advance It is desirable to send deputations of Indians to foreign countries to study new developments, but it is not necessary to postpone any part of the activities under the Plan on the ground that previous training is required for them There are hundreds of men in the country who, after a few weeks preparation and study, will be able to handle with perfect success all the problems and operations arising out of the Plan and there are many ways of obtaining the services of specialists, and technical and practical information required from expert agencies and from foreign countries.

A Five-Year Plan was adopted in Soviet Russia because the authorities there were able to carry out a survey and had sufficient data to enable them to prepare reliable forecasts and estimates of what could be accomplished in five years Since our survey is not based on any preliminary public enquiry, it has been found convenient to adopt a Ten-Year Plan By carrying out an economic survey for about three years, a Five-Year Plan may be prepared for the whole of India to take the place of the Ten-Year Plan after the latter has been half through The Ten-Year Plan may be discontinued at the end of the first quinquennium and a new Five-Year Plan put in train from the sixth year Similarly, although the Central Plan may be a Ten-Year one, there is no objection to the provincial plans being prepared for five years at a time from the very outset The All-India Ten-Year Plan will provide the basis and the material for each provincial Five-Year Plan

Since the Economic Plan outlined in these pages will be fulfilling the declared intentions of Government, there should be no hesitation or delay in making a beginning Any other equally reasonable plan adopted will include at least 75 per cent of the proposals put forward in these pages, if the plan is to satisfy Indian aspirations and the views of economic experts trusted by the people If the Government of India are, however, unable or are not permitted to carry out a plan on the scale recommended, it is the duty of the leaders and economic experts in the country to advance their own independent proposals along lines recommended in this book and press for their acceptance by Government from a thousand platforms all over the country

CHAPTER XX

A SELF-DEVELOPING INDIA

The Principal Suggestions Restated—In a Misleading Atmosphere—Nation Building—India Self-Sufficient and Self Improving—If Britain Helped—The People and the Work before Them—Picture of a Reconstructed India

THE PRINCIPAL SUGGESTIONS RESTATED

WE have come to the end of our task It is difficult to present a proper resumé of so vast a subject but to give the reader a clear perspective of the problem, its trends and its proposed solution, a brief summary of the principal suggestions offered may not be inappropriate at this stage

In the opening pages of this book, attention was invited to the fact that the country laboured under a two-fold disability, one due to the continued inattention in the past to keep her in step with the outer world, and the other to the effects of the recent world trade depression

Two grave consequences have followed one, the neglect of industries, and the other, mainly as a result of that neglect, the crowding into agriculture of about twice the population that it can reasonably bear These, in turn, have been responsible for further untoward results, such as, lack of technical efficiency in the people and absence of touch with modern business practices and machinery

Other untoward consequences of past policies have been succinctly stated in Chapters XI and XVIII The net result of all this has been that the huge population of India has not been receiving the training and equipment that civilized peoples usually receive, and a vast amount of human energy and creative power which, if rightly trained and directed, can produce wealth and income for the people is running to waste before our very eyes No prudent nation, placed in the position in which India finds herself to-day, would view the situation without grave alarm

The most reasonable thing to do to meet the situation which is daily getting critical is to adopt the two measures, which have come to be popular of late and which are being successfully introduced and worked in some of the Western countries These are —

(1) A National *Economic Plan* for Five or Ten years at a time, and

(2) An Organization like the *Economic Councils* to work the Plan and to be responsible for the country's economic activities and problems generally

On account of the rise of tariff walls everywhere, planning at the present time has become a necessity for the nations of the world A plan is primarily meant to remedy accumulated deficiencies or supply speedily many of the wants of a country The second measure, the organization, is intended to provide the agency necessary to give effect to the plan and to control and regulate the economic policies and activities from time to time in the best interests of the country

If these two measures, namely, the economic Plan and Organization, are to be successfully started and worked, there must be created, in the first instance, the atmosphere in which they can thrive Nations which have succeeded with measures of this type have had national governments to lead them, the rulers and the ruled have belonged to one political unit and one nation and not, as in India, to two different political units and two different nations No constructive policies or measures can be built up, if necessary action against this fundamental weakness is not provided for in the first instance

The Indian public have good reason on their side to be impatient for a reasonably sound form of Responsible Government at once and a complete Dominion form of Government within a period of 25 years from the date of promise Responsible Government was promised to India by an announcement in the British Parliament in the year 1917 His Majesty's Government could not have meant then that it would take more than a quarter of a century to implement their promise

A peaceful way—and perhaps the only peaceful way—of solving the problem would be to invite the British Government to forego, gradually but according to a pre-appointed schedule, all the monopolies and special privileges at present enjoyed here in the economic sphere by its people—the like of which do not, or have ceased to, exist in a Dominion like Canada or Australia—on receipt of compensation for all immediate losses occasioned thereby, say, for a period of 20 years, at an yearly rate of Rs 10 crores Subject to this payment, all the contemplated safeguards in the new Constitution, which are not recognized in the British Dominions, should be removed within 10 years and the entire Defence Forces transferred to Indian control within 15 years, at the latest

Assuming that Responsible Government is conceded and an organization of Economic Councils such as is suggested in these pages is introduced, the next earliest move should be to put into operation the measures recommended for the relief of Unemployment (*vide* Chapter XVII) This is suggested because occupations in the country are unbalanced and the resulting lack of employment is responsible for much of the distress and suffering which exists to-day. These conditions are driving vast numbers of people, including the educated classes, into apathy and despair

The present unequipoised distribution of the population among occupations, mostly primitive in character and scope, should be steadily rectified on a settled plan and schedule This process should go on continuously till about half the population now dependent on agriculture is transferred to industries, trade and other occupations and professions

The entire Indian public should be won over to the conviction that economic activities are the source of all progress and that the most essential of them needed at the present time is industrial development Propaganda should be organized for the purpose so as to take (in the words of the late Lord Morley) moonshine out of the heads of the people and put sunshine into their hearts From what has been said before, intensive industrial development is bound to prove the most efficacious cure for the present-day ills of India's enormous population

It would not be reasonable to say, as some indeed have already said, that money cannot be found for the plan The developments being of the nature of an investment, Government credit could and should be utilized for the purpose There is no more legitimate use to which such credit could be put

Nor can it be urged that the plans and programmes suggested are either extravagant or impracticable Similar developments, but of a far more radical character, have been and are being pushed forward, with breath-taking courage, by nations like Japan, the United States of America, Canada and Italy, let alone the phenomenal activities of the newly awakened people of Soviet Russia

The European community in this country have welcomed the adoption of a planned economy for India. The economic organization proposed here is not in principle very different from that recommended by Sir Arthur Salter, the League of Nations expert The special features of the scheme recommended in this volume are the introduction of a representative element in the Economic Councils and the provision that, save in emergencies, the final approval of the Councils should be a *sine qua non* to the sanction of every important policy or measure initiated by the Central and Provincial Governments

IN A MISLEADING ATMOSPHERE

With regard to the proposed economic organization and plan, Government have admitted that both these measures are needed, but the late Finance Member of the Government of India seemed to be of the opinion as previously remarked that Sir Arthur Salter's report was unsuitable and since one or two Provincial Governments had set up Economic Committees, the result of such experiments should be awaited The question of economic planning must be put off because an economic survey was necessary, survey was to be put off because Government wanted expert guidance as to the best method of conducting it The survey may take three years and in the meantime three Indian officials are to be sent to England to receive training in statistics, and an addition of two or three appointments may be expected to the present cadre of three Foreign Trade Consuls So far as the public are aware, these are the only practical proposals about which Government appear to have made up their minds to solve the Indian problem at this time of acute economic distress To say that Government are really without a policy and things are drifting is perhaps to state the blunt truth

When people are hungry for bold policies of advance, some of the Government policies seem not only not favourable to people's interests but in some respects positively misleading For example, they appear to have convinced themselves that the people must be content with agriculture as their principal occupation Some high authorities have even gone to the length of holding that it is not possible for India to become an industrial country! Such prophecies cannot be falsified so long as there is no policy, no effort, no move in that direction

Recently the Government of India evinced some interest in the matter of affording help to industries and convened two all-India conferences of Provincial ministers and officials for the purpose The proceedings of these conferences were treated as confidential The practical results announced so far are, that a Central Bureau of Industrial Intelligence and Research is about to be started on which Rs 5 lakhs is to be expended within the next three years and that sericultural research and hand-loom weaving would engage the attention of the new Bureau Heavy industries, the greatest need of the day, have been left severely alone, and long-range proposals, if they have any, for the economic development of the country, are kept undefined and shrouded in mystery Nor have they propounded any scheme or policy that might have meant a real lead to the people in the industrial domain

It is in regard to industries and finance that Government policies have wrought incalculable harm to Indian progress

As these pages are going to the press, the newspapers report the address of a broad-minded Englishman (Mr Justice Stone of Madras) in which he referred pointedly to the situation in this country and remarked that "there was much scope for industrialization" in it and he instanced the case of China which "in spite of her mineral resources, fertile soil and hard-working people, was the poorest country in the world for no other reason than the lack of industrial expansion" For the same reason, in international comparisons of economic achievements, India seems to be competing with China for the lowest place

With reference to Finance, the following passage taken from a recent Japanese publication[27] will show the extent to which financial policies and credit were utilized during 1933–34 to help industry and trade in that country —

"The Government budget deficits were spent for two principal purposes The 'arms replenishment' programmes of the Army and Navy, and the relief of agricultural villages The Army and Navy budgets resulted in the granting of important contracts to thousands of factories, large and small These contracts were the basis for the most remarkable credit expansion movement in Japan's economic history .. The money advanced for the relief of agriculture also helped but not in so direct a manner .. Japan, by holding down currency circulation, as severely as possible, is keeping domestic purchasing power from rising more rapidly than necessary By this process it is maintaining the high domestic purchasing power of the yen and the great competitive ability of the country's industries in foreign markets For the present, Japanese industry and commerce are making money Unemployment is falling Its effective load on the economic body is almost eliminated The Government's low money policy has had excellent results It has allowed

[27] *The Japan Advertiser Annual Review, 1933–34*

enterprise to convert old high-interest obligations at economical rates It has allowed the Government to meet its rising indebtedness without too great cost "

Government can help people in their business in many ways by utilising its credit for the purpose The prices of commodities within the country can be influenced by the judicious control of currency circulating within the country By proper adjustment of the means of payment for imported goods, it is possible to maintain approximate parity with gold We have seen Japan has been following these policies Before the present slump began, it was reported that the United States of America was accustomed to do about $ 80 billion worth of business with $ 4 or 5 billion in cash It is, therefore, evident that the control of money power is most essential to advance the country's industries and trade and that, without it, responsible government will bring no real advantage to the country.

The truth is that, on account of the existence of the conflict of interests referred to, the Government of India are unable to follow a consistent policy or to practise any thorough-going methods It is not the fault of the estimable gentlemen who recently constituted, or do now constitute, the Cabinet of the Government of India The fault is with the *system* under which they have to carry on

Commissions and Committees are often appointed to meet the demand for investigation of public questions But such bodies are generally made up of men likely to look at questions—at any rate that is the popular opinion—from a point of view liable to create misapprehension in the public mind Comprehensive treatment of any subject is usually avoided by strangely restricted terms of reference These commissions and committees seek light, not from the British Dominions or other advanced self-governing countries, but from evidence gathered within the country itself from sources many of which are ill-informed or prejudiced, with the result that their recommendations, when they issue, are usually non-national and of very limited constructive value

The recent Communal Award has set people by the ears Government have also introduced the communal principle in selecting recruits for the public service A feeling has been generated that intelligent communities are a public danger, that majority communities when they come to power are out to oppress the minority ones, and that in making appointments, it is not inconsistent with the future efficiency of the public services to select average, or below average, men, when Government can confessedly get superior men for the posts This is having a demoralizing effect on the country's national life as a whole, and is bound to lower before very long the prestige of Indians as a race in the higher administrative and other fields of Governmental action

The Dominion form of Government is without question the promised future constitutional status of this country but references to the Dominion experience and precedents are rigidly excluded in Government documents and publications

NATION-BUILDING

The people of India have too long ignored the claims of nation-building The attempts so far made have been feeble to develop the principle of nationality and to work out the country's destiny on broad lines

Reference has already been made more than once to the three fundamental nation-building activities, namely, education, industries and military training.

The progress of these important activities should be watched and promoted from year to year, and even from quarter to quarter, with zealous care When Responsible Government comes into existence, it would be a great gain to the country if the Ministers in charge of the Government departments connected with these activities, are required once a year to prepare comprehensive reviews of the progress achieved Such reviews should be given the widest publicity to stimulate public thought and effort

Broadly stated, the three classes into which all nation-building activities may, for our present purpose, be divided are (1) political, (2) economic, and (3) social and all others The individual citizen should have a clear conception of his duty or responsibility for each of these three classes of activities The responsibility has to be exercised in three spheres, namely, (1) local, (2) provincial or regional, and (3) national

By proper organization, up-to-date methods and united effort, the country can achieve many great national objects which other countries have already attained The people have too long ignored the claims of nation-building They are divided, they fight shy of initiative and they get no inspiration from any quarter

This seems a piteous situation for a nation of 350 million to get into, eking out its existence without policies, plan or purpose for the country as a whole or for any important sections of it

India Self-Sufficient and Self-Improving

By self-sufficiency within the country is meant that India should not import products, which she can with some effort manufacture for herself This sort of economic nationalism is at present extensively practised in all advanced countries There is, however, no desire to isolate this country But India cannot in her present stage move faster than the United States of America or Canada towards internationalism Economic nationalism is a necessary stage in passing towards internationalism By importing manufactured goods, which can be made locally, the labour population of India is being deprived of occupations of which it is sadly in want If Indians go on importing indiscriminately and make no effort to manufacture locally, they will continue to be dependent on outside countries for many necessary requirements, and will be exposed to great risks in emergencies, even as a normally self-sufficient country like the United States of America was during the late War The people should not lose sight of the fact that India is becoming visibly poorer under the operation of the present unnatural policies

India has sufficient resources to provide herself with all her elementary needs—food, clothing, shelter and transport facilities—by the labour of her own people Under the Ten-Year Plan proposed, it should be treated an emergency measure to provide for the manufacture of the more important capital goods needed in the country like steel, electrical machinery and supplies, textiles, automobiles and many kinds of chemical products If there were the intention and the policy in the government of the country to provide the higher types of manufactured goods, their production would be speedily attempted in every case, either at once, or after a short preparation, which need not exceed three years at the outside

India must be ruled by national policies, if she has to escape from her present low economic position So long as Great Britain was a free-trade country, she insisted on India also being one such Happily, the United Kingdom has abandoned this attitude If India were a free-trade country to-day, Japan would be flooding the Indian market with her cheaper products and England would be the first to lose in the bargain The Japanese goods have been competing successfully to-day in the Indian market, both with local and British goods, because the country is not, even yet, sufficiently protected

When the writer visited the United States of America for the first time in 1908, that country was sparsely populated, her resources were abundant and no restrictions were then imposed on immigration Since then, America has begun to control immigration, has increased the use of machinery and developed mass production methods The War enabled her to sell her products to European nations at specially high prices and, by those sales and other measures, she greatly improved her position and raised her standard of living to a level never before attained, in any part of the world And, to-day she is loath to lower that standard Canada, too, has, by following the policies of her neighbour, attained a high measure of prosperity The natural resources of India are more akin to the resources of these two countries than to any of the States of Europe, except Soviet Russia The best course for India, now, is to follow the policies and lines of development pursued in the recent past by the United States and the Dominion of Canada, both of which are at present in the van of progress

A Ten-Year Plan, once introduced, will lead to the habit of planning, as a means of meeting every large want, national, provincial or local in the economic sphere The people of each province or region, through the agencies provided under the Plan, will study the shortcomings and wants of the area and endeavour to supply them by their own effort They will keep watch and make sure that the collective work of the people in the area is giving them sufficient income to feed and clothe the population and maintain it at a reasonable standard of comfort If the income is not sufficient, they will induce their fellowmen to work harder and produce more and better goods and services Also, the agencies will ensure that instruction in all practical sciences and arts needed for efficient management of agriculture, industries, trade, defence and other activities is imparted to an adequate proportion of the population and on the requisite scale All the many deficiencies, inequalities and abnormalities noticed in the present public life of this country, some of which are not even freely and fully discussed at present, will come under review during the periodical stock-taking under the Plan The Plan will be constantly reminding the public of the duties and activities expected of them to provide for the immediate as well as the future needs of the region they inhabit

If the practice of planning, that is, of exercising forethought in respect of economic needs, comes into favour, if some authority or body is held responsible both for suggesting remedies, when deficiencies are noticed, and for taking action when wants are felt, the rapid progress of the region will be automatically secured

Self-development will become a practical reality, if every province and region comes to have full control over its resources As in the United States, the provincial governments should become wholly autonomous and there should be no outside direction or control in respect of the development of their resources Under autonomous governments, the provinces should have full incentive to raise the literacy of their population, multiply their industries and push forward production of every kind At present there is a dead level of uniformity maintained in relation to elementary education in the British Provinces It has been recently brought to notice by an official of the Bombay Municipality that the proportion of literate population to the total in the country has risen only from 6 to 8 per cent within the past one hundred years According to the 1931 Census, the proportions of literate population to the total in Madras, Bengal and the Punjab were 10.8, 11 1 and 6.3 per cent , respectively, and for all-India 9 2 per cent , while the corresponding percentage in each of the three Indian States of Baroda, Travancore and Cochin was at least twice as high These States have been able to raise the level of literacy, because they were free to follow their own policies in this respect.

Every province, the entire country, should be rendered in this way self-sufficient and self-improving The practices of the British Navy may be studied with advantage in this connection It is said that, though for general purposes the Navy is under the control of the Civil Government, yet in the actual operations of purely naval matters it looks after itself Even though Parliament is apathetic, the Cabinet hostile, even though the whole of England is asleep, the Navy can keep on, making itself more and more efficient "because the Navy to a large extent is a self-governing, professional, self-improving institution" To a country which has lost all spirit of adventure even in thinking, this example of a self-improving British Navy ought to be a refreshing object lesson

If Britain Helped

Whenever any important economic reform or development is required, we ultimately come up against the political difficulties inherent in the existing constitution The remedy seems clear Since political and economic policies are inseparably inter-locked in the present-day practices of the Government in India, some device should be found, some satisfactory readjustment of relations should be worked out to safeguard all reasonable British interests instead of allowing them to block the way of the Indian people to political reform and economic progress A compromise or understanding on the lines already suggested seems necessary for peaceful progress (*vide* Chapter XVIII)

After these many years of deliberation and discussion, what the character of a sound constitution should be is well known With the readjustment referred to above, if the strength of the Legislatures and the nature of the franchise are settled to the satisfaction of the people, a responsible cabinet might be expected to automatically come into existence which in due course will be best fitted to serve the country's interests The proposed economic organization and plan can be developed and brought into operation in about six months time from the date the measures are taken in hand It would be necessary to suitably adjust the machinery and methods of the new Constitution to facilitate the satisfactory functioning of this organization

The new Government will require time to build up its defence arrangements The British Government can help to nurse the new Government for ten or fifteen years, till a proper democratic *party* system of Government is firmly established They could help every national effort at reform and development because, under their protecting influence, opposition and impediments to progress would be at a minimum

It is an attitude of this kind on the part of the British Government that the country would welcome.

The memories of such help would go far to promote good-will between the two nations in the years to come The United Kingdom should look for increased business and trade for its people in this country in future not by restricting the scope of activities of the indigenous population to primitive occupations done in a primitive way but by assisting them in the development of new industries and occupations and by increasing the total volume of business in the country for which there is immense scope The people should now have opportunities to build up wealth There will be room for British trade and also for the services of the British people if rendered in a spirit of equality and friendliness India, under such an arrangement, is likely to become a new source of strength—commercial and political—to Great Britain in the years to come

The conditions are favourable at the present time to build up a new political and economic order but if a decision on the constitutional problem is further delayed, if special interests are encouraged and class jealousies become acute, if racial discrimination is allowed greater play, disunion and discard are bound to grow, minority communities are sure to assert themselves, and progress is certain to be impeded interminably Once internal commotion gets a start, there is no knowing how long it may take to establish a stable democratic government in the land There is already a strong tendency towards socialism and pronounced leanings are noticeable in some elements of the population towards communism, and a wise government would, it is expected, take time by the forelock and improve upon existing conditions in a manner which may mean continued good relations between, and benefit to both, Britain and India for generations to come There is no reason why, with a little prudential restraint on both sides and with mutual concessions on really fundamental points, such a consummation should not come about

THE PEOPLE AND THE WORK BEFORE THEM

We have sketched a tentative plan and an organization on the lines adopted by modern nations They may prove useful at least to pave the way for the preparation of an alternative plan and organization more acceptable to the business and political representatives of the people The scheme has been outlined in its broad features to facilitate action without delay The scheduled figures may have to be revised after utilizing the information available in Government records, with the aid of departmental experts and leading business men in the representative professions That, however, is a matter of detail The vital point is that the Government and the leaders should, it is felt, think seriously on the need for planning for collective action and get ready to organize and act in a manner that might help to advance the nation on lines well understood and well tried elsewhere

If the Government remain silent and make no move in the matter, a new situation would certainly be created The question would then be as to what should be the duty of the people and their leaders in regard to the ideals and objectives to which shape has been given, in however inadequate a fashion, in these pages It cannot be that the people can afford to give up the objectives. The people and their leaders should not lose faith in themselves but endeavour to carry out as many of the objectives of the Ten-Year Plan as possible with their own unaided resources

If Government help be not immediately forthcoming, it is suggested that a National Economic Council consisting of about half-a-dozen elected representatives be established, the men being chosen by some form of plebiscite or by means of a meeting of merchants, industrialists, financiers, etc , from all over the country convened for the purpose, so that the Council may be truly representative of the views of the majority of the nation Every Province should likewise have a Provincial Council constituted in the same way The District and City Councils, however, need not undergo any material alteration

Each such Council (National or Provincial) should be maintained by means of subscriptions or contributions from the public, the initiative regarding the collection of funds being taken by one or more of the existing public bodies or associations like the Chambers of Commerce

The main purpose of the Councils will be to place before the public the ideals and objects to be pursued in the economic sphere and to assist and guide them to increase production and income Provision should at the same time be made also for promoting leisure, culture and recreation with a view to increase the comfort and enrich the normal life of the working population

This is a machine age, an age of collectivism, an age of economic nationalism There should be policies and propaganda to make the people adjust themselves easily to the changing conditions Well-equipped industries, efficient managers, trained technologists and skilled workmen constitute the true wealth of the country. It would be an immense advantage in the coming time if arrangements are made for the people to obtain training and guidance to work with definite policies and well-thought-out plans

If each of these Councils did nothing more than issue, once every three months, a brief statement of advice, they would be doing incalculable service to the cause of economic advance The more important policies and activities which the nation should adopt or follow should be concisely embodied in such a statement. By doing this, the country will receive authoritative guidance and thereby much conflict of views and waste of effort would be prevented

If half-a-dozen acknowledged leaders—men and women—could come together in this way and think for the Nation, they could suggest lines of advance, guide the people and encourage them from time to time along right lines, a continuity of policy would be secured and the country helped to achieve its destiny It is undeniable that the people of this country have culpably neglected nation-building and are paying heavily for the omission It is up to them to realize the defect in their position and put forth the necessary talent, energy and action to remedy it A small sum of Rs 1½ lakhs collected and placed once a year at the disposal of the Central National Economic Council would, it is felt, prove sufficient to keep it in funds and help it to carry on its advisory duties efficiently, successfully and without break of continuity from year to year In the same way, perhaps, the provision of a sum of rupees three-quarters of a lakh or a lakh would secure the establishment of a thinking centre for each Province in the shape of a Provincial National Economic Council.

When the National Council gets a start, and the people take to the new dispensation, as they are bound to, when they see that it means a new era of progress of self-development and of national advance, even the few—including governmental authorities who might have held themselves back at first—will be drawn into the work, for, at times, in the progress of a nation a stage is reached when it carries everything before it, and the position would be so strengthened that a return to the *status quo ante* would be impossible It is but a truism in a case of this sort—a national struggle for progress—that relief should first come largely through individual personal efforts, then through the co-operation of individuals engaged in like enterprises or occupations; and finally through the co-operation of large groups, each one recognizing its dependence on other groups and all coming together for the purpose of common national good It is this third stage we are at to-day and its accomplishment will be the work, to put it in a nutshell, of the National Economic Council

The Plan outlined involves an indefinitely large number of decisions and efforts For a purpose like that, an organization that can command national confidence, that will listen and be listened to with respect throughout the length and breadth of the country, that is in close touch with the thoughts of the masses, and that will help towards the maintenance of a continuity of policy in national economic affairs, is necessary A body with a Plan, however much we may dislike it for particular reasons, is preferable to "a group sauntering down the road complaining of the economic weather and wondering when the rain will stop" A conscious will, a completed design, and a capacity to circumvent seeming difficulties is what we should expect from the Economic Councils charged with the high duty of furthering national well-being for national ends

In accomplishing this aim and end—the aim and end of regenerating the national will for accomplishing national well-being—India will be acting not only for herself but also for the world at large An India economically strong—that is, industrially efficient, educationally high and in collective co-operative effort thoroughly modernised—would prove a source of strength in the new stage of human development itself That stage is now coming, and it cannot, indeed, be long delayed The age of new Capitalism—of balance, order and discipline, of co-operation within and between nations—is fast on us and it is the duty of India to drop off her age-long apathy, deficiencies and defects, and evolve a Plan of work that will help her to retain the best features of the individualism to which she has long been so deeply attached and yet build up to advantage that system of collective effort without which economic salvation to-day is all but impossible To solve this problem of problems, the ideals of sacrifice, surrender and service should be accepted in the place of mere individual gain, personal profit and single objective That is the role that awaits new India

Picture of a Reconstructed India

The Ten-Year Plan embodies all the principal reforms and developments needed in the immediate future for building up the economic life of the people If the operation of the planning system proceeds uninterruptedly for a couple of decades on the scale and in the spirit indicated, the three fundamental wants of the country, namely, education, industries and military training, will have been adequately supplied, and very notable progress made towards economic recovery and nation-building The country will have been industrialized in the sense that the United States of America, Canada, Japan and Soviet Russia are to-day. Two or three new heavy basic industries, owned by large public companies or firms or by the local governments themselves, will have been established in every province Many medium-scale industries and a great variety of minor and cottage industries will have sprung up Agriculture will have come to be more profitably practised on scientific lines New methods of intensive cultivation and cottage industries will have been developed to supply most of the staple wants of the population

Many new reservoirs, large canals and numerous minor tanks will have been built and model farms established amidst expanses of smiling fields The rivers will be protected and will be carrying clean water

Transport and travel facilities will have been greatly extended Thousands of miles of new roads will have been laid out and old ones improved, particularly in rural areas The railways and air services will have been greatly extended, and the engines, machinery and plant required for them supplied from factories successfully operating within the country Docks and harbours will have been extended and substantial progress made in carrying Indian trade in Indian bottoms Many new hydro-electric plants will have been installed and the country covered with a net-work of wires carrying electric power all over the land for lighting, industries and lift irrigation

Both individual enterprise and collective effort will have been brought to bear on production, and enthusiasm maintained in the management and workers both by lure of profit and ideal of service

The school-going population will have been trebled or quadrupled The Universities will have trained an adequate number of picked men in the theory and practice of all the highest sciences, professions and arts These men and others who have had foreign training will be attending to the management and overhead work of numerous industrial, commercial, financial and other enterprises

Two or three National or All-India Councils will have come into existence for watching world activities and progress and advising the Government and the public as to how to keep abreast of the times

Whenever any class of beneficent activities shows a falling off in efficiency, an alarm would be raised automatically under the operation of the mechanism set up The agitation would be maintained till the deterioration noticed is arrested and progress in development restored

All large economic wants and deficiencies, whether local, provincial or national, would be under investigation, and efforts would be made to supply the same from time to time to the limit of the resources of the area concerned or the country as a whole

Investigation and research will be maintained, and also adequate statistics, for measuring progress in all fields of scientific and human activity

One of the National Councils referred to will be charged with the duty of maintaining a proper balance in the country's public activities, business pursuits, political strength, social standards and cultural efficiency

The life of the people will be organized on lines vastly more improved than now Unemployment, poverty and suffering would have been gradually brought under control and there would be a progressive tendency to make the country a better, lovelier and happier place to live in

APPENDIX

CONTENTS

EXPLANATORY NOTE ON STATISTICAL TABLES.

The ten Tables, which follow, give in a short compass, the essential statistics bearing on the economic condition of India They compare India with five or six countries, which are in the van of progress, in the matter of the pursuit of industry and trade and in economic activities generally

The Government of India's statistics deal essentially with data pertaining to the routine needs and details of the administration, but are incomplete as regards production, silent as regards income and wealth, and inadequate for comparing the country, in an economic sense, either with her past or with other contemporary countries Where data for India are found insufficient or lacking, rough figures, mostly estimates, have been entered in the Tables in their place

The Tables give comparative statistical data for India and the progressive countries mentioned under the following main heads —

- I Vital Statistics
- II Occupational Statistics
- III Revenue, Public Debt, Income and Wealth.
- IV Production
- V Agriculture
- VI Industries
- VII Foreign Trade
- VIII Transport
- IX Banking
- X Education

The most recent figures available have been used, save in cases where, for obtaining material for comparison, some earlier year or years had to be preferred Also the latest reference books have been consulted A list of the publications from which the data and information have been obtained, or which have been consulted in compiling the Tables, is printed at the end of this note

Attention is invited not so much to the absolute size of the figures included in the Tables, important though they may be, as to their ratios which may be accepted, more as illustrative than as exhaustive, of the general position indicated in the book

The League of Nations has begun to publish comparative statistics of the kind attempted in this book, but that body has admitted that "in many cases, however, close comparability is difficult to achieve owing to certain differences in the character of the various national data relating to the same subject and differences in the methods used in compiling them" This remark applies also to the accompanying Tables It cannot be said that the figures under any main head or subject in the Tables always represent identical conditions for all the countries with which comparisons are instituted In a few cases, where no information or data were available and it was thought estimates might mislead, the columns have been left blank

For facilitating international comparisons foreign money has been converted into Indian currency at rates of exchange which were current in the year to which the figures pertain

Taken as a whole, the Tables set forth data with whose aid broad conclusions can be drawn with confidence as to the position and standing of this country in the various departments of its economic life

STATISTICAL TABLES

I. VITAL

Country	Year	Area (Square miles)	Popu	
			Total	Urban (Percentage of total)
1	2	3	4	5
India .	1931	1,808,679	352,837,778	38,979,211 (11.0)
The United Kingdom	1931	94,278	46,178,884	31,948,168 (80.0)[2]
The United States of America	1930	3,685,382	122,775,046	68,954,823 (56.2)
Canada ..	1931	3,510,008	10,374,196	5,572,058 (53.7)
Germany .	1930	180,985	64,776,000	40,191,588 (62 0)
France .	1931	212,659	41,860,000	19,984 766 (49 05)[4]
Japan .	1931	147,593	65,366,500	33,324,000 (560.)[5]

[1] Figures in column 10 do not in every case relate to the year in column 2

[2] For England and Wales only

STATISTICS.

lation	Density per square mile (Persons)	Per 1,000 of total population		Expectation of Life (Years)[1]
Rural (Percentage of total)		Births	Deaths	
6	7	8	9	10
313,858,567 (89 0)	195 5	32 9	24 5	26.7
7,999,765 (20 0)[2]	490	16 3	12 5	37 6[3]
53 820,223 (43 8)	33 3	18 9	11.3	56.4
4,802,138 (46 3)	2 95	23 9	10.7	
24,584,412 (38 0)	357.9	17 5	11.1	49.04
20,750,131 (50 95)[4]	197	17 4	16 3	50 5
26,413,000 (44 0)[5]	443	32.35	18.17	44 5

Relates only to England

In 1926

For 1925

II. OCCUPATION

Country	Year	Total Population	Working Population		Agriculture, Fishing, etc			Industry, Minin Quarries		
			Total	Percentage of 3	Total	Percentage of 3	Percentage of 4	Total	Percentage of 3	
1	2	3	4	5	6	7	8	9	10	
		(000)	(000)		(000)			(000)		
India	1931	352,838	154,390[1]	43 8	103,762	29.4	67.2	15,707[2]	4.4	1
Great Britain	1921	43,176	19,357.3	44 8	1,380 9	3 2	7 1	9,141.8	21 2	4
The United States of America	1930	122,776	48,832.6	39 8	10,752.4	8.8	22.0	15,475 6	12 6	3
Canada	1931	10,377	3,924 5	37.8	1,225.3	11 8	31 2	978 0	9.5	2
Germany	1925	63,181	32,009 3	50 7	9,762.4	15.4	30 5	13,239 2	20.9	4
France	1926	40,744	21,394 1	52 5	8,199 9	20.1	38.3	7,114.8	17.5	3
Japan	1930	64,450	29,220 5	45 3	14,689.2	22 8	50.3	5,717.5	8.9	1

[1] Two-thirds of the working population, being agricultural, has regular employment c

[2] The population employed in mines, plantations and organized industrial establishme

STATISTICS

Trade and Transport			Public Administration			Liberal Professions			Others		
Total	Percentage of 3	Percentage of 4	Total	Percentage of 3	Percentage of 4	Total	Percentage of 3	Percentage of 4	Total	Percentage of 3	Percentage of 4
12	13	14	15	16	17	18	19	20	21	22	23
(000)			(000)			(000)			(000)		
10,254	2 9	6 6	1,835	0 3	1.2	2,310	0.7	1 5	20,517	6 1	13.3
4,008.4	9 3	20 7	1,141 5	2 6	5 9	845 5	2.0	4.4	2,839.2	6.5	14.7
11,975.6	9 7	24 5	1,057 9	0 9	2 2	3,425 8	2 8	7.0	6,145.2	5.0	12 6
693.1	6 7	17.7	116 7	1 1	2 9	243 3	2 3	6 2	668.1	6.4	17.2
5,273.5	8 3	16.4	648 0	1.0	2.0	1,301.4	2.5	4 1	1,784 8	2 8	5.7
3,640 9	8 9	17 0	476 7	1.2	2.2	764.6	1 9	3.6	1,197.2	2 9	5 6
5,891.2	9 1	20.2	2,051 1	3 2	7.0	.	..	..	871.5	1.3	3.0

r about half the year

iving 10 or more employees, numbered 25,005,280

III REVENUE, PUBLIC DEBT,

Country	Revenue (Central, Provincial and Local)			Public	
	Year	Total	Per Head of Population	Year	Total
1	2	3	4	5	6
		(Rs Crores)	(Rs)		(Rs Crores)
British India	1932-33	268[1]	10	1932	1,212
The United Kingdom	1933	1,334[2]	290	1932	10,197
The United States of America	1930	2,732[3]	222	1932	5,413
Canada	1931	205	197	1931	555
France	1933	460[4]	115	1931	5,166
Japan	1932-33	459[5]	76	1932	940

[1] Central and Provincial, 1932-33, Local, 1930-31

[2] Imperial 1933, Local 1931-32

[3] Federal 1933, State 1929

INCOME AND WEALTH

Debt	National Income			National Wealth		
Per Head of Population	Year	Total	Per Head of Population	Year	Total	Per Head of Population
7	8	9	10	11	12	13
(Rs.)		(Rs. Crores)	(Rs.)		(Rs. Crores)	(Rs.)
45	1922–23	2,223	82	1930	12,000	441
2,217	1931	4 995	1,002	1925	29,432	6,371
440	1928	24,533	2,053	1928	1,12,316	9,366
533 6	1930	1,319	1,268	1929	8,344	8,023
1,230	1928	2,618	636	1928	18,857	4 581
145	1928	1,471	271	1924	13,645	2,308

[4] Represents only State revenue.

[5] Imperial 1932–33, Prefectural 1932–33, Cities 1931–32, Towns and Villages 1931–32.

IV. PRO

Country	Production		Primary		
	Total	Per Head of Total Population	Agriculture	Forests	Fisheries
	(Rs Crores)	(Rs)	(Rs Crores)	(Rs Crores)	(Rs Crores)
India	2,500	71	2,032	28	3.3
The United Kingdom	2,452.8	531	286.1	2.7	24
The United States of America	12,317.7	1,003	2,105	565.6	22.7
Canada	885	851	222	84	13
Japan	1,408.53	234	340.5	28.9	34 3
Germany			666.7	.	.

[1] The figures in this Table do not all pertain to any particular yea

[2] Only Rs 146 crores of this is the estimated value of product

DUCTION[1]

Production		Secondary Production			
Total	Per Head of Total Population	Industries	Mining	Total	Per Head of Total Population
7	8	9	10	11	12
(Rs Crores)	(Rs)	(Rs Crores)	(Rs Crores)	(Rs Crores)	(Rs)
2,063 3	59	408[2]	28 7	436.7	12
312.8	68	1,890	250	2,140	463
2,693 3	219	8,857	1,333	10,190	830
319	307	489	77	566	544
403 7	67	955.2	49.6	1,004	167
	111.1	1,733.3			288.9

but to one or the other of the years between 1924 and 1931

of large-scale industries

V. AGR

Country	Area (Million Acres)						Pop		
	Total	Under Cultivation	Under Irrigation	Under Food Crops	Under Commercial Crops	Under Forests	Employed in Agriculture	Supported by Agriculture (including actual workers)	Percentage of Population employed in Agriculture to Total Population
1	2	3	4	5	6	7	8	9	10
							(Millions)	(Millions)	
British India .	669.3	261 9[2]	49.7	209.6	48 06	87 9	78	192	28 8
The United Kingdom	60.3	33.6		5.5	0 45	11.9	1 3	.	3 06
The United States of America	2,358 6	955 6	19 6	243 8	54 3	628.8	10 5	30 4	8.5
Canada	2,246 4	140.9	1.3	46 7	0 68	736	1.08		10.4
Germany	115 8	103 7		29.5	1.4	32 1	9 8	14 4	15.4
France	136 1	108.7		27 2	1.0	27.2	8 1		19.9
Japan .	94 5	23	7.4	12 4	0 52	49 7	14	.	21.4

[1] The statistics in this Table are not for same year for

[2] 32 8 million acres out of this were sown more than once.

CULTURE [1]

…ation		Agricultural Holdings		Capital Invested			Production			
Percentage of Population employed in Agriculture to Total Working Population	Acreage per Head of Population employed in Agriculture	Total Number	Acreage per Holding	Total	Per Head of Total Population	Per Head of Population employed in Agriculture	Total Value	Per Head of Total Population	Per Head of Population employed in Agriculture	Live Stock
11	12	13	14	15	16	17	18	19	20	21
		(Millions)		(Rs Crores)	(Rs)	(Rs)	(Rs Crores)	(Rs)	(Rs)	(Millions)
60.4	3 3	55	5				1,508	59	196	213 9
6.7	26	0.59	55				286 1	62	2,201	51.4
21.5	87	6.3	157	15,901	1,290	14,544	2 105	175	1,931	181
27.65	140	0 71	198	2,048	1,909	18,020	222	213	2 035	17 4
30.3	12	5.1	21				666 7	111 1	680	52.3
37.85	13							.		37.4
48.3	4 2	5.6	4.2				340 5	57	362	3.9

: refer to various years between 1925 and 1931

VI INDUS

Country	Number of Establishments	Number of Workers	Gross Value of Products	Net Value of Products
1	2	3	4	5
			(Rs Crores)	(Rs Crores)
India	9,422	15,361,933	800	408
The United Kingdom	107,500[2]	7,700,500	4,269	1,925
The United States of America ..	174,136	14,110,652	19,444	8 857
Canada .	24,020	644,439	952 5	489
Japan .	59,887	5,459,031	1,905	933.33

[1] The figures in this Table do not all pertain to any given year but to one or the other of the years between 1926 and 1931

[2] The indigenous capital is estimated at Rs 300 crores

TRIES[1]

Net Value of Products per Worker	Net Value of Products per Head of Total Population	Capital Invested	Value of Exports of Manufactured Goods	Percentage of Column 9 to Total Net Production
6	7	8	9	10
(Rs)	(Rs)	(Rs Crores)	(Rs Crores)	
265	12	700[2]	43	10.5
2,500	412	7,067	587	30.6
6,327	721	23,000	895	10.1
7,647	470	1,445	81	16.6
1,761	158	1,009[4]	241	25.8

[1] Includes also commercial establishments

[2] Authorized

VII. FOREIGN

Country	Year	Total Trade (Imports and Exports)	Total Trade per Head of Population	Im		
				Total	Food Stuffs	Raw Materials
1	2	3	4	5	6	7
		(Rs Crores)	(Rs)	(Rs Crores)	(Rs Crores)	(Rs Crores)
India	1929	584	17	253	40	23
	1932-33	265	7.6	133	15	20
The United Kingdom	1929	2,747	597	1,628	714	453
	1932	1,495	324	937	500	219
The United States of America	1929	2,653	214	1,204	266	646
	1931-32	1,011	84	480	128	222
Canada	1929	957	920	461	48	89
	1932	316	304	161	21.4	32 6
Germany	1929	1,866	296	915	250	471
	1932	680	105	305	98	138
France	1929	1,165	284	626	142	378
	1932	531	127	320	118	142
Japan	1929	595	90	295	36	211
	1931	318	47	165	12	54

TRADE

ports			Exports					
Manufactur-ed Goods	Miscellane-ous	Percentage of 8 to 5	Total	Food Stuffs	Raw Mate-rials	Manufactur-ed Goods	Miscellane-ous	Percentage of 14 to 11
8	9	10	11	12	13	14	15	16
(Rs Crores)	(Rs Crores)		(Rs Crores)	(Rs Crores)	(Rs Crores)	(Rs Crores)	(Rs Crores)	
173	17	68	331	68	156	84	22	26
95	3	71	132	37	55	38	2	29
446	16	27	1,119	74	105	765	175	68
210	8	22	555	63	90	383	19	69
264	28	22	1,449	221	540	688		47
130		27	531	88	218	225		42
298	25	64.7	496	205 5	137	147	6.5	29.7
95.2	11 8	59	155	47.9	30 6	63.8	3.7	41.3
148	46	16	951	46	191	643	71	67
47	2	16	375	13	67	293	2	78
107		17	539	65	134	338	1.4	63
00	..	10	211	31	49	131		62
46	2.3	16	300	21	129	125	25	45
24	75	14	153	12	67	61	13	40

VIII TRANS

Country	Merchant Vessels (Total Gross Tonnage)	Automobiles in Use		Railway Mileage	Road Mileage
		Motor Cars	Motor Cycles		
1	2	3	4	5	6
India	271,820	174,450	15,729	42,753	253,125[1]
The United Kingdom	19,672,000	1,558,075	734,123	21,162	190,252
The United States of America	13,442,000	26,697,398	110,757	261,816	3,009,066
Canada	1,463,000	1,222,731	9,427	43,173	422,942
Germany	4,164,000	715,044	792,075	36,257	
France	3,556,000	1,544,057	441,503	25,964	393,845
Japan	4,255,000	95,719	24,332	13,363	591,484

[1] British India only

[2] The actual figure is 9,274

PORT.

Posts (Number of Offices)	Telegraphs (Number of Offices)	Telephones (Number of Instruments)	Waterways (Length in Miles)	Broadcasting (Number of Receiving Sets per 1,000 of Population)	Aviation (Passenger Miles Flown)	Electricity Output (Million K W.H.'s)
7	8	9	10	11	12	13
23,983	4,675	56,894	4,008	.03[4]	144,095[2]	1,852[4]
22,919	12,542	2,054,249	4,853	94	1,604,000	16,600
48,159	23,490	20,098,059	26,410	98	50,000,000	115,000
12,427	4,661	1,402,861	2,700	50	4,073,552	16,400
60,950		3,247,012	7,689	61	6,750,653	25,500
•		1,113,000	6,204	36 6	5,849,000	14,400
11,296		715,020		14.7	1,063,626	14,100

Including 5,495 passenger miles

[4] Approximate.

IX BANK

Country	Year	Banking Offices		Banking Capital and Reserve	Bank
		Total Number	Per Million of Population		Total
1	2	3	4	5	6
				(Rs Crores)	(Rs Crores)
India .. .	1930	882	2 5	25.46	227.66[1]
The United Kingdom	1932	12,557	273	316.5	3,226.5
The United States of America ..	1931	22,071	179	3,540 6	13,787 7
Canada .. .	1931	4,176	417	113.7	836
France[2] ..	1929	2,061	49	48.9	510 5
Germany .	1928	2,166	33	212.3	1,084 8
Japan[3] ..	1929	6,670	103	357.3	1,407.5

[1] Includes Rs 68 11 crores deposited in Foreign Exchange Banks in India.

[2] The figures against France under Columns 8 to 11 refer to the year 1931

ING

Deposits	Savings Banks Deposits				
Per Head of Population	Postal	Accounts, Postal	Total including other classes of savings	Per Head of Population	Exchange rate
7	8	9	10	11	12
(Rs)	(Rs Crores)		(Rs Crores)	(Rs)	
6 4	37.02	2,477,613	73 4	2 1	
698	385 7	9,865,817	1,232 9	266 8	£ = Rs 13.3
1,123	95 4	770,859	6,677 3	543 7	$ = Rs 2.74
804	6 85	80 098	34 1	32 8	$ = Rs 2.74
122	348 9	9,829,022	523.1	125 1	(1929) Fr = Re 0 107 (1931) Fr = Re 0 115
167			1,091 5	168 1	Rms = Re 0.684
215	346.9	38,332,773	581 6	88 9	Yen = Rs 1.37

[3] The figures against Japan under columns 8 and 9 refer to the year 1931

X. EDUCA

Country	Literacy: Year	Population: Total (Million)	Population: Literate (Million)	Percentage of Literate Population to Total Population	Scholars under: Year	Total Number
1	2	3	4	5	6	7
All-India	1931	353	28	8		
British India	1931	272	22 7	8 5	1930–31	12,689,086
The United Kingdom[1]	1921	42.7	32 5	76 1	1930–31	8,719,134
The United States of America	1920	105 7	79	74.5	1930–31	29,156,286
Canada	1921	8 8	6 3	71.6	1931	2,542,747
Germany	1925	62.4	50.2	80.5	1931	10,430,774
France	1926	40.2	32 2	80.1	1930	6,371,439
Japan	1925	59.7	42.8	71.7	1930–31	12,428,519

[1] Figures in columns 2 to 5 refer to Great Britain only

TION.

Instruction	Expenditure		Elementary Instruction		University and Collegiate Instruction	
Percentage of Total Population	Total	Per Head of Population	Total Number of Scholars	Expenditure	Total Number of Scholars	Expenditure
8	9	10	11	12	13	14
	(Rs Crores)	(Rs)		(Rs Crores)		(Rs Crores)
.						
4.67	28 32	1 04	9,362,748	8 14	92,028	3 92
18.8	149 81	32 4	6,186,973	86 21	61,712	56
23.7	801 4	65	23,534,000	347	971,000	374.17
24.4	49.72	48	2,005,652	42 1[2]	41,168	6 6
16 07			6,771,404		131,081	..
15 3	..	.	5,576,312		91,910	..
19	71 5	11	9,923,877		143,503	.

' Including vocational and other grades of instructio

PUBLICATIONS CONSULTED.

The following is a list of the *Annuals* and other publications from which the data and figures given in the Tables have been obtained An abstract of publications consulted for each Table is given at the end

Serial Number	Name and Year of Publication
1	*Statesman's Year-Book*, 1906, 1915, 1925, 1930, 1931, 1932 and 1933
2	*Indian Year-Book*, 1931, 1933 and 1934.
3	*American Year-Book*, 1931
4	*Liberal Year-Book*, The United Kingdom, 1930
5	*Labour Year-Book*, The United Kingdom, 1930
6	*Canada Year-Book*, 1931, 1932 and 1933
7	*Japan Year-Book*, 1931 and 1932
8	*Japan Times Year-Book*, 1932 and 1933
9	*Europa*, 1929
10	*Whitaker's Almanack*, 1932 and 1934
11	*Year-Book of Education*, 1933
12	*Chicago Daily News Almanack and Year-Book*, 1932
13	*Census of India*, 1921 and 1931, Vol I
14	*Statistical Abstract for British India*, 1919-20 to 1929-30, 1920-21 to 1929-30 and 1932
15	*Abstract of the Population Census of India*, 1931
16	*Government of India Report on Education in India*, 1929-30
17	*Education in India in* 1930-31 (1933)
18	*Joint-Stock Companies in British India*, 1927-28 and 1930-31
19	*Review of the Trade of India*, 1932-33
20	*Statistical Year-Book of the League of Nations*, 1931-32, 1932-33, and 1933-34
21	The League of Nations' *Memorandum on Public Finance*, submitted to the First International Economic Conference, Geneva, May 1927.
22	League of Nations' *International Year-Book of Agricultural Statistics*, 1930-31
23	*Commercial Banks*, 1913-1929 (League of Nations)
24	*Statistical Abstract of the United Kingdom*, 1913 and 1917 to 1930
25	*Statistical Abstract for the British Empire*, 1924-30.

Serial Number	Name and Year of Publication
26	*Statistical Abstract of the United States of America*, 1931 and 1933
27	*The British Census of Production*, 1924
28	*Macmillan Committee Report on Finance and Industry*, 1931
29	*Annual Report of the Comptroller of Currency United States*, 1930
30	Rajani Kanta Das, *The Industrial Efficiency of India*, 1930
31	Shah and Khambata, *Wealth and Taxable Capacity of India*, 1924
32	Jathar and Beri, *Indian Economics*, Vols I and II, 1931
33	H G Moulton, *Japan, An Economic and Financial Appraisal*, 1932
34	Colin Clark, *The National Income, 1924-31* (1932)
35	F Cyril James *England To-day*, 1932
36	G D H Cole, *British Trade and Industry*, 1932
37	O P Austin, *In These Eventful Years*, Vol I, 1924
38	Frank Yeigh, 5,000 *Facts About Canada*
39	P Barrett Whale, *Joint-Stock Banking in Germany*, 1930
40	J R Cahill, *Report on Economic Conditions in France in 1928* (1928)
41	H E Fisk, Article on "New Estimates of National Income" in *American Economic Review*, March 1930
42	T E Thomson in *American Economic Review*, December, 1932
43	*Bankers', Insurance Managers' and Agents' Magazine*, June 1933
44	*Encyclopædia Britannica*, 14th Edition, Vol X, 1929
45	*Agricultural Statistics of India*, 1929-30
46	*Financial and Economic Annual of Japan*, 1930

ABSTRACT OF PUBLICATIONS CONSULTED

Table Number		Serial Number of publications, in the above list, consulted
I	VITAL STATISTICS	1, 2, 6, 7, 8, 9, 10, 13, 15, 20, 24, 30 and 33
II.	OCCUPATIONAL STATISTICS	1, 6, 8, 13, 15, 20 and 33
III	REVENUE, PUBLIC DEBT, INCOME AND WEALTH—	
	Revenue	1, 6, 7, 8, 14, 21, 24, 26 and 33
	Public Debt	1, 6 and 33
	Income	6, 33, 34 and 41
	Wealth	6, 12, 33, 35 and 37
IV.	PRODUCTION—	
	India	31
	The United Kingdom	1, 24, 27 and 34
	The United States	1, 3, 26 and 42
	Canada	1 and 6
	Japan	1, 7, 8 and 33
	Germany	44
V	AGRICULTURE	1, 2, 6, 7, 13, 22, 26, 32 and 15
VI.	INDUSTRIES	1, 5, 6, 7, 8, 14, 18, 26, 28, 30, 32, 33, 36 and 46
VII	FOREIGN TRADE	1, 2, 6, 7, 8, 19, 20 and 38
VIII	TRANSPORT	1, 7, 8, 10, 14, 20 and 40
IX	BANKING	1, 6, 7, 8, 11, 18, 21, 23, 25, 26, 29, 39 and 43
X.	EDUCATION	1, 6, 7, 8, 11, 16, 17, 20, 24, 25 and 26

INDEX.

PAGE

P—*Contd*

R